ALL TEACHERS WISE AND WONDERFUL

By Andy Seed and available from Headline:

All Teachers Great and Small

ALL TEACHERS WISE AND WONDERFUL

A further memoir of lessons and life in the Yorkshire Dales

ANDY SEED

headline

First published in 2012
by HEADLINE PUBLISHING GROUP

1

Cataloguing in Publication Data is available from the British Library

978 0 7553 6216 5

Typeset in Adobe Garamond by Palimpsest Book Production Limited, Falkirk, Stirlingshire

Printed and bound by CPI Group (UK) Ltd, Croydon, CR0 4YY

Headline's policy is to use papers that are natural, renewable and recyclable products and made from wood grown in sustainable forests. The logging and manufacturing processes are expected to conform to the environmental regulations of the country of origin.

HEADLINE PUBLISHING GROUP
An Hachette UK Company
338 Euston Road
London NW1 3BH

www.headline.co.uk
www.hachette.co.uk
www.andyseed.com

To our parents, Mike, Sue, Trevor and Lisette.

Anyone who thinks they recognise themselves in this book but can't remember the events described need not worry that they're suffering from amnesia. While the events described in this book really happened, the characters are based on amalgamations of real people, rather than particular individuals, with the exception of Andy and Barbara Seed.

Acknowledgements

There are many people I wish to thank for helping to make this book possible. My special appreciation goes to Kate Shaw, Carly Cook and to my Yorkshire-born (and therefore understanding) editor, Emma Tait.

My family have been a great support, as always: my wonderful wife Barbara, along with Joe and Amy, Ben and Naomi, not forgetting Jane and Julian Winstanley, Jenny and James Briggs, and Jennifer Vesci in Switzerland.

Lots of friends have spurred me on after reading *All Teachers Great and Small*, and I would like to mention (in no particular order): Sheila and Richard Brown, Libby and Greg Pearson, Joy and Pete Whitfield, Mike and Ros Laycock, Paul Price, Vicky Humbles, Penny and Roger Powell, Debbie Wood, Kristl and Matt Kirk, Ken and Jackie Burns, Mandy and Karl Avison, Jean Wardman, Dave and Deb Ward, Jean Denney, Andrea and Stephen Dennis, Ian and Diane Middleton, Eddie and Wendy James, Carolyn and Chris Rorke, Eileen Davis, John Rice, Linda Murphy, Marion Cuthill, Andy and Katey Dean, Ellen Stott, Heather Russell and the Coates family: Martin, Fran, Michelle, Becky, James and Bryan. Thanks, too, to the crowd at The Blacksmiths Arms in Sunny Swinton.

Other kind people who gave me invaluable help, perhaps

unknowingly, are Ros Akers, Margaret and Dave Helliwell, Julia Elliott, Joanne Miller, John Miller and Albert Calvert.

Finally, I received great encouragement from everyone at Elim Ryedale Church and would especially like to thank Andy and Andrea Boxall, Bryan and Amanda Barrett, Sara Abbey, Jeff and Liz Bentley, Colin and Lesley Bessant, Bob Booth, Steve and Sandra Camps, Mark and Nettie Camps, Dave and Sue Davies, Val and Peter Fox, Ruth Hardy, Cliff and Diane Hicks, Becky Ibbotson (as long as she doesn't mention dresses), Richard Jesse aka Jock MacTavish, Terence and Sue Maw, Hazel and Andrew Pearson, Alan and Inez Pratt, Claire and Tom Robinson, Trevor and Babs Smith, Tony and Janet Walton, John and Ann Weatherill, and Nigel and Dawn Wright.

Please forgive me if I've missed anyone from these lists.

Contents

Prologue

Bernadette

Everything was ready. There were sheets of clean, white cartridge paper on each table and pencils were sharpened. The class of eight- and nine-year-olds were sitting still and listening, twenty-two eager faces looking forward to their first Art lesson of the new term. I had planned the afternoon carefully and chosen a familiar subject: shoes. Everyone was going to draw his or her own shoe, and so I began to explain how to go about this; I wanted good results.

'Drawing is all about looking, really. If you look hard, you'll see lots of detail on every shoe.'

I asked for a volunteer to lend me a shoe for demonstration purposes. A tall, bespectacled girl at the front nearly exploded with eagerness to oblige. She stood up and swiped at her raised foot in one frenzied movement, taking several involuntary hops towards me while trying to put up her hand at the same time. She yanked off a shoe and used it to break her fall as she crashed into my chest, winding me severely.

'Thank you, Bernadette,' I wheezed. The rest of the class guffawed as she disconnected her slender frame from my front and sidled back to her place, trying to hide the intense blush beneath her sandy hair. I attempted to recover my composure and regarded the shoe for a moment. It was a heavily scuffed and worn, brown lace-up of the deeply unfashionable 'sensible' type. I picked it up gingerly; I had a suspicion that there may have been something distinctly unpleasant lurking on the sole, but I didn't look. At least it wasn't a boy's shoe – a colleague had warned me never to tie little boys' shoelaces for them, even if they really couldn't manage themselves. She had once done so, wondering why the laces were wet, and then realised that the child had just returned from the toilets. I put the shoe down on a piece of paper on my desk and waited for the class to settle.

'As I was saying, it's all about looking carefully, children. If you want to draw this shoe really well, you need to put in all the small things, as well as get the shape right. You need to draw the little stitches, and the lace holes, and the pattern on the edge of the sole there, too.'

I looked up. About one-third of the class were listening. Bernadette had taken off her sock and was picking between her toes with her pencil; she blushed again when I looked at her. A loaded clear of the throat and call to pay attention allowed me to go on.

'There's one more thing that I want you to try and do when you draw your shoe, Class Three. When I look at Bernadette's shoe, what can I see that most of you can't?'

A voice at the back whispered, 'Doo-doo.' I chose to ignore the remark but, apart from this, the question was met with silence.

'I mean, which part of the shoe can I see that you can't see?'

A hand went up. 'The front?'

'But you can see the front, can't you?'

'Not really, Lee's head's in the way.'

I soldiered on. 'Because I'm much nearer the shoe and I'm standing almost above it, I can see a different part to you – which part do I mean?' There was another silence and several children looked confused. A number wore furrowed brows.

Eventually another hand went up – it was Bernadette. 'The bottom?'

'Bernadette, do you really think I can see the bottom of your shoe?' She shrugged, leaving me unsure as to whether she was serious or not. My voice was now becoming agitated so I gave the answer. 'I can see the *inside*.' Several children looked completely amazed and those near the front craned forward, as if they needed to verify for themselves that this piece of staggering information was really true.

Fifteen minutes had now passed and not a single pencil mark had been made on a piece of paper. 'What I'm getting at, everyone, is that you must draw exactly what you can see: so if you can see the inside, draw the inside.'

Another hand went up, that of a serious-faced boy at the back of the class. 'But none of us can see the inside of the shoe from 'ere, Mr Seed.'

I tried hard not to look or sound as tense as I was. 'Yes, Guy, but you're each going to draw your own shoe – on your own desk.' A general 'Ohhh' of understanding rose up from the class; I obviously hadn't been making myself clear. Another question followed.

'Will we all tek off us shoe then, like Bernie?'

'Yes.'

'But there'll be a bummer of a stink, Mr Seed.'

The tide of mumbling was now rising steadily and so I attempted to regain control and get the activity started.

'Right, everyone, listen, please. Even though I said that you should draw the inside of the shoe if you can see it, don't concentrate on that: you are going to be looking at it from the outside, after all. Well, you'd better all start.'

There was a huge scraping of chairs and a great rumpus as twenty-one shoes were removed and plonked on the wooden classroom desks. There were black plimsolls, and heavy leather boots, shiny patent buckle-ups and tattered hand-me-downs, all in various shades of muddy greys and browns. The noise level rose once more as neighbours' shoes were admired or ridiculed, or as others were slid across the tabletops for sport. After a few barks and looks of disapproval, I settled the children down yet again and made sure that everyone was sitting still with pencil in hand.

Given that my new class was bright, I had thought that this activity would be easy, but I was rapidly discovering that nothing in teaching is ever straightforward. The range of individual approaches to drawing was amazing: a number of children produced a sketch of a stylised shoe without once looking at their own footwear. Another group didn't seem to realise that it was possible to turn the paper round and contorted their bodies gymnastically in attempts to follow the shoe's curved outline with their pencils. Others spent more time rubbing out than drawing, until their paper became a crumpled grey fog and they asked for more. Some kept moving the shoe they were observing so that their drawings took on the look of an exploded diagram from a textbook.

At first I began to despair that any good-quality work would be produced at all, but as time went on and I made my way around the room, it was clear that there were several talented artists among the group. Delicate sketched outlines became filled with sharply observed pattern and line; some employed skilful shading to add depth to their work and others became absorbed with the challenge of describing every crease and seam of leather and rubber.

As children began to notice their neighbours' splendid drawings and hear my words of delight and encouragement while I toured the desks, others found inspiration, and the general quality of the pictures increased dramatically. My mood gradually changed from frustration to delight, and I could envisage a wonderful wall display of brilliantly observed shoe drawings, perhaps good enough to grace the entrance hall of the school.

I was just about to congratulate everyone on their artwork when I noticed an empty chair next to a studious, red-haired girl called Nina. It was Bernadette's.

'Have you seen Bernadette, Nina?' She was concentrating so hard on her picture that she hadn't even noticed me.

'Er, no, I don't know where she is.' None of the other children on the table had information either. I scanned the room and checked the stock cupboard, but there was no sign of her. Perhaps she had gone to the toilet, but it wasn't like Bernadette to leave the room without asking. I was baffled.

It was at this point that something caught my eye through the window on the far side of the room. The classroom was a 'mobile' – a temporary, prefabricated affair, separate from the main building, which had been brought in fifteen years previously when the numbers of children in the school were at a peak. It had long windows on three sides, set high into the flimsy walls, and at one of these I now stood, staring in disbelief.

At first I wasn't sure what it was: a flash of light-brown materialising through the glass for a fraction of a second, but after it appeared three or four times in rapid succession, I realised that it was hair. The top of someone's head. I walked forward for a better view of this odd phenomenon, hoping that none of the children in the class would become distracted from their work. I was about halfway across the room when it shot into view again: a human head pogoing outside the classroom. I moved nearer still – it popped up again and this time I could see that it was, unmistakably, Bernadette. What on earth was she doing? By now, a few children had noticed my concern and word passed around the room with the speed of light that Mr Seed had seen something strange outside. Chairs started scraping and bodies were raised for a better view. I silenced the initial hoots of laughter with a growly 'Sit down!' and skipped through the door to intercept the bouncing child before a riot broke out.

At first, she didn't register my appearance and I watched her for a moment. On the grass beside her was her pencil and a piece of paper resting on a large atlas. She was just winding up for another leap: knees bent, arms back, facing the classroom. She sprang upwards with clenched teeth and spine arching backwards for maximum effort, obviously straining to see through the window. Her landing was less graceful, and she hit the grass with a clomp of long arms and legs before diving towards her picture and sketching in a few scribbly lines. She was, I noticed, still wearing only one shoe.

'Bernadette, what exactly are you doing?' She twisted around and reddened for the third time that afternoon.

'Am drawing ma shoe, Mr Seed, like yer said.'

'Where is your shoe, Bernadette?'

'It's on ma desk.'

I could see a line of sniggering faces at the window, crouching and ducking desperately as I blasted a glare at them.

'But why are you drawing it from here?'

'Well, yer told us to draw the shoe from the outside.'

At this point, words failed me. I looked around for another adult to witness this peculiar episode, fearing that no one would believe me when I told them, but not a soul was there. I picked up Bernadette's paper and asked her nicely to return to the classroom. On the way through the door I took a glimpse at the picture – it looked like one of Dali's nightmares.

Back in the room I considered once more whether Bernadette was just being naughty or trying to gain attention, but the innocent look of concern on her face when I had stepped outside told me that this wasn't the case. I had been a primary school teacher for two years now and I should have known that if there is even the slightest possibility of misinterpretation then at least one child will grab it and run with it, however preposterous the result.

'Welcome to the new term and your new class,' I said quietly, shaking my head and laughing.

Chapter One

Sheena

It was a glorious September morning as I drove from our home in Applesett to the school where I worked in Cragthwaite: six miles across the stunning, broad valley of Swinnerdale, one of the treasures of the magnificent Yorkshire Dales. On days like this I had to remind myself constantly that we actually lived here, amid this spectacular scenery with its soaring hills, wooded waterfalls and characterful stone villages.

I thought about my young son Tom, just fourteen months old, at home with my wife Barbara. What a wonderful place for a child to grow up. We'd only lived in the dale for two years but we felt settled and deeply content to be part of this curious, old-fashioned community, seemingly set apart from the rest of the country.

The proud little village of Cragthwaite came into view as I rounded a bend and I looked forward to another day at the school. I remembered this moment two years ago when I approached each day with trepidation, having to work under the fearsome Howard Raven, a dour, backwards-looking headmaster who seemed to reserve special disapproval for everything I did as an apprehensive newly qualified teacher. But now the place was transformed. The new head, Joyce Berry, was much more than a new broom that had swept away the depressing cobwebs of the past; by the sheer warmth of her personality and enthusiasm for children and learning, she had lifted the whole community, giving a once cold, unfriendly school a welcoming, lively atmosphere, even if one or two of the staff participated reluctantly.

My own teaching group was Class 3, the second oldest of four, and they were a quite delightful clutch of eager, smart and responsive children, the eldest of whom I had taught the year before. As with my previous two classes, this mixture of eights and nines was also a blend of locals and off-comers – as outsiders were called by the old indigenous families – including the children of many farmers: sheep, dairy and beef cattle still being at the core of the local economy.

I parked the car outside the front door and looked at the 1970s school buildings: they were incongruous amid the old stone houses and farms either side but somehow it didn't matter because the rising green fells all around presented such a beautiful panorama that one's eyes were quickly drawn away towards the crags, the ribbonwork of dry stone walls and the sweep of distant hills up the valley.

The door was blocked by the considerable bulk of Pat Rudds, the caretaker, who was rubbing at the glass with a cloth.

'Morning, Pat, beautiful day.'

She stood up and rubbed her back. 'Now then, Andrew. Aye, it is a grand day; just a shame I've no time to enjoy it. It's only ten past eight and me ankles have started already.'

I smiled inwardly thinking that no school week had properly

begun until Pat Rudds had referenced her ankles. Inside, the head-teacher's door swung open as I passed and Joyce Berry emerged in her silk paisley scarf, flicking through a pile of papers and back-heeling the door shut. She looked up and gave me a characteristic smile.

'Good weekend, Andy?' As always, she stood close. 'Staff meeting in two minutes,' she added before I had time to reply.

'Yes,' I said, watching her disappear. I went straight to the staff-room where I knew I would find Val Croker, the deputy head, and Hilda Percival, the Class 2 teacher, in a grump. They disliked these newly instigated early Monday morning meetings, short as they were, and made sure that everyone knew it.

Val, the Class 4 teacher, was already there, drumming her fingers on an armrest. She was in her fifties, squat with red hair and was the most no-nonsense person I had ever met. She grunted a kind of hello and then raised her eyebrows towards Hilda who fussed into the room, as always, muttering and shaking her head. She was the oldest member of staff by a distance; tiny, wrinkled, prickly and Cragthwaite's foremost wag.

'Well, I've only got a hundred and fifty-eight other things to do on a Monday morning, so I don't suppose it'll make much difference to sit here and find out some more,' she grumbled without saying hello.

'What's wrong with the bloody staff meetings we have after school on Wednesdays, I want to know?' added Val. 'I'm in a bad enough mood at this time on a Monday anyway.'

Joyce breezed in at that moment and we all wondered if she'd caught the end of Val's moan, although Val's stony face suggested that she didn't care and Joyce wasn't giving anything away, being quite aware of the senior teachers' feelings. The contrast in their personalities often made for good entertainment and yet their professional relationship worked well, with the head's warmth and enthusiasm complementing Val's practical logic.

Joyce smiled, as always. 'Right, well, good morning, everyone. I see we haven't got Emma yet – has anyone seen her?'

Hilda glanced at her watch. 'She'll be just getting out of bed about now, I reckon.' But before anyone could reply, Emma Torrington rushed through the door and sat down with apologies and a sigh. In her late twenties, Emma taught the youngest infants in Class 1 and was not the school's most organised individual, seemingly transported from the psychedelic urban sixties to the bluff Yorkshire eighties.

Joyce gave her a moment to settle and then quickly moved into full flow. 'OK, lots of things to tell you about this morning. First, Andy has a new girl starting today called Sheena, so everyone keep an eye out for her, please, and make sure she feels welcome.'

'Where's the family come from?' asked Hilda, always keen to know what was going on.

'Hauxton. Single mother with a few problems as far as I can gather. They've moved into one of the council houses in the village.' We all wondered what had brought them to rural Swinnerdale, but Joyce pressed on. 'We have lots of things coming up this term so make sure you've all got them in your diaries. The Inter-school Road Safety Quiz is being held here on the eighteenth of November and there's an HMI visiting in early December – no date yet.'

Val looked up. 'An inspection?'

'Not a full one, just a morning visit by one HMI to check up on reading.'

'But I guess you'll want the school looking nice,' said Emma.

'That would be very good,' said Joyce.

I didn't like the sound of inspectors at all. 'Do they check up on our teaching, then?'

'Only the newest members of staff,' added Hilda, wickedly.

Joyce ignored her. 'Not this time, so nothing to worry about, but it goes without saying that I'd like everyone on best behaviour.' I watched Emma scribble 'HMI' in huge red letters in her diary. 'Also, don't forget, everyone, the new vicar starts with assemblies on Wednesday mornings later this term and he'll be dropping by to say hello. He's only young so let's not scare him, please.' Joyce looked down but I couldn't help a sideways glance at Val, who maintained a steady half-scowl.

A minute later, Joyce seemed to have reached the end of her list and Hilda made to get up but the head put a long-fingernailed hand up. 'I'm afraid there's just one more thing.' We all suppressed a groan. 'It's a new school year and I really would like the school tidied up a little. I didn't want to ask you to do it in the holidays or during the first week but now I would really appreciate a bit of help to spruce the place up – it is a mess in places.'

'But surely that's why we have Pat?' said Val, making no attempt to mask her disgruntlement. 'She may moan for England but she's a good enough caretaker and cleaner. We have enough to do without becoming janitors 'n' all.'

'I know, I know, you're quite right, Val, and Pat will be doing most of it, I've given her a list, but I'd rather we tackled the areas containing resources, just in case things get lost.'

'Like tempers, perhaps,' whispered Hilda audibly.

'Andy, will you do the PE equipment in the hall, please? Val, the cloakrooms and corridors, Emma and Hilda, the stock cupboard, and I'll do the shed – there's lots of junk in there I want to throw out.' We all sensed another skip was on the way. In her eighteen months at the school, Joyce had established a reputation as being somewhat overenthusiastic about clearing out.

'What about Sue?' asked Emma, referring to the classroom assistant who worked in Class 1 and was often referred to as The Wondrous Mrs Bramley because she did countless useful things in the school without being asked.

'Oh, it's all right, she can do everywhere else,' said Joyce, now ushering us to our classrooms as the clock registered quarter to nine. On the way outside I chuckled at the thought of the poor children in Class 4 having to face Miss Croker this morning. Personally, I found the meetings really helpful, not having the best memory in the world, and I could only admire Joyce's refusal to be discouraged by Val and Hilda's grouchiness. She would win them round eventually.

My mobile classroom was empty, all the children having chosen to play outside in the sunshine, and there was no sign of the new girl. Within five minutes the ancient handbell rang and Class 3 filed in, some smiling, some panting, some worrying and some slouching. I had already learnt their names and knew who lived in Cragthwaite and who was bussed in from outside, who was a local and who wasn't, but I needed to find out what they knew, what they could do and, more importantly, what they couldn't. I felt after two years in the classroom that I was now on top of the job. After the calamities of my first probationary year, I had become a real teacher: I was in control, managing behaviour well, keeping all of the children learning across all subjects and providing inspirational activities.

The first lesson after the register and assembly was Maths and I'd planned it carefully. The topic was 'weight' and the children had to find five objects in the room, estimate their weight in grams and then check it using scales. As I had been taught at college, I organised the activity at three different levels to cater for the varying abilities of the class. I had the bottom group working with objects under 100 grams and using a simple balance with metal weights. The middle children worked up to 500 grams and used kitchen scales, while the brightest group worked with items over 1 kilogram and had to use two different sets of scales.

After what I felt was a clear, comprehensive explanation of the task, I set the groups off, confident that each child would know what to do and get on with it. Within a few minutes twenty-two children were busy gathering objects, holding them and making estimates, writing down measurements, reading scales and handling weights. I toured the room helping those who were struggling, checking on learning and encouraging accuracy and neat writing. The children work diligently and quietly, despite the amount of moving around.

I was reflecting on what an excellent Class 3 this was going to be when the door opened and the school's mouse-like secretary, Eileen Marsett, walked in, followed by a large girl of about nine.

'Ah, this must be Sheena,' I said walking over to greet her.

'That's right,' said Eileen. 'She's just moved to the village with her mum who says sorry they're late this morning.' Every child in the room stared across at their new classmate.

'That's fine, no problem, thank you, Mrs Marsett,' I said.

Eileen left and I smiled at Sheena, who doggedly kept her eyes down and held a flat expression. She certainly was a hefty girl, bigger than most of the boys even, and possessing of a wild spray of dark hair that looked like it hadn't been washed for many moons.

I asked the class to stop work. 'Now, this is Sheena, everyone, and she's joining our class from today. I want everyone to be extra welcoming to her – she doesn't know any of you and it's difficult coming into a new school like this.'

A small, doe-eyed girl put her hand up. It was Hazel. 'She's moved in nex' door to us at 'ome, Mr Seed. She can join our group in Maths.'

I nodded. 'Well done, Hazel, that's really kind. Now, everyone, carry on with your work.'

I put Sheena in the middle group and called over the mature and reliable Nina from the top group to show her what to do while I found her a pencil and a worksheet. She sat down, maintaining her stony face and saying nothing. Perhaps she's nervous, I thought to myself.

The door opened again and Eileen returned, sidling up to me with a furrowed brow, holding a green dinner register. 'I'm so sorry to disturb you again, Andy, but the dinner money doesn't add up: we're 60p over. Can we just go through your register?'

'Er, yes, of course.' Collecting each child's dinner money on

Mondays was not my favourite task but, knowing how important it was for Eileen to balance the books, I went over to my desk with the school's long-suffering secretary.

'Oh dear,' she said, apologising as always. 'I know it's a burden during lessons.'

'No, it's fine,' I lied.

After carefully checking each child's lunch arrangements in the register we discovered that I'd put down Bernadette for one dinner too few and Eileen smiled.

'Oh, while I'm here,' she said in a whisper, 'can I tell you about Sheena?' She nodded towards the door suggesting the need for confidentiality and we stepped outside for a moment. 'I've put her down for free dinners but I just wanted to tell you that her mother is, well, a bit worried about her settling.'

'Did she say why?'

'Not really, she's a strange woman . . . I did try to ask but she was in a real hurry to get away to work.'

'Right, er, where does her mum work?'

'At least she told me that: at the pub in Chapelgarth – she's a cleaner, just doing mornings. Her sister-in-law works there, according to Hazel's mum.' We discussed whether that might be the reason that they moved to Swinnerdale and I was just about to ask if Eileen had found out anything about Sheena's father when I noticed a rising level of noise from inside and knew that I couldn't leave the class unattended any longer.

Stepping back into the classroom I was struck by a cacophony. There were children shouting and pointing, and almost all of them were on their feet.

'RIGHT, EVERYONE SIT DOWN!' My bellow did the trick and calm returned. As I looked around the room, I noticed something very strange.

'Alvin, why are you in your vest?'

The anxious boy immediately blushed. 'She made me take my jumper off.' He pointed to Sheena, who responded quickly.

'I wanted to weigh it.' It was the first time she had spoken. I was just about to condemn this action when her victim put up a shaky hand.

'Yes, Alvin?'

'She wanted me to take off my trousers, too.'

I was momentarily dumbfounded. 'Sheena, you simply can't do things like that.' She was tight-lipped and I sensed a defiance that I'd never previously come across in a nine-year-old. I looked around. 'So what was all the other noise about?'

Nina raised a hand. 'She, er, Sheena took all the weights so nobody could weigh anything else using a balance.'

I scanned the new girl's face to see if this was true. 'I needed them, di'n't I?' she said, dismissively. 'I were weighin' the record player.'

'That's not very sensible, Sheena. What if it had fallen off?'

'It did,' said Bernadette.

I checked the floor and saw the evidence: a trail of broken pieces of plastic and wood. Before I could speak, Sheena shrugged: 'It were a rubbish old one anyway.'

I decided to deal with the situation later as no one was getting any work done, but the remainder of the lesson fell into disarray. Three children came over to me and asked if they could move to a different group from Sheena because she was annoying them, then Bernadette told me that the new girl had scrunched up her worksheet and thrown it in the bin. When I went to check, I found Sheena arguing with two boys over some scales. Just as I approached she shouted at them to get lost, then stomped off to the book corner. Once again, the whole class stopped work to stare.

Mercifully the bell rang for playtime and I let everyone out right away, except for Sheena. It was only half past ten and I felt worn out already.

I tried the quiet approach, sitting down next to her in the book corner. 'Now, what's the matter, Sheena? You seem very upset.'

At first she just looked down, shook her head and mumbled incoherently.

I tried again. 'Is there something you want to tell me?'

'It's a schhpmn schuur.'

'Pardon?'

'This is a stupid school.'

'I don't think it is, Sheena.'

'I do.'

I tried a few more openings to get her to talk but she didn't want to say anything so I let her go outside with a gentle warning to try and stay out of trouble. Perhaps some fresh air and a run around would do her good.

I hurried to the staffroom for a cup of tea and wondered whether to tell Val about my new pupil before deciding to go outside just to make sure Sheena had settled down. In the playground there was a mob of children thronging around Emma, who looked quite flustered. When the bell rang, I discovered what I feared: Sheena was at the centre of things.

Bernadette rushed to tell me, 'She pushed two children, broke a hoop and threw a Sylvanian family on to the roof.'

'What, a whole one?'

'Yes, even the baby.'

I was wondering if I could get the toys down when Bernadette continued, 'They belonged to a girl in Class Two who wouldn't let Sheena play.'

'Perhaps she should have let Sheena play,' I said, knowing full well that this was completely unreasonable.

'Sheena said they were babyish and used a rude word.'

'How rude? No – don't repeat it!' Her lips had formed a 'tw' sound and I vainly hoped it was 'twerp', although I was reliably informed by Nina later that it rhymed with 'cat'.

I really wasn't looking forward to English, which was next after break, but I managed to get through the lesson by sitting next to Sheena and giving her one-to-one help. She needed it, too: her reading and writing were desperately poor.

At lunchtime I sought out Val, who knew the answer to most primary school dilemmas. She'd evidently heard from her class all about my new addition.

'So, you've got trouble, have you? Well, now's when you earn your corn – just make sure she's sorted out before she reaches my class.'

'But she won't listen to me. She's aggressive, loud, rude, a bully, argumentative and just, well, totally disruptive.'

'So what have you tried?'

'Being nice to her: that didn't work. Shouting at her just makes her sulk and become totally uncooperative, and she needs loads of help with her work. None of the other kids are getting a look-in.'

'Hmmm, one of those . . . Has Joyce looked at her file? I wonder what her last school has to say.'

I went to find out and Joyce told me that she did have 'behaviour issues' but nothing that sounded too bad. I was just about to ask whether she knew anything about Sheena's home background when there was a thumping boom and the door flew open. A vast, red-faced figure filled the frame: Mrs Hyde, the school's redoubtable dinner lady.

Joyce exhaled. 'Please, Mrs Hyde, you really should wait when you kno—'

'I aren't waitin' this time because I've 'ad enough! That new lass is refusing to return her tray. And she's really upset Mrs Harker in t'kitchen – she said her Spam fritters taste like puke.'

Joyce went off to lecture Sheena, who gave no response at all, and I wondered how I would get through PE in the afternoon. She didn't have a PE kit and refused to wear a borrowed one from lost property. Bending the rules, I said she could join in without one but she preferred to sit at the side of the room, trying to trip children up as they ran past. Towards the end of the lesson I saw her surreptitiously write with biro on the bench where she sat. It said: *I ate this shcool.*

She didn't write a word in RE, which followed, and spoiled the story at the end of the day by whispering and shuffling continuously. In a few hours I had told her off more than my previous class in an entire term. I went home despondent and so did the rest of Class 3.

As I drove up the side of the long village green in Applesett, my heart was lifted by the sight of a car outside our house, the unfortunately named Craven Bottoms. It belonged to two friends, Pete and Natalie, who were staying with us for a couple of nights, on their way from Nottingham to Scotland. With my mind whirring over what to do with Sheena, I'd quite forgotten that they were coming to stay with us.

I put my key in the lock and saw a small shuffling shape through the clouded glass, accompanied by a sound I loved to hear.

'Dada, Dada.' I picked up our crawling son Tom and planted a kiss on his soft round cheek. He rewarded me with a lovely smile.

'How is my gorgeous boy? Have you learnt to walk yet, crawler?'

Barbara appeared from the kitchen. 'Not yet but he's not far off – keeps standing up and thinking about taking a step.' She gave us both a hug.

I smoothed my hand over her tummy. 'How's the next one?' It had only been a week since we'd discovered that Barbara was expecting our second child.

'I actually feel quite good. Anyway, how was your day?'

'Don't ask.'

'What happened?'

'I'll tell you later,' I said, grimacing. 'Where are Pete and Natalie?'

'In the living room looking at photos. It wasn't anything serious was it?'

I shook my head. 'No, just a new girl who's a bit difficult, that's all.'

She smiled. 'Oh, you'll soon have her sorted out – go and sit down with Pete and Nat while I get Tom a drink.'

Pete and Natalie were friends from university, both possessing a naughty sense of humour, and their presence was just what was needed to lift my spirits. They'd evidently been given a tour of the village by Barbara.

'Andy this place is amazing,' said Natalie. 'You never told us it was this beautiful.'

'It's not bad, is it?' I said, grinning.

'Not bad?' laughed Pete. 'It's got a waterfall! I wanted to spend all day there building dams. Used to love that stuff as a kid.'

'Yeah, I can't wait until Tom's a bit older and can paddle through the beck.'

'The beck?' said Natalie. 'Is that the stream?'

'Oh, yeah, sorry – I'm turning Yorkshire!' It was true that since moving from Cheshire my vocabulary was gradually changing.

'Pub looks good, too. How's the darts going?' said Pete.

'Well, I'm getting better but still feel a bit strange being with all those giant builders and farmers.'

Natalie then said she'd like to climb the looming hill behind the village, Spout Fell, before they left us. 'The view must be amazing.'

'It is but it's eighteen hundred feet high and takes a good hour to get to the top. And I'll be jealous because I have to work tomorrow.'

Pete looked sheepish. 'Yeah, sorry we couldn't come Saturday and Sunday but that's the way it is with the candle shop: got to be open all weekend or we'll be broke.'

'Ha! We're broke anyway,' said Nat.

Barbara came in with Tom who immediately dived towards my lap. 'Oh, I haven't told you that we can go to the pub quiz in Skirbridge tonight – Iris said she's happy to babysit.'

We spent a few minutes telling Pete and Natalie about our wealthy neighbours across the green, Iris and Don Falconer, before sitting down for a huge bowl of spaghetti Bolognese. They laughed at the various village characters we described including ninety-two-year-old Sam Burnsall, who drove around at night with no lights on, motormouth Mrs Dent at the shop and the cheeky rogue John Weatherall, our local builder.

'Did he do your kitchen, then?' said Pete.

'Yes, although, you "helped" didn't you, dear?' said Barbara looking at me.

We retold the story of finding and renovating the house, explaining how we could only afford it because it was such an ugly duckling of a place among the solid stone cottages that ringed the village's great sloping green.

'Aw, it's not ugly, exactly,' said Natalie. 'It has character, that's all.'

I looked at my watch. 'Hey, we better get ready for the quiz. I'll drive then you two can have a drink.'

With Tom settled off to sleep and our maternal friend Iris installed, we headed off to the Skirbridge Force Hotel. It was a large comfortable pub next to the old bridge across the River Swinner where it dropped over a series of wide stepped cataracts before meandering into the lower part of the valley. Pete handed me a pint of dark Twissham Bitter.

'Hang on, I'm driving,' I said, only half-protesting.

'You can have one, surely?'

'I suppose so, and it is fabulous beer.' I took a long gulp, eager to forget the day that had gone before. It was even better than I'd remembered. At that moment there was raucous laughter from the bar and one of the men snorted in delight at his friends' reaction to the joke he'd just told.

I sat down with the others and Barbara noticed that I'd already drained half my glass.

'I've just had an idea,' she said, looking pleased. 'Why don't we leave the car and walk back tonight and then you can have a drink. You look like you need one.'

'Well, we could do but . . . well, it's three miles and I've got to work tomorrow,' I said, hoping fervently that everyone would dismiss my objection.

'That's a really good idea,' said Pete. 'The beer here is sensational, and I can drive you back in the morning to pick up your car on the way to school.'

Natalie knitted her brow. 'Hang on, mister. Don't forget Barbara's expecting and those three miles looked quite hilly to me.'

'Oh, I'll be fine,' said Barbara. 'It was my idea, after all, and I'm only a few weeks pregnant – it's not like I'm carrying a big pudding yet!'

'Well, if you're sure,' said Natalie.

Barbara nodded. 'It's a shame I can't drive since I'm not drinking anyway.'

We all agreed that Barbara needed to learn soon, then Natalie looked over to me.

'How's the job going anyway, Andy? Barb says you've got a new starter in your class.'

'She's a nightmare.' I really didn't want to talk about Sheena but I knew that Natalie was thinking about going into teaching and wanted to find out what it was really like.

'I thought you'd sussed this teaching lark; on the phone you said what a brill job it is and how you'd got the kids doing some great work last year.'

'I thought I had sussed it but I'm beginning to think I haven't got a clue. I just don't know what I'm going to do with this girl tomorrow.'

Barbara put an arm around me. 'Don't worry – it's only the second week of term – and you've had tricky kids before and brought them round.'

I was just about to say that this one was different when a short, burly man stood up and shouted, 'Welcome t'the Skirbridge Force 'otel Quiz!' His Yorkshire accent was as thick as treacle.

I looked around and noticed that there were just two other teams sitting round tables, clutching pens and gathering their answer sheets. One of them, judging by their familiarity with the landlord, was made up of locals, while the other seemed to be a group of tourists. There was also a gregarious couple, sitting on stools at the bar who were clearly taking part. We organised ourselves and waited for the first question.

The landlord and quizmaster, referred to as Gun by the locals for some reason, cleared his throat, 'Number One: how many moons does Saturn have?'

My teammates all turned towards me. 'Well?' said Barbara.

'I'm not sure. We don't study space in my class and I've never really been into astronomy.'

'You mean you don't know,' said Pete, looking faintly disgusted. 'I thought you were a teacher.'

'I think it might be two,' I said, trying to sound as if I had some idea.

'Isn't it Mars that has two?' said Natalie.

I nodded sagely, 'Er, yes, I think you're right.'

'Maybe it hasn't got any,' said Pete. 'Could be a trick question.'

'Shall we put one?' said Barbara. Before anyone could reply, the second question was on its way.

'What was Pucky Knee's last opera?'

'Eh?' called out Pete, a little too loudly.

One of the tourists lifted a hand. 'Could you please repeat the question?'

'What was, erm, Pukey Nigh's last opera?'

'You mean Puccini, Gun.' It was a bald fellow from the locals' team, who winked towards us as he said it.

Natalie's shoulders were bobbing. 'I've got all Pukey Nigh's albums.'

'Shhh, he'll hear you,' said Barbara, stifling one of her snorts.

'Was it *Madam Butterfly*?' said Pete, who seemed oblivious.

'What about *Don Giovanni*?' I added.

'That was Mozart.'

'I think it was *Turandot*,' said Barbara, composing herself.

Pete nodded enthusiastically. 'That's it.' He wrote the answer before anyone could disagree.

After ten questions, featuring only minor mangling of the English language, we were told to swap papers with another team for marking. The cheery, bald local came over and introduced himself as Ray.

'Enjoying the quiz? We only come for the entertainment of Gun's elocution.'

The landlord cleared his throat again. 'Reet, answers.' He looked like he was going to enjoy this bit. 'Question One: Saturn 'as fourteen moons.'

'Not very close with one then,' grumbled Pete.

One of the tourists' team, a smartly dressed woman, half-stood up and said, 'Actually, the answer's seventeen. Three more were discovered by the Voyager probe a few years ago. Your source must be out of date.'

'I've always said the sauce in this place was out of date,' quipped Ray.

Gun refused to be flustered. 'Sorry, love, but the rule in this pub is that the answer on t'card is correct. Question Two . . .' The woman sat down with pursed lips. I glanced across to see Ray smiling and shaking his head. It was obviously a familiar scenario.

After Round One we had scored seven, which put us in equal first place. Pete was excited and sprung up to get some more drinks. 'Do we know what the prize is?'

I noticed the joke teller at the bar drain his glass then slap Gun on the back and say goodnight before heading outside. Gun helped himself to a lager then continued with the questions: 'Which city replaced Colchester as the capital of Roman Britain?' We all agreed it was London and suddenly realised that we were really enjoying the evening. The second round passed quickly and once more we swapped our papers.

'You're doing a bit too well, you lot,' said Ray, smiling. I suspected that his team usually won.

'Right, answers: the capital of Roman Britain after Colchester was Londinium,' boomed Gun.

'Can we have London?' said Pete.

'No, Londinium only.' There was clearly no arguing with him, despite protests from all four teams.

'Huh, at least we all got it wrong,' said Pete. When our papers came back we were one point in the lead.

Round Three began. 'Which UK business first used the term "the customer is always right"?'

Quick as a flash Ray quipped, 'Well it certainly wasn't the Skirbridge Force Hotel.'

We guffawed loudly and then spluttered into our drinks as Gun went on a wild spree of mispronunciation.

'Which Greek goddess fell in love with the youth leader?'

'What?' said Natalie, her mouth open. He repeated the first part then stopped.

'I mean fell in love with the youth *Leander*.'

We had only just recovered when he asked about the Green Witch Observatory, closely followed by a question about the perfume 'Channel Number Five'.

The tide of our giggling was matched by a torrent of grouches from the tourists, who had fallen out of contention. We were now four points ahead of Ray's team with one round to go. Pete was bouncing and turned towards Gun, who looked down at his papers.

'Right, to finish we're 'aving thirty questions on James Bond.'

'What? Thirty!' I said, a little too loudly, causing Barbara to elbow me in the ribs.

Gun ignored my remark but Ray leant over, 'That's nothing – we once had fifty questions about dogs on TV.'

Pete looked at each of us. 'Right, come on, who can do James Bond? Someone must be a fan.' Each of us shook our heads.

'I've seen most of them,' I said, 'but I just get them all mixed up.'

'That's because they're all basically one film,' said Natalie. 'And a bit of a rubbish one at that.' We muddled through and managed twelve correct answers. The locals scored an amazing twenty-eight.

'Sorry, chaps,' said Ray. 'It's my speciality – 007.' We congratulated them, Pete grudgingly, and watched Gun throw them five pounds' worth of drinks vouchers. It had been an excellent night out. I looked at my watch: it was ten past eleven.

'Come on, we'd better get going,' I said, getting up. 'It's going to take us an hour to walk back and I have to be up early for work.'

'Never mind that, what about poor Iris?' said Barbara.

We turned off the main road and headed down towards Applesett. There were no pavements here, nor street lights, and we were shrouded in the thick blackness of a country night.

'I can't believe how dark it is,' said Pete. 'We could be anywhere.'

'There's only one road so it must be right,' I said.

Barbara was just in front of me. 'But we do need to watch out for cars. None of us thought to bring a torch.'

We plodded on, our progress slow, and each of us now feeling the cold. As we walked my thoughts turned to Sheena. What on earth was I going to do with her? I cast my mind back to the things that Eileen had said earlier in the day. The poor girl's home situation was in all likelihood difficult and her mother was obviously worried about her. But what approach should I take?

As my mind wrestled with the problem two lights appeared in the distance heading our way. I warned everyone and we watched two intense beams trace out the contours of the road as a car rounded bends and crested hills. We heard the engine and tucked ourselves against the dry-stone wall on the other side of the lane before being blinded by the headlamps. The small saloon passed us travelling quickly then stopped a little further on. It was a police car.

An officer climbed out and walked towards what he evidently considered to be a very suspicious rabble of four motley characters out late at night wearing dark clothes. He pointed a powerful flashlight towards us.

'Could you explain what you're up to please?' I recognised the voice immediately. It was the man who I'd seen in the pub just a couple of hours earlier. I'd noticed him downing a few beers, too.

'We're just, er, walking home,' said Barbara, wisely acting as spokesperson since she hadn't had anything to drink.

'Yer what?'

'Walking home. We live in Applesett.'

'Oh, er, I see. Where have you been? Nobody really walks round here.'

'The pub in Skirbridge for the quiz.'

'Right . . . and you walked there all the way from Applesett?' I could see him eyeing me with a hint of recognition. Barbara explained about the car and the policeman listened open-mouthed. I wondered how much he'd had to drink himself.

'Well come on, then,' he said. 'It's cold out here and I'm not having you run over. Hop in and I'll give you a lift back.' We smiled at our fortune as we climbed into the Escort, although I couldn't help praying that no one would be out in Applesett to see us arrive home in a panda car.

Chapter Two

Chris

'Do you need anything from the shop?' called Barbara from the living room. 'I'm just nipping out to get some cheese.'

I wandered out of the kitchen clutching a much-needed cup of tea after a wearying day at school. 'Can't think of anything, but why don't you ask Mrs Dent about driving instructors?'

'I already have: I passed her on the green this morning while I was taking Tom out. She said there isn't anyone local.'

'So what do people do round here?'

'She says they all learn driving tractors or messing around in an old banger in someone's field. They'd never dream of paying for lessons.'

That certainly sounded like the Dales to me. 'Looks like we'll have to try one of those two in Ingleburn.'

'Why don't you ask Val? She lives there, doesn't she?'

The deputy head at my school was an amazing fount of local knowledge, it was true. She'd been at Cragthwaite Primary for twenty years after moving into the area from the North East. I made a mental note to speak to her and wondered how much extra it would cost for the instructor to make the fifteen-mile return journey here to Applesett. Barbara popped her head back in through the doorway.

'Oh, forgot to tell you that Mrs Dent also hilariously asked why I needed to learn to drive when I could just dial 999 and get a lift.'

I groaned, recalling how the curtains had twitched four weeks earlier when we'd arrived back at home in the police car after the pub quiz, and how the shocked face of our babysitting friend Iris had appeared at the window. Iris was a lovely person but villages were villages and by the next morning Mrs Dent at the general store had circulated the news that we'd been rounded up late at night by the law on a drunken rampage through the countryside. Well, it made us more interesting to the locals, I told myself at the time.

Two days later I was standing in the minuscule front garden of Craven Bottoms holding Tom. He was now able to walk and was desperate to get down and waddle on the soft grass. It was late on a cool October afternoon and we were waiting for Barbara to return from her first driving lesson. I was really glad that she had finally decided to learn: it was essential in a rural place like this.

I surveyed Applesett with its tapering green set on a great long slope between two small valleys. The grass was circled by grey-brown stone houses, each one solid and uncomplicated, roofed in thick slabs. The tiny Victorian school with its steeply pitched slates stood proud, as did the noble little chapel opposite. Then there was the whitewashed pub in the heart of the village, the shop a few doors down and a scatter of barns, tractors and blue Land Rovers and red pickups. A fat pony chained to a stake chomped away near the top of the green, making a curious pale circle in the grass. And framing everything were the hills, from the hazy far slopes of Swinnerdale, the main valley, to the great squat bulk of Spout Fell behind us, rising up like a rock custodian.

I put my wriggling son down on the lawn and stepped back a few paces, holding out my arms.

'Come on, Tom, walk to Daddy.'

He smiled with a gurgle then took a teetering step forward, falling over in the process.

'Oops!' he chirruped, before pushing himself back up and wobbling forward, his hands stretching towards me. He stumbled forward the last two paces, quickening to reach me, and fell into my arms with a dribbly chuckle.

'Clever boy!' I gave him a tight squeeze and a kiss and wished I could explain how much I loved him. Having children was just inexpressibly wonderful.

'Aye up, is this young gentleman walkin'? I saw that, I did.' I recognised the voice right away – it was Billy Iveson, a retired farmer who lived a few doors down from us. He passed this way every single day, taking his old collie for a walk up Buttergill, the tranquil cul-de-sac dale that ran behind the village.

'He certainly is, Billy. Isn't he clever?'

'He is that – I've not seen such canny walkin' for nigh on ages.'

'Bihyee,' said Tom, waving. The old man took off his flat cap and waved it, breaking out into a broad toothless grin.

'Would yer like some field mushrooms, you lads?' he asked. 'I'm off ter do a bit o' gatherin'.' I nodded enthusiastically, remembering how tasty the last bag was, just as a brown Austin Allegro crawled up the road towards the house.

Billy signalled a goodbye and Tom gave a babble of excitement as Barbara climbed out of the small ugly car. I went to make her a coffee and asked how it went.

'Well, I don't think I'm a natural, let's put it that way,' she said. 'It could take quite a few lessons.'

I tried not to sound too perturbed. 'That's a shame cos at seven pounds a time we're struggling.'

'I know but it was harder than I expected. All that stupid clutch stuff . . .'

'Oh, you'll soon pick it up, and then perhaps I can take you out in the Alfa.'

'Hmmm, we've only been married three years – let's not think about ending it so soon.'

I decided not to push the idea. 'Er, what's Mr Potts like as an instructor, then?'

'Well, for a start he has a handlebar moustache. Secondly, he insisted on giving me his life story as we went round and, thirdly, he wears sandals with socks.'

'So I don't need to worry about you driving off together somewhere exotic?'

'Not in a brown Allegro, no.'

Chris Lund walked across the classroom slowly. He was eight years old, a pale boy who was always blinking, and I'd asked him to come and read to me at my desk. He looked fidgety.

'Don't tell me, Chris, you've forgotten your reading book.'

'Sorry, Mr Seed.'

I wasn't surprised. Chris Lund never remembered his reading book. In fact, Chris Lund never remembered anything. His coat was frequently left on the field at playtimes, his PE kit stayed at home and important letters to his parents would be found in the cloakroom, abandoned, like so many of his belongings.

His mother despaired of him. I'd got to know her quite well in the first five weeks of the autumn term, since she appeared in the classroom most days with items that Chris had left behind. I recalled her shaking her head that morning after she'd handed him his bag, along with a bundle of written reminders.

'He's in a world of his own, that lad. Why can't he be like his big sister? I never had no trouble wi' her.'

'I'll see what we can do to improve things, Mrs Lund.'

But, despite his absentmindedness, it was hard not to like Chris: he was quiet and good-natured. His work was generally good, too, although the content was often different from everybody else's because he forgot what he was supposed to be doing.

The other staff's views were mixed, as I discovered at break.

'I think he's a lovely little boy,' said Emma, who was wearing something like a floral kaftan. 'Yes, he's forgetful but he was never any bother in my room as an infant – he used to play so nicely with everyone.'

Hilda, the staffroom's senior matron, shook her head. 'Well, he doesn't pickle my sandwich. You just said he played nicely – well, just try getting him to learn some spellings or remember a rule.'

'Well, he still smiles when he sees me; I think he's sweet.'

I was about to add my piece when Val walked in and asked if

anyone wanted a cup of tea. She made her own with two teabags and sat down next to me.

'How's Sheena this morning, then?'

'I don't know, actually – she's been in Joyce's office.'

'What, all morning?'

'Yes, she's sitting with her for English on Wednesdays so I can get something done with the rest of the class.' The peace had been blissful.

'Bloody hell . . . so things are still bad when she's in the class?'

I nodded. 'She doesn't concentrate on anything and just can't seem to stop herself from meddling with whoever's near her.'

'Is Joyce getting her mother in?'

'I think they've spoken on the phone once but she's quite elusive.'

'Doesn't surprise me . . . Oh, by the way, everyone, Joyce asked me to remind you all that some of those "tidying the school" jobs still haven't been done, ahem.'

My heart jumped. I'd completely forgotten the hall! Hilda looked a bit sheepish, too, so at least I wasn't alone.

After the home-time bell I went straight to the hall and got to work. It really was a mess – how could I have forgotten? After all, I'd seen Joyce empty out the shed, throwing away piles of old school-fair games and ancient garden tools. I'd even picked up a pair of wooden stepladders that she'd left for the bin men to take. There was nothing wrong with them so I'd squeezed them into the Alfasud and taken them home.

I decided to blame Sheena. The girl had thrown my job into turmoil in the last few weeks and I just couldn't seem to get anything else done. My life was a constant stream of dealing with the repercussions of her misdemeanours. It was only thanks to Joyce's kind offer that I had kept sane. Nothing I tried in the classroom seemed to make any difference.

I looked at the stack of cluttered PE equipment that had been dumped in the hall store area among chairs, benches and dining tables. Normally, I would have found such a task tedious but I was actually quite glad to do something simple and straightforward: bean bags didn't argue, hoops didn't sulk and sponge balls didn't start fights. But it *was* a huge mess.

I decided that the only way to tackle it was to empty the whole storage area. I drew back the curtains fully and started to lift out the crates and boxes of games apparatus. Next I pulled out all of the tables, leaving a trail of woolly dust. Finally, there were the tall stacks of chairs pushed against two walls. I wheeled them out using the chair barrow, including the old ones at the back that we never used. And that's when I saw it: a large, heavy, wire cage with a kind of hefty metal box inside. Heaving the last two stacks aside I moved in for a closer view. It was a kiln.

At home, Barbara was making good progress with her driving lessons and began to get quite excited at the prospect of being able to go shopping with Tom on a Saturday.

'Can't you cycle to work, darling, so I can have the car in the week?'

'Of course, I'll just need eight panniers for all the marking and planning documents. It'll be a doddle up those hills in the rain.'

'I wasn't serious. But I'll be able to drop you off when I need it.'

'Hmmm . . . Well, depends how good you are.' I gave her a cuddle. Tom tottered into the room sucking his thumb and twisting a finger through his wispy hair.

'What's with this hair-twiddling, Thomas?' I said.

But he wasn't listening. He'd heard the chug of a tractor outside and toddled at maximum pace to the big bay window where he pointed excitedly. 'Duh-duh, duh-duh!'

'You are duh-duh crazy, squidgy boy,' said Barbara, picking him up for a better view of the red Massey Ferguson as it throbbed past.

The following Sunday we were in Applesett chapel for the morning service. As usual we had taken a selection of small toys and board books in order to try and keep Tom amused while the preaching was taking place, but as the organ sounded for the first hymn he was distracted by something at the front of the pews. I picked him up and leant forward for a better view. There was a young family who had their hands full with four small children. The mother was holding a plump baby and sitting between her and her craggy husband were two bright-eyed girls in cotton dresses. But Tom was interested in the other child, a boy of about three who was playing on the carpet at their feet with a clutch of model tractors. It was unmistakably a Dales family, although I'd never seen them before.

'Dud-duh,' exclaimed Tom, drowned out by the warble of voices discharging a long Wesleyan verse. All through the hymn he kept up his pointing and looking across. Barbara held him for a while then put him down with his favourite book, which he prodded with disinterest. At the end of the song he was gone. I nudged

Barbara while a church elder read out the notices. She glanced around unable to see him. I leant forward and saw a small body waddling across the carpet in front of the communion rail. Several members of the congregation gave a quiet titter as Tom ignored the speaker in the pulpit and approached the small boy playing with the tractors.

The boy, ruddy-faced like the rest of his family and wearing a miniature woollen jacket, eyed up Tom for a moment, then pushed a tractor towards him. Tom sat down and picked it up, immediately blowing out his cheeks to make the requisite engine noise. Fortunately, the elder's booming voice drowned him out. The mother looked across to see the invader's origin. Barbara lifted a hand and the woman smiled back warmly to indicate that she would keep an eye on him.

I did sometimes find staying awake in these services a challenge. The speakers were varied, the church operating a circuit of part-time travelling preachers, but most were ancient and lacking the sparkle of communication needed to bring their message alive. But this time, the young father sitting next to Tom stood up and moved to the pulpit.

He introduced himself as Adam Metcalfe, and it was clear that most people in the chapel knew him quite well. He was rugged and handsome, with the glowing skin of an outdoor worker. He cracked a joke about his family growing again, which made the audience chuckle, then proceeded to talk around his theme: how a tree is known by its fruit. He explained that, being a hill farmer, the fruit he tried to produce were lambs and how a good strong lamb revealed a lot about the mother. I found him quietly compelling to listen to; he had a simple straight manner and spoke with a kind of modest wisdom that seemed genuine and borne from his own experience working with animals on the high fells.

After the service, we edged forward to pick up Tom and thank the Metcalfe family for child-minding so generously. Adam was standing by the front door shaking hands and chatting to the worshippers as they filed out. The mother introduced herself as Ruth and her children as Beth, Hannah, Robert and David, their plump baby.

'Do yer live in the village, then?' she asked.

'Yes, just next door,' I said. 'We've been here two years now.'

'It's a grand spot, is this.'

'Where's your farm, then?' said Barbara.

'Oh, it's right up Reddle, quite a way.'

'Where's Reddle?' I asked. I'd never heard of it.

'Oh sorry, I should have said Rawdale, that's the proper name, but we just call it Reddle. It's up past Kettleby, on the road to Wherton.'

'Oh right, that's a long way,' I said.

'It's about twenty miles or so,' said Ruth, who was distracted by a tug on her dress from Robert. He was concerned that Tom still had a hold of one of his tractors.

'Be kind and let him hold it a bit longer,' she said. 'You've still got all the others.'

I picked Tom up and held out my hand to see if he'd give me the toy.

'That's a John Deere, that is, young man.' It was Adam. 'You can come and see my real, *big* tractor if you like.'

'Ooh, he would love that!' said Barbara. Tom stared at the farmer's wind-hewn face.

Adam smiled, 'Aye, you can come and sit in the cab, little fella.' Tom just gawped with huge eyes and I took the opportunity to furtively wrest the toy tractor from his grasp. Everyone laughed.

We talked to the family for some time and Adam explained how his farm was the second highest in the northern dales with very poor land and that life was a constant battle to make a living. But he said it without even a hint of resentment or weariness; there was something immensely likeable about this man. Ruth herself was gentleness personified and both possessed in abundance that mix of old-fashioned graciousness and wry humour which we found so appealing in Swinnerdale's natives.

We exchanged phone numbers and said we'd call to fix up a visit to the farm. Ruth offered us lunch on the day and we headed back home feeling warm inside.

The following day, back at school, I went to see Val in Class 4.

'Why didn't anyone say there was a kiln in the hall?'

'Because it's never been used, that's why. I'd forgotten we had one.'

'Does it work?'

'I've no idea, The Beak wouldn't let us touch it.'

It was no surprise that Howard Raven, or The Beak as the previous head of the school was known, wouldn't have approved of such a thing.

'Well, there's only one way to find out,' I said. 'I'll ask Joyce if it's OK to give it a try.'

Val's mouth formed a grimace. 'Oh, you and you're flamin' creative activities. My class'll be moaning at me to do pottery now.'

I smiled, having learnt that scowling was her normal friendly mode. 'Sorry, Val.'

'Well, go on, push off and burn the school down with the kiln.'

'Er, actually, there's just one more thing.'

'What?'

'Have you got any clay?'

Joyce was typically enthusiastic about the kiln.

'Ooh, we could have displays of ceramic crafts! I bet that would go down well with the HMI. I'll order some glaze and clay tools. Do we have any clay?'

'Yes, Val gave me some. But we don't know if the kiln actually works yet.'

'Well, go and switch it on then.'

'Er, OK. Erm, isn't it a bit dangerous to have something that hot with the children around?'

'Don't leave it on, you noodle, just see if the switches and elements work,' she said, struggling to hide her vexation.

'Oh, right.'

'If we use it, it'll have to be put on overnight, then we'll get Pat to switch it off first thing when she arrives in the morning. It has that cage thing round it anyway – we'll be fine.'

I hurried off, blushing a little, but excited about trying some pottery with the class. Once the children had gone home I cleared a space around the kiln and switched it on. It came to life, giving off a strong whiff of cooked dust.

I drove to Ingleburn after school and called in at the library. That night I read *A Beginner's Guide to Pottery* from cover to cover. One of the projects was making a piggy bank, beginning with two simple hand-made pots joined together. I became quite excited about the idea.

The following morning the day started, as it often did, with a complaint about Sheena. It was from Chris.

'Mr Seed, she pushed me over into them rose bushes. Me arm's all scratched.'

'I'm sorry, Chris, I'll have a word with her.' I checked his wounds, which were fortunately superficial, then went in search of Sheena, calling her into my room.

'Sheena, don't you get fed up with being in trouble?'

She shrugged and stuck out a lip, 'It's not always ma fault.'

'Chris says you pushed him over.'

'He pushed me first.'

'Are you sure? That doesn't sound like him.'

'No one likes me 'ere.'

'Well, if you were kinder to people then maybe they would.' I stopped, suddenly realising that I'd had this exact conversation four times already. I shook my head and looked down. A blue folder on my desk gave me an idea. I recalled how Joyce had in the past suggested giving difficult children responsibility as a way of showing trust and building them up.

'I tell you what, Sheena. How would you like to do a special job for me? The dinner register here needs taking to Mrs Marsett in the office every day. I usually pick different people to do it but how would you like to be the person who does that every day?' She gave me a glance and made a small grunt.

'It's important and other children would like to do it. But I'm asking you. What do you think?'

She gave a half-shrug, 'OK.'

Well, it was something.

A few days later, I was sitting next to Sheena in the classroom, as usual, but with four of the small tables pushed together. Eight children, including Bernadette and Chris, were enthusiastically rolling small pieces of clay on wooden boards.

'Right, we're going to practise making different shapes. Let's start with rolling a ball.' I felt confident, having tried it out first at home, much to Barbara's amusement. The children all managed it well, Sheena included. Next we went on to small, pea-sized spheres, then flat discs, then sausage shapes, and finally cubes, tapping the clay against the boards to make flat sides. This they found much more challenging.

I noticed the rest of the class were chatting a little too freely, having been left to finish some collages from the previous week. I left the clay group and toured the room briefly, ensuring that everyone was working.

Two minutes had passed when Chris tapped me on the shoulder.

'Yud better come back, Mr Seed. Sheena's flickin' clay peas at everyone.'

He wasn't telling fibs. Sheena was conspicuously the only one at the table who had no clay peas left. Not only that but she'd discovered that, if wet, they would stick to the windows. She slumped low into her chair as I gave yet another reprimand. Before I could finish, the door opened and Joyce walked in looking stern.

I took Sheena's clay away and went over to the door to talk to the head.

She kept her voice low. 'This is the second day that things have been going missing from children's lunchboxes in the hall: chocolate bars and crisps.'

'Oh dear, I can guess the problem.'

'Mmm, I don't think the experiment with her taking the dinner register is working.'

'Are you sure it's her?'

'I found the evidence in her coat pockets just now.'

The fun of the clay session ebbed away. 'Right, what do you want to do?'

'I'll sort this out – you look busy.' She switched her voice to authoritative mode. 'Sheena, I'd like a word with you please in my office, now.'

The following day after school I took some of the small clay shapes the group had made, now dried hard, and put them in the kiln. I moved the chairs away from it, locked the heavy door and switched it on before going to find the caretaker Pat Rudds.

She wasn't happy, as usual. 'I don't want to 'ave owt to do with that big oven thing.'

'All you have to do is switch it off in the morning, Pat. It's easy.'

'Well, I'm sure that in't in ma job description.'

'Please.'

'Well, show me 'ow to do it, then.' She shuffled towards the hall, complaining about her ankles. My spirits were rising once more.

The following day I waited until school had finished before inspecting the clay shapes. The kiln was still slightly warm when

I pulled the big handle to open the door. To my complete amazement, inside were pieces of red-orange pottery where once had been soft, dusty clay. Only one shape was broken. They were hard and brittle. I scooped them up and hurried to show Val before stopping and rushing to show Joyce.

The following Saturday, I took Tom for a toddle to the waterfall at the bottom of the village while Barbara was out having another driving lesson. When we returned she was back at the house, greeting us chirpily.

'How are my favourite men doing?' Tom rushed to her for a hug.

'He had great fun throwing leaves into the water from the little bridge. How did your driving go?'

'It was good – I really feel I'm getting the hang of it now.'

'Great, where did you go?'

'Ooh, we went all the way to Hauxton. I didn't like the hills, though.' I wasn't surprised; it was one of the steepest towns in the country. 'In fact, Mr Potts nearly pooed himself when we were going down Castlegate. He said "brake" but I pressed the accelerator by mistake. Then he screamed, "No, the other brake!"'

We laughed and Tom joined in, which amused us even more.

'Pottsy says I do need to practise my reversing round corners, though, before I can start to think about a test.' She looked at me, knowing what I was going to say.

The next day we left Tom with Iris and headed out in our rusty Alfasud towards the village of Shawby where there was a small estate of new houses.

'It's the best place for reversing, I think – really quiet.'

Barbara didn't answer, she was still in a grump after we had argued over who should drive. I told her it was ridiculous that I should drive there since she was the one who needed the practice. She countered that she didn't know the car and that she didn't want to drive along the main road in Swinnerdale before she was used to it.

I gave in and drove but when we reached the road for Castle Heywood I turned off. This was the tiny village we'd lived in when we first moved to the Dales. We loved the place dearly and when the road crested next to the great, square, gaunt castle I stopped the car.

'Look, you know how quiet it is here – there's hardly any traffic ever. Why don't you drive the last bit to Shawby on the back road?'

'Well, I suppose I could but you'll have to promise to be *really* patient with me.'

'I promise. It's only about a mile and a half anyway.'

We swapped seats. 'It feels very different,' said Barbara. She looked in her mirrors, held the handbrake and pressed on the accelerator. The noisy, flat-four engine screamed. She gave a 'Whoops' and I forced myself to hold my tongue. The car crept forward and we were off, pootling along the village's rough-stone road.

'There,' I said. 'Easy-peasy.'

Barbara didn't reply. She gripped the steering wheel with white knuckles and stared ahead as if in a trance. We left the village at a full fourteen miles an hour and entered the narrow back lane to Shawby, bordered by tall trees. I prayed that nothing would come the other way. The road began to dip and I recalled that it followed a sharp bend, too, where it traversed one of the fast becks tumbling down the side of the valley.

Barbara slowed to five miles an hour. 'I don't like this, it's too steep,' she muttered through gritted teeth.

'It's fine; just keep your foot on the brake – the middle one, that is.'

I wondered what time sunset was as we crawled around the bend and began to climb the hill on the other side. The engine was making a lot of noise again.

'I think you're in first, Barb. You should be in second here.'

'I'm not changing gear. Just look at that drop there – I hate these kinds of roads even when someone else is driving.'

I had to admit that the road did fall away very steeply here in the deep cleft cut by the stream. 'Don't worry, just keep going and we'll soon be there.'

We heard the unmistakable noise before we saw it. A big, blue, Ford tractor pulling a heavy trailer of muck. It chugged around the bend towards us, taking up most of the road before stopping abruptly. Barbara gave a little shriek and slammed her foot on the brake. I was glad it was the right brake.

'Now what are we going to do? I can't reverse down here. I knew it was a stupid idea for me to drive!'

I tried to sound calm. 'Don't panic. It's OK, I'll help you manoeuvre.' I could hear her breathing quickly. 'Right . . . the tractor can't reverse up the hill with that trailer, so . . .' I looked at the driver, a young man with a baseball cap. He slowly rolled the big machine forward and to the edge of the road.

Barbara clasped the steering wheel even tighter. 'What's he doing?'

'He's edging forward so that you can pull in tight to the left against the bank. He obviously thinks he can pass us.'

'Well, he must be stupid: that thing's enormous.'

I didn't want to admit it, but it was a big duh-duh. 'Look, the road does widen a few yards ahead and he's a local who's probably done this lots of times, so it must be possible.'

'Yes for someone who isn't learning and driving a car for the first time ever!' The pitch of her voice was hurting my eardrums.

'All right, don't worry. All you've got to do is creep forward a few yards and keep to the left. At least we're away from the drop on this side.'

The last words seem to reassure her and she sounded a little calmer. 'Right, what do I do?'

I noticed her right foot was still rammed against the brake pedal. 'OK, it's a hill start – I'm sure you've been practising those with Mr Potts – you need to put the handbrake on hard then take your foot off the pedal.'

She gulped and gave the handbrake lever a yank. As she lifted her foot the car began to roll backwards.

'Aaarrrghhh!' she screeched. The tractor driver looked pleased and stole forward a few more yards. Barbara slammed her foot on the pedal again causing the car to jolt furiously. In the panic I'd forgotten that the Alfa's handbrake had never worked properly. I was just used to it.

'I'll do it,' I said, and gave it a mighty heave. Barbara was virtually crying. The tractor driver looked bemused.

'Try again,' I said, attempting to sound calm. The same thing happened.

'Stupid car!' she bellowed. 'It can't go forward and I can't go backwards.'

'What about if we change seats and I drive?' I said.

'Oh, that'll be easy, you demmick! The brake pedal will just stay down by itself, will it?'

I admitted it wasn't my best ever idea. 'Well, OK, we're going to have to go back but I'll steer. All you have to do is take your foot off the brake a bit.'

Barbara made another series of growly noises then agreed it was the only option. I took the wheel and, at the speed of a drowsy slug, began to crawl back down the hill. Another car came up behind us and Barbara let out a further wail but the driver saw what was happening and moved right back out of the way.

After what seemed like an age we reached the bridge at the bottom where the road widened, and we pulled in tight to the verge. The tractor roared past with the driver shaking his head and laughing. I waved the other car past. In silence we swapped places and I drove back to Applesett. I was going to protest that Barbara hadn't practised her corner reversing, but thought better of it.

Back at school I sat down with the clay group once more. As well as hefty Sheena and mousy Chris, there was the gangling, eager Bernadette, small and busy Hazel, and a pudgy, exuberant chatterbox by the name of Eddie.

The whole class had now taken turns to make basic shapes and the time had come to tackle the first proper project – the piggy banks. As before, I had taken a lump of clay home and had had a go at making one first, following the illustrated directions in the library book, and it had worked a treat; even Barbara was impressed with the finished porcine money box. I said I'd get it fired in the kiln and bring it back for Tom.

On this occasion, I had Sheena opposite me, so I could watch her carefully, and Chris next to me so I could regularly remind him what to do. The rest of the group was more than competent and each of them started shaping their two clay pinch pots enthusiastically. I had brought my own piggy bank in so they could see what they were aiming for.

'Do we 'ave to do a pig?' asked Sheena, who for once was concentrating well.

'Well, I suppose you could make another animal, as long as it has a round body,' I said.

'I'm gonna mek a tiger then. Or I might do a rat.'

'My uncle shoots rats,' said Bernadette.

'The horrid man,' said Eddie, crumpling his nose. I immediately regretted not saying no.

'Right, everyone stop please and put your pots down.' To my surprise they did, so I quickly demonstrated how to join the two pots together with wet clay to make a hollow body. I told them to carry on, then glanced at Chris who was busy patting one of his pots on a wooden board to make a flat edge for joining. He stopped then turned to me.

'I've forgotten what to do next.'

'You rub some water on the top edge, Chris, to make it wet and sticky.'

He did as instructed then stopped.

'I've forgotten what to do after that.'

'Do the same with the other pot.'

He did so quickly.

'I've for—'

'Push the two pots together gently and twist until they're joined.' I watched but didn't wait for him to speak. 'Then smooth across the joint with a wet finger.'

I looked around and the whole group had done an excellent job so I showed them how to make the legs and snout from a ball of clay rolled into a long sausage and cut into five. I was a bit wary of giving Sheena a knife, even if it was a plastic one.

'I don't know 'ow to do a tiger, so I think I'll do a pig,' she said.

I smiled. 'Good idea.'

Once the appendages were attached, the children began to get excited as their models started to look piggy-bank-shaped. I repeated the stages for Chris as the others waited impatiently.

Eddie was desperate to embellish his animal. 'Can I give mine shoes, Mr Seed? Or possibly a nice jacket?'

I gave him a suitable glare then showed the group how to make the tail and ears, and finally add marks for nostrils and eyes using a blunt pencil. When finished, they looked magnificent.

'Hey, I've made a pig!' said Chris. 'Oink, oink!'

I smiled – moments like this reminded me that they were still young children.

'But 'ow do we get the money in, Mr Seed?' he added.

'Whoops, I've forgotten the slot. This is quite tricky – someone pass me a knife.' They watched in silence as I carefully cut a narrow rectangular opening in the top of my demo pig.

'How do you get the money out?' asked Chris.

'Ahh, that's a good question,' I said. 'It can be done using a kitchen knife in the slot. You hold it upside down and the coins slide out. But it's not easy.'

'My mum says you 'ave to smash the pig,' said Hazel. There was general wailing from the group.

'I love my little piggy,' said Chris. 'No way am I gonna break it.'

'Course you don't have to break it,' I said, wishing I'd thought harder about the extraction of savings.

Chris looked up, 'Do we 'ave to put a slot in it, Mr Seed? I just want mine as a pig, not a money bank.' A couple of other children agreed.

'Well, I don't see why you can't do that. They are fantastic pigs.' A little cheer erupted from the group and the rest of the class leant over to admire their work. It was a triumph. Even Sheena was proud.

Three days later the models were dry and the children asked if they could be fired. I declared they were ready and, after school, cautiously carried them to the kiln, arranging each pig inside with great care. I couldn't wait to see them transformed into real pottery. I shut the door gently and switched on the power. The light turned red and the kiln hummed into life. As previously, I arranged the old chairs protectively around the kiln and went to ask Pat Rudds to switch it off in the morning.

Bernadette rushed up to me in the classroom the following morning and asked if the pigs were ready.

'Sorry, Bernadette, but I did explain yesterday that I won't know until late afternoon. The kiln's only just been switched off and it takes all day to cool down.'

'Awww,' she wailed, and dashed off.

The rest of the day was a typical one with Class 3: a battle of wits between me and twenty-three children, each determined to find new and inventive ways to spell words incorrectly, avoid punctuation, forget multiplication tables and confuse countries for continents.

I watched Sheena like a hawk as she continued her programme of disruption now the novelty of clay work was gone. I reminded myself continuously to give attention to the quiet, bright children as well as the noisy, demanding ones, and asked at least 459 times for someone to tidy away detritus.

Then, at 3.27 p.m., just a few moments before the bell for the end of school rang, a small miracle happened.

Chris came up to me and said, 'Will the pottery pigs be ready now, Mr Seed?'

It was the first thing he'd ever remembered.

I gave a grin as broad as a plate and, knowing that he lived in Cragthwaite and usually walked home alone, asked if he could wait behind a few minutes. He nodded, unsure whether to be excited or anxious.

Chris followed me to the hall and I explained that I was so pleased he'd remembered the piggy banks that he could have the special honour of being the first to see them. I moved the chairs back and felt the cage for heat: it was at room temperature. He waited expectantly, rolling on to tiptoes as I opened the thick door of the kiln.

'What's the matter, Mr Seed?' He saw my face drop.

I couldn't disguise it. Inside the kiln were hundreds of pieces of shattered terracotta. I lifted some of the shards to see if a whole pig had survived underneath but it was not to be.

'I'm really sorry, Chris,' I said, letting him peer inside. His face was surprisingly stoic. 'I don't know what happened. We'll make some more.'

Then I realised. Only some of the models had slots; the others were just hollow sealed orbs. The air inside must have expanded and caused them to explode. That was it – the book had actually warned that this must be avoided.

I looked at the silent boy, a fragment of dead pig in his hand. 'I should have told you to make a hole in it, Chris. I forgot.'

I thought about apologising again as the irony hit home but stopped, reassuring myself with the thought that by tomorrow he wouldn't remember a thing.

Chapter Three

Vanessa

October was drawing to an end and Swinnerdale became sheathed in mist and damp as the temperature dropped with autumn's fall. Each house chimney bordering Applesett's green vented a rising plume of grey wood smoke, pervading the village with the evocative smell of the season.

Mrs Dent in the village shop was quick to remind us that the village bonfire was a week on Saturday.

'Your little Tom'll love the fire but I'm not so sure about the fireworks.'

'We kept him inside last year when he was only a tiny tot but I think he'll enjoy being out this time with all the people on the green,' I said.

Barbara looked doubtful. 'Those fireworks are very loud.'

'Well, we should give it a try – we can always go in if he doesn't like it. I don't want to miss the food, though.'

'Oh, you've got to be there,' said Mrs Dent. 'Everyone in the village will be out, as usual.'

It was true: the dale's huge open spaces were in complete contrast to the closeness of the people. We found the village's sense of community immensely comforting.

Over the next few days we became reacquainted with most of the older children in Applesett: there were frequent knocks on the door accompanied by cheeky calls of 'Penny for the Guy!' The Guy, a degenerate figure flopping back in a rusty wheelbarrow, was kitted out in ancient farming clothes and stuffed with hay. The children were delighted with the handful of coins they were given and ran off, only to return a few hours later to ask if we had anything to go on the bonfire. I was tempted to give them the teetering stack of new curriculum documents that Joyce had suggested I take home for a little light reading but instead handed over the last few fragments of the old kitchen cupboards that we'd ripped out and which had been lying around outside.

As the week went on, a pile of wood began to grow in the centre of the green: the children spent hours touring the houses, farms and fields, frequently pulling huge logs and branches great distances to build the fire. This, we'd come to learn, was a proud tradition of Applesett's younger generations and was known as trailing.

Finally, the Saturday before the fifth of November arrived, bringing a clear sky and the first really cold day of the year. By five o'clock it was dark, but the dusk's normal tranquillity was replaced by great excitement as children rushed about and the fireworks were set in place at the bottom of the green. By the time Barbara, Tom and I were togged up in coats, hats and gloves, a huge inferno was roaring in the centre of the village, just two hundred yards from Craven Bottoms. Tom's big brown eyes were wide and he cooed at the scene, pulling to draw nearer in his little red wellies.

Thronging silhouettes of people stood around, warming themselves and catching up on news. As Mrs Dent had said, virtually the whole village was there – over a hundred and fifty people, a huge crowd for Swinnerdale, all standing on the rough grass on a biting winter's night, as had been done for centuries.

'Now then, you two. Hello, cheeky.' I turned round to see John Weatherall, the wiry local builder, complete with flat cap and hobnail boots. 'Byyy, it's bracing toneet. Make sure you get summat hot to eat – you especially, Andrew – I want you in tip-top condition for next week's match against Abbothwaite.' As always, he was talking darts.

'No worries, John, I'm famished.'

Barbara went off to talk to Iris, who was wrapped in a huge sheepskin coat, along with Don and their amicable son Stewart, while I looked around in search of a bite. Alec Lund, a tree trunk of a farmer and another member of the darts team at The Crown, was chewing something. He lifted a beer glass to his lips and drained it in a trice.

'I'll 'ave a pint if yer going ovver t'pub, Seedy,' he said, spying me.

'I'll get you one if I go in,' I laughed, always nervous about crossing Big Alec, who had now turned to talk to old Sam Burnsall from the top of the village. I tried to recall if they were related; most local people in Swinnerdale were and countless times it had been explained to us who was whose father-in-law or third cousin, and who used to live where. It was one of the charms of the Dales but also one of the hurdles for incomers: however long you stayed, you would always be an outsider.

Barbara returned with Tom, who was now ready for a carry, and several more people came over to talk to us, including Billy Iveson, whose mushrooms had fed us royally, and the saintly John and Mary Burton, farmers from nearby Buttergill.

'I saw you made friends with Adam and Ruth Metcalfe tother Sunday,' said Mary, whose rosy cheeks looked redder than ever with the reflection of the fire.

'Yes, they invited us over to their place,' said Barbara.

'Grand folk are t'Metcaffs,' rumbled John in his great bass voice. I looked him in the eye, aware that when we met I usually found myself staring at his giant hands, which were the largest I had ever seen. At that moment someone came round with a huge tray of hot dogs and, seconds later, conversation became impossible, as a great rattling bang behind us signalled the start of the firework display.

Tom had been looking groggy at this point but the explosion made him jump and when a second blinding flare detonated across the sky he began to wail. Barbara gave me a 'told you so' look.

'I'll take him home,' she said. 'I've never been that keen on fireworks anyway.'

'Er, right, OK,' I said sheepishly, not liking to admit that I adored them.

'Don't worry, you stay here and enjoy yourself.' She disappeared into the darkness with Tom still blubbering.

I wandered across to see who was running the display and saw the shadowy figure of John Weatherall moving about with a glowing taper. It was a splendid scene, not least because the bigger rockets and explosions of fire lit up the sleeping black masses of the hills around us, delineating the village's snug valley setting and adding further drama to the night.

The following morning, Barbara and I brought Tom out again to look at the remains of the fire. A huge pile of ash was smoking quietly in the centre of a ring of dirty, trampled grass. A man wearing slippers suddenly appeared from a house near the pub and skipped over to the fire. He was carrying two silver objects, which, to our amazement, he dropped into the smouldering ashes of the bonfire.

'Reet, that's lunch sorted,' he said, then looked at us and smiled at our bewilderment. 'Jacket tatties – lovely.'

He then scuttled back to his house before carrying out another bizarre piece of behaviour: as he reached the small metal gate outside his front door, he stopped, lifted it off its hinges and carried it inside. Just as Barbara and I looked at each other ready to guffaw, the man's head popped out of his open doorway and called up to us, 'Don't forget to take yours off, too – it's Mischief Night tomorrow!'

'What on earth is Mischief Night?' Barbara asked me.

'Oh, you don't have it in the South, do you, lucky things, and we were away last year. It's always on the fourth of November and it's a kind of excuse for kids to run around being naughty, really – they throw eggs and knock on people's doors, then run away, that kind of thing.'

'And steal people's gates?'

'Well, they don't steal them exactly – more kind of hide them somewhere annoying or funny.'

'You seem to know a lot about it.'

'Well we had Mischief Night where I grew up.'

'But I'm sure you didn't do any of those things, Andrew Seed.'

'Me? Er, of course not . . .'

Vanessa Ingleby despaired of me. A slender girl with long, dark hair and green eyes, she was only eight years old, but among the brightest characters in Class 3, and she made me nervous. One of the reasons for this was that she never allowed me to get away with anything. If I ever made the slightest mistake with something I said in class, or if I got a person's name wrong, she would gleefully correct me as if she were the teacher. Alas for me, this happened fairly frequently. Worst of all was if I made a spelling mistake on the blackboard. Vanessa was always ready to challenge dubious-looking words that I had written. She was amazingly self-assured and never afraid to express her strong views on any other given subject; her two favourite issues being the care of animals and girls' rights.

Vanessa, one of the class's few incomers, was also keen on acting, being something of a drama queen herself, and often asked me when we could do a play or act out some sketches. Unfortunately, my track record with plays in school wasn't the best and I cringed thinking back to the play about a ghost my very first class had performed, and the calamitous panto which I had overseen during that Christmas at Cragthwaite.

But I did agree that theatre was an excellent way to develop confidence and speaking skills so I ordered some BBC drama lesson tapes to play in the hall, which I hoped would be a lot easier than putting on a play. The first tape was called 'Jungle Hunters' and was based on the theme of Amazon Indians searching for food. I used that Monday afternoon's PE session to test it out and was quietly relieved that Sheena was absent, something that happened quite regularly – her mother's notes would simply say that her daughter was 'badly'.

The session began well: the children loved the music and I enjoyed having the luxury of a professional drama teacher giving the instructions on the tape while I observed the children's responses. Within minutes, the whole class were absorbed in their roles as rainforest natives, fetching water, digging edible roots and making bows and arrows. Even some of the more reticent boys joined in the ritual dance in preparation for the mimed big hunt to follow. The tape was excellent: every child crept when told to creep and jumped when told to jump. They particularly enjoyed working themselves into a frenzy for the animal hunt.

'Stamp your feet in rhythm with the music,' said the tape. They did.

'Begin slowly to move in a circle, chanting as you go.' The class obliged.

'Shake your spears aggressively, practising your throwing action!' Twenty-one invisible spears were raised and waggled. It should have been twenty-two but Vanessa conspicuously kept her arms down by her sides as she stomped. I stopped the tape.

'Vanessa – why aren't you shaking your spear?' She shot me a look which would have withered a desert cactus.

'Mr Seed, I'm a *vegetarian* hunter.'

Part of me wished that we were performing a class pantomime:

she would have made a perfect ogre's wife in *Jack and the Beanstalk*. When the programme finally ended, every child having eaten unfeasible quantities at the climactic pretend feast, I sat the class down and asked the children what they thought they had learnt. Only Vanessa raised her hand.

'Yes, Vanessa?'

'You've left the tape on.'

That night back at home I sank into the settee, exhausted. This half-term seemed to have been much more difficult than any of the others. Barbara snuggled up to me, which helped immensely.

'Tom's in bed. Let's light the fire and have a quiet night,' she said.

I reached over to her tummy. 'How are you feeling, anyway?'

'Well, I've not been sick yet – I actually feel quite good.' She looked it, too, with her thick brown hair shining and her skin radiant.

After half an hour, I had a beautiful fire going in the grate and we both settled down into the soft comfort of the settee with a drink and a book to read. It was bliss after the clamour of the day.

Then the sound began. It was a gentle but persistent tapping – the noise of a hard object knocking against another in the distance.

'Can you hear that?' said Barbara.

'Yes, sounds like someone tapping on the wall.'

'But it's not a hand – it's something hard and tinny.' We stopped talking and listened again. *Tik-tik-tik* it went, hardly stopping at all. It seemed to be coming from the window. I went over and opened the curtains. I could see nothing but blackness speckled with a few lights from houses across the green.

'How odd,' I said. 'It's definitely something tapping on this window but I can't see a thing.'

'Go out and have a look, will you?' Barbara wasn't scared; she was just mystified, as I was. The noise stopped for a few moments, then continued. I put on my shoes and went to the front door. Outside, it was much warmer than Bonfire Night had been two days earlier, but it was equally dark and I couldn't see anything clearly. There was certainly nothing outside the window where the noise seemed to be coming from, and I couldn't hear a sound.

I was just about to return inside when I heard the *tik-tik-tik*, as before, but slightly louder. I went over to the window. Against the light from the room inside I was able to see the cause of the tapping, and most peculiar it was. A tiny black button was hanging from a dark cotton thread, attached to the window frame and dangling just in front of the glass at the top of the pane. I went closer, and was amazed to see that the cotton was not simply a single short piece. The thread from the button was looped over a drawing pin at the top of the window frame and continued to stretch out away from the house and over the stone garden wall at the front. It was difficult to pick it out in the gloom, but someone was clearly tugging the cotton and causing the button to tap lightly against the window. I was just about to say something when two words came to mind: Mischief Night. I had forgotten all about it. I looked down the path and saw that our gate, which I hadn't removed as our neighbour advised, was gone. Just then I heard voices from behind the wall, or rather, the unmistakable sound of children sniggering. I crept back inside.

Barbara barely believed me and wanted to go out and look.

'Hang on,' I said. 'Not yet, let's give them a surprise, too.' Barbara rolled her eyes, a frequent response to my batty ideas.

'Don't do anything silly, Andy.'

But I wasn't listening. In the kitchen I found a bucket under the sink and half-filled it with water. Then I quietly crept out of the back door and round the side of the house so as not to disturb the mischief-makers. When I reached the front corner of the small garden wall I peeped round. Three hunched figures in dark clothes sat with their backs to the wall, whispering. One of them sounded vaguely familiar. Another one was casually tugging at a long piece of black cotton. The *tik-tik-tik* continued.

I almost laughed out loud at their cheek and guile. A bit of water would sort them out. I picked up the bucket and tried to twist my body into a shape where I could give it a real heave over the sapper trio five yards away. Just as I was in mid-swing, one of the children looked up and gave a mild squeal of fright. In a split second, I doubted my act of watery justice and pulled back the handle of the bucket. About two-thirds of the water went straight up in the air and landed on my head. A small fraction hit one of the children, who were all now scrambling frantically to flee the bucket-wielding madman by the wall. They escaped swiftly, leaving behind a long piece of cotton, a button and more than a shadow of recognition in my blurry eyes.

The following day at school, I began the morning in class with a discussion.

'Hands up who enjoyed Mischief Night last night?' Lots of arms shot into the air, accompanied by more than a few culpable smiles and sideways glances. 'It was a shame it was so wet.' The children looked perplexed. Nina spoke up for them.

'But it didn't rain last night, Mr Seed.'

I smiled and looked at Vanessa, whose lack of eye contact said everything. This was one mistake that she wasn't going to point out.

Chapter Four

Mervyn

'You go up to Kettleby, through the town and turn left on the road towards Arkleton. Follow that fer about five miles and when the road starts to climb after the bridge you'll see Black Busk Farm on the right.'

I'd written down Adam Metcalfe's telephoned instructions carefully and we were now on the way, travelling up Swinnerdale on a cloudy Sunday in early November. Dales' miles always seemed to be long miles and there was plenty of time to admire the scenery as we travelled through the broad green valley towards the great brown folded hills of the higher fells.

Tom sat quietly in his seat, thumb in mouth, twiddling his hair, and Barbara half-snoozed, as she often did on car journeys. We passed a farmer in a red pickup just as he stuck out a slow arm to greet someone in a field. All around, the trees scoured by autumn winds reluctantly surrendered their last few leaves.

After twenty minutes we passed Kettleby's clustered shops and cafes, and ascended the road to Reddle. We'd left behind the soft meadows and quiet woods of the lower dale; here the land was higher and wilder with bleak hills carpeted with rushes and scrubby heather. The road climbed and twisted and climbed some more, opening up startling views of dark sweeping hills and valleys divided by blocks of dense forest. The majority of the few scattered buildings in this little-known dale were derelict: ramshackle barns and gloomy houses with thick walls.

I slowed down as a farm came into view, and Barbara looked up. We recognised the Metcalfe's old Vauxhall and pulled in next to a rugged stone house huddled between sheds, trailers, machinery and piles of fencing and old gates. A tilted sign said 'Black Busk'. There was just a single tree – a naked ash, bent and lean. We stepped out of the car and were assailed by a numbing wind. This was a different world.

Ruth Metcalfe's warm smile ushered us into the house and past the three eldest children who were sat on a battered sofa watching a TV screen containing white fuzz ghosting with barely discernible forms. The sound suggested it was a cartoon.

'The booster aerial keeps blowing down,' said Ruth. 'Cuppa tea?'

Adam came in from outside and greeted us with twinkling eyes. 'Welcome to Reddle – you found us OK, then?'

'It took a lot longer than I expected,' I said, 'but I really enjoyed the journey.'

Tom was straining to get down and pad about. 'Is it OK to let him wander?' asked Barbara.

Adam gestured towards the door. 'Well, why don't we take him out to see me tractor right away while it's not raining?'

Tom looked very excited so we scooped him up and followed Adam into the wind past a barking collie and a jumble of old tyres.

'Duh-duh, duh-duh!' gabbled Tom, jiggling and making his best diesel noise.

'Aye, this is my old Zetor,' said Adam, slapping the side of a sturdy red tractor. 'Do you like it, little man?'

Our son just stared, his wide, brown eyes bigger than ever.

'I think he's too excited to speak,' chuckled Barbara.

We walked around the tractor, then Adam opened the door and climbed inside.

'Would you like to come and sit in the cab, Tom?'

Again he just stared. I lifted him up towards Adam, who gently placed him on his knee. Tom reached for the steering wheel and we all smiled watching his disbelieving face.

'You're in a duh-duh!' said Barbara. 'Oh, why didn't I bring a camera?'

'Shall we switch on the engine?' said Adam to Tom. 'Make it brum?'

Tom was in too much of a reverie to respond so Adam turned the key and brought the motor chugging to life. The little tot jolted with shock and then burst into a violent wail. Adam quickly switched off the engine and passed him down to Barbara.

'A bit louder than he thought, mebbe,' he said, smiling.

Half an hour later I was striding up a rough hillside with Adam, who had offered to show me round the farm. Barbara wanted to come, too, but she couldn't put down Ruth's baby son David who was charming her with a beaming chuckle.

'Thes a grand view o' the place from up here,' said Adam, pacing up the steep valley side as if it were flat.

'It's amazing,' I panted, already out of breath and struggling to keep up. I watched my footing carefully on the lumpy ground which was full of rushes and boggy dips. A good thing I'd brought wellies.

'Is it mainly sheep you have, then, Adam?' I could hear bleating up above.

'Aye, mostly Swardles with some Leicester crosses. I have beef cattle, too, but not on this side – thes not enough grass.'

It was extraordinarily sparse here and I wondered how on earth he could make a living on such bleak land. Adam noticed I was breathing heavily and so we stopped and took in the panorama. There were big brooding hills in every direction, with wild, bare fells beyond. The farm buildings were dwarfed by the scale of the valley; there wasn't another house for miles, apart from a ruin across the opposite side of the dale. What struck me most was the emptiness – there was hardly a tree in sight and only a few scrubby fields of grass below vast swathes of open moorland dotted with straggly sheep.

'There was a family living in that place fifteen years ago,' said Adam, pointing to the ruin. 'Hard to believe, isn't it?'

'But it's just a pile of stones now – what happened?'

'They moved out; couldn't survive with the bit o' rented land they had. The place just fell down. That's what the weather does here.' He smiled and carried on. 'A funny thing happened there ten years ago, though, when it was still standing. The farmer who took on the land couldn't find his bull – a cow and a calf were missing, too. He came to ask me if we'd seen it and we found them in that house, upstairs. The bull's head was sticking out of the window. The silly beasts had broken the door down, gone in and climbed the stairs to a bedroom but they couldn't get out. They won't go down stairs.'

I laughed, wishing I could have seen it. 'How did he get them out?'

'I had to go and get my two big brothers and we went in and pushed them down the stairs. It wasn't easy, I can tell yer.'

We carried on upwards towards the ridge before Adam abruptly turned to the side and headed for a small, dank pool of black water. I followed him and saw what he had spotted: there was a bulge of matted grey wool at the edge of the water and a black, horned face with panicky eyes. A sheep was half-submerged in the boggy mud at the side of the pool.

'Daft yow,' said Adam, leaning towards the now bleating animal. 'They never learn.'

He planted his feet well apart, the front one on a dry tuft of rushes, and leant towards the sheep. It made a frantic effort to escape the situation, waggling a front leg, but it was held fast by the peat bog's glutinous grip. With astonishing strength I watched Adam grasp the ewe's leg and a handful of fleece and heave the frightened animal out of the mire in a single movement. It jumped forward, its wool filthy with black mud, and scurried away through the heather, trailing globs of ooze.

'Would it have died if you hadn't found it?' I asked.

'Oh, aye. Sheep have a talent for dying, especially on this farm.'

Adam wiped his hands on a lump of moss and pointed to the crest of the hill just above us. 'I'll show you something interesting when we get to the top.' I smiled – it was all interesting to me.

When we did reach the ridge the land flattened out and we

came across a long, half-broken dry-stone wall. There were huge, flat rocks up here and the wind bit at our faces. I followed Adam through a gate and across the hilltop. A further valley opened out before us, a smaller dale than Reddle and another place I didn't know existed.

'That's Haggem,' said Adam. 'Or Haggholme, if you want to spell it. It used to have nine farms and now there aren't any. All the land's just ranched.'

'The dale that died . . . When did that happen?'

'The sixties mainly. The last one went in the seventies and the land was sold off. There used to be meadows with barns all the way along it. There was even a little school at one time.'

'You obviously know it well.'

'I should do – I managed Slack Gill Foot at the top of the valley when I was twenty: a thousand acres and not a single tree. I had the whole dale to meself . . .'

'How did you do that on your own?'

'I was young, fit, foolish . . . I did all the walling meself but the land is poor. See that hillside yonder?' He pointed at a steep incline across the valley.

'Er, yes.'

'I tried to go up that on a Honda three-wheeler – it was before we had decent quad bikes. I fell off and it bounced all the way down, about four hundred feet.' He laughed at the memory.

'Was it wrecked?'

'No, but it didn't do it any good.' He looked up at the gloomy sky. 'We'd better head back now, thes not much light left.'

On the way down, Adam told me about his plans for the farm,

how he hoped to rent some better land towards Arkleton where decent grass grew, expand his flocks and herd, and maybe put up some new buildings eventually.

'My priority is a four-wheel drive, though,' he said, almost wistfully. 'That old Cavalier I have'll hardly get up the road with a trailer. Then there's the house – that needs a spot o' renovation.'

Looking at the barren land and hearing about how other hill farmers had deserted the dale, I couldn't believe that he had such big plans. 'It must be exciting to have a vision like that.'

'Aye, well, I'm only twenty-seven and I've been mightily blessed so far. I have four brothers to help me, too.'

There was something quite extraordinary about this quiet, rugged man and I felt a strange little thrill at the prospect of becoming his friend.

The house was empty when we returned so Adam suggested we look in the barn next door. 'They'll be playing in the hay.'

He was right, the two older girls were jumping off bales while Robert and Tom played with toys on the floor. Ruth was jiggling the baby.

'Barbara wants to come and see some lambs in spring,' she said, struggling to make herself heard among the shrieks of the leaping girls. 'Bewished, you two!'

'Well, lambin's in April – we start later than everybody else – and you're welcome to come then,' said Adam.

Barbara hunched her shoulders in excitement. 'Oh, I'd love that; I used to work with livestock at Farm Club at my school.'

'Oh, if you don't mind gettin' mucky you can come as often as you like!'

'Well, I'll be driving soon so maybe Tom and I'll be able to visit when Andy's at work.'

Ruth nodded. 'Yes, please, it does get a bit isolated here. And Robert would like the company, too.'

I gazed round at the huge, dusty cobwebs along the barn's roof beams and the feed bags, steel drums and implements that were piled all around. Adam saw me looking.

'Bit of a scrow in here, isn't it?'

'A what?'

'A mess. That's what me dad used to call it.'

'What's through the trapdoor?' I asked, noticing a mysterious opening in the floor.

'That's the baulks.' He saw the confusion on my face and smiled. He was enjoying himself. 'It's a kind of cellar fer storing stuff. Well, that's what we called it, anyway. You drop bales through the hole.'

'And what are those?' I asked, pointing to four huge bulging bags hanging from a joist.'

'Fleeces. We get next to nothin' for them, sadly. Great fun to play in, though: as kids we used to hide inside and turn the lights off then wait quietly. Then one of ma brothers would flick the switch and we'd shoot all the rats wi' catapults.'

'Can I do that, Dad?' said Robert, looking up.

'In a few years, mebbe, Bob lad. We've got the cats for now.'

On the drive back to Applesett we talked about the day while Tom fell asleep in his seat.

'Ruth's such a lovely person,' said Barbara. 'Talented, too – she showed me these woven things made out of wool that she dyed herself. They're beautiful.'

'I really like Adam as well, he's like all the other Dales farmers but there's something different about him. But I just can't fathom how they survive on that farm: the land is awful.'

'With four kids, too. I wonder if they have any other income?'

'I don't think so; not from what Adam said. Everything's against them but they have such huge plans. It's unbelievable.'

Barbara chattered about how excited she was to be able to go back there and see the animals and get to know Ruth more but I wasn't really listening. I was thinking about Adam's struggle against adversity on the bleak Reddle hills and how it put my small troubles with Sheena into perspective. It just didn't seem possible that one young girl could prevent me from doing my job properly and yet that was how it felt. Adam had countless acres of desolate land to work, miles of crumbling wall needing repair and hundreds of brainless sheep to contend with but he didn't really complain at all. Was I blowing it out of proportion? Perhaps it was my attitude that was the problem.

Val Croker strode into the staffroom like a snorting rhinoceros and threw down a notepad on the table. Emma, Hilda, Sue and I looked at each other: it was a dangerous place to be at moments like this.

'That pillock Mr Foylan . . .' she muttered.

'What's he done?' asked Hilda, unable to resist.

'Wasted my bloody time, that's what.'

'Who is Mr Foylan?' I whispered to Sue, the classroom assistant.

'He's the Road Safety Officer,' she whispered back, her eyes still on Val.

Hilda put down her coffee. 'Come on then, Valerie, you've got to give us the dirty details now that you've mentioned it.'

Val stayed on her feet, arms on her hips. 'Well, you know it's the Road Safety Quiz next week?'

'What, the inter-schools thing?' said Emma.

'Yes, the one that Joyce has so very kindly asked me to organise here for Kettleby, Ingleburn and Applesett primaries.'

'Oh, I see . . .' said Hilda. 'Has our delightful Mr Foylan put his foot in it, then?'

'I'm going to put my flamin' foot in him when I see him,' growled Val, 'and not in a very nice place.'

Hilda rubbed her hands. 'Ooh, he's really upset you! What did he do?'

Val finally sat down. 'Well, the quiz is four teams of four kids from each school, as you know, and I've spent the last two bloody weeks coaching my chosen Brains Trust quartet from the top juniors because Ingleburn always win and I'm fed up with it and since it's being held here I thought it would be good if we took the cup this year . . .'

We all looked at her. 'Yes, and?'

'Well our lovely neighbourhood Road Safety Officer only rings up this morning and says that he's changed the rules and he wants two lower juniors in each team now, with less than a week to go!'

'I see,' said Hilda, evidently disappointed.

Val ignored her. 'So, I've not only wasted a load of time but I've got to tell two of the kids that they can't take part now, poor buggers.'

I suddenly twigged that it wasn't just bad news for her. 'And I've got to find two smart children from my class and give them intensive training on the Green Cross Code, I suppose.'

Val gave me an expressionless look. 'Right, afraid so. He says it's "to increase traffic awareness among younger pupils".'

'Well I think this is all really unfair,' said Emma, standing up in a rattle of cheap jewellery.

'Me too,' said Sue. 'It's not as if any of us have time to waste.'

Hilda chuckled, 'Well, Andy, you'd better hold an emergency meeting of the Tufty Club.'

I half-smiled, pondering how she found humour in every situation except those that adversely affected her.

I looked to Val, 'So, does it have to be a boy and a girl? And can it be anyone in my class or one from each year group?'

'Don't ask me. Our road safety man has probably changed the rules again since this morning. You'd better ask him.'

I knew that Val would be more help once she'd calmed down. 'What's the best way for me to get hold of Mr Foylan?' I asked.

'By the neck, I would have thought,' said Hilda just as the bell rang.

Some children are popular with their peers and, for various reasons, some are not. Mervyn Sowerby most definitely fell into the latter category, sadly for him. I couldn't really explain it; he wasn't an unfriendly boy, nor did he possess a disagreeable personality. He just didn't seem to have many or even any friends among the other members of Class 3.

Perhaps it was something to do with his appearance. He was undeniably a peculiar-looking eight-year-old, being tall, gawky and always dressed in what looked like charity shop cast-offs. Then there were his eyes, which were very close together, and his spiky hair like a frightened cat's.

Mervyn was often alone in the yard at playtimes and I usually made an effort to talk to him. I felt sorry for the boy and encouraged others to spend time with him but we both knew the truth that you can't make someone like another person. The other children didn't disdain him; they just didn't play with him.

Perhaps that was one of the reasons I selected him for Cragthwaite Primary's Road Safety Quiz Team. But there was another. I'd mentioned the quiz to the class and explained how I needed two volunteers to represent the school; two people who would have to work very hard over the next few days to learn all about the Green Cross Code and much more.

Every child put up his or her hand enthusiastically, except Sheena, who predictably pulled a face and muttered, 'Borrrring.'

I scanned the faces. Bernadette? I recalled what happened when the class drew their shoes. She was out. Chris? Having the world's worst memory was not the ideal attribute for this event. Vanessa? Well, she was always pointing out other people's mistakes – perhaps she could put her brimming self-confidence to good use here. And it might also redeem her after Mischief Night. She was in.

I looked at Mervyn. He was desperate, but there were cleverer children and I knew that Val really wanted us to do well. Then he spoke up. 'Mr Seed, my sister 'as been doin' cycling proficiency and I've been helpin' her learn all the road signs – I know them all.'

It was a good case and his pleading eyes, close together as they were, tipped the balance. Perhaps if he did well it would make him more popular, I thought.

'OK, Mervyn, you can be the second team member.'

He waved clenched fists in celebration amid groans from the remaining children.

During the lunchtime break I borrowed a Junior Highway Code from Val and called Vanessa and Mervyn into the classroom to start the necessary cramming. I was just explaining how the quiz would work when Joyce walked in.

'Are these our new road safety experts then, Mr Seed?' she said, grinning at the two children.

'Yes, Mrs Berry,' I replied, hoping that it was a fleeting visit.

'We're going to learn the Green Cross Cold,' said Mervyn eagerly. Vanessa gave him a look and I could see her wondering what she'd let herself in for.

Joyce nodded. 'Well, I'm sure you'll make a great team, you two. It certainly would be good to have that big shiny trophy in school, wouldn't it?' She winked at me and mouthed the letters 'HMI'. Vanessa watched closely, her mind whirring to decode this clandestine signal. 'Well, I'll leave you to it,' she said and walked back to the door.

Vanessa turned to me. 'What—'

'Never mind, Vanessa, we need to get started,' I said, opening the booklet at the page headed 'Crossing the Road'. 'Right, Mervyn, where should you never cross the road?'

'Ingleburn,' he said confidently. 'It's really busy on a market day.' Vanessa cackled. I tried to remain calm.

'Near the brow of a hill or on a blind bend are two places. Vanessa, what's the other?'

'Between parked cars.'

'Good.' At least something was right. 'Now, let's see if you can finish this list of safe places to cross a road: subway, footbridge, traffic island . . .' Mervyn's hand went up.

'Yes?'

'Mr Seed, what's a subway? And I've never heard of a traffic island.' My heart sank: I'd quite forgotten that rural children have no experience of these things. There wasn't a single zebra crossing or footbridge in the whole of Swinnerdale. Come to think of it, there were no traffic lights either . . .

The day of the quiz arrived and my hopes weren't high. Mr Foylan, a short, bespectacled man with monster bushy eyebrows was busy setting up the hall. Out of the classroom window I could see a minibus arriving, bringing the teams from the three other primary schools in the dale.

In the past few days Val had made it clear that she wasn't really bothered about Cragthwaite winning the quiz any more, despite Joyce's unsubtle hints. She was still sore with Mr Foylan and I smiled when Hilda asked Joyce if she could bring her class in to watch the quiz; it was clear that she just wanted to see what Val would say, or do, to the County Road Safety Officer.

'Oh, I want the whole school in to watch,' said Joyce. 'They can give our team a cheer.'

When Joyce had gone, Val looked at me. 'What are your two like, then?'

'Vanessa's not bad but Mervyn is, er, hit and miss.'

'I've not done any more revision with mine – we've wasted enough time on this already.'

'I'm bored with it, too, especially as I've been going through the Highway Code with Barbara for her driving test as well.' It was true – at home we'd reached the point where we were so fed up with traffic signs that we started making up new ones: 'low-flying pedestrians', 'no caravans over three foot six', 'uneven cyclists' and, my favourite, 'elderly people merging from the left'.

At five to ten we all filed into the hall. Four tables were set up along one side and behind each were four twitchy-looking children. Mr Foylan had his own desk near another wall and he directed the audience to the middle.

'I see he's not put any chairs out for the staff,' muttered Val, passing some out.

I saw Sheena slide across the floor and crash into Bernadette. 'Sheena, you come and sit next to me, please,' I said sternly.

'Awww, do I 'ave ter?' The teacher from Kettleby raised her eyebrows. I just pointed to the floor next to my chair, resolute. Reluctantly Sheena slid over.

Joyce welcomed everyone with her usual beaming smile, then passed over to Mr Foylan who explained that there would be three rounds with ten questions per team in each round.

'The team members can confer,' he announced. Mervyn looked blank. I glanced at Val, who looked up at the ceiling. 'Right, the quiz will now commence. The first round is on crossing the road. Question One, for Applesett: Give two examples of a safe place to cross the road.'

I recognised some of the children from my own village in the Applesett team. There was Mark, John Weatherall's son, and Mrs Dent's niece Alice was there, too. They answered: 'A pelican crossing and where there's a lollipop lady.'

'Correct, one mark,' said the Road Safety Officer, keeping the straightest of faces. The Applesett children jiggled with delight.

Our team was next: 'Why should you not cross the road between parked cars?' Mervyn started to speak but Vanessa elbowed him. She'd clearly remembered my instruction to let the two older children from Class 4 check that they all agreed on the answer. They didn't, and a heated thirty-second conversation followed in audible whispers. Emma failed miserably in her efforts not to laugh.

Val leant towards me, 'Bloody hell, this is going to take hours.' Sheena glanced up, clearly delighted that she'd heard Miss Croker swear.

'I'm going to have to hurry you,' said Mr Foylan.

'Because you can't see if traffic is coming,' said Vanessa, ignoring the others.

'That's close enough,' said the arbiter, jotting down a score for Cragthwaite.

At least we've got one, I thought. Ingleburn, looking confident, had no problem with their question and the hulking upper-dale children from Kettleby answered theirs correctly, too.

The pattern continued with the other schools doing well and ours spending a lot of time arguing over each answer. Mr Foylan was losing patience and Joyce didn't look too impressed. Val was drumming her fingers and I knew she was desperate for a smoke. The second round was about cycling and the Cragthwaite children didn't exude confidence when their first question arrived.

'What sort of clothes should you wear when cycling?'

They leant in to form their now-familiar huddle for a discussion. Mervyn just couldn't get the hang of whispering quietly.

'Shorts?' he proffered.

'No, I think he means bright colours, so you can be seen,' said a Class 4 boy.

'So is the answer yellow or pink?' said Mervyn. The others ignored him.

Vanessa looked agitated. 'What about a helmet, does that count as clothes?'

'Dunno,' said the girl from Val's class. 'Shall we say illuminous?'

In the end they ran out of time. After two rounds we were seven points behind the leaders Ingleburn. Joyce snapped at a couple of very bored infants who had decided to lie down, and I reined in Sheena who was flicking the contents of her nostrils at Class 2. As the morning descended further, only Val seemed unperturbed; she was enjoying the sight of the Road Safety Officer lose his composure as Cragthwaite delayed the quiz schedule.

'Right, we need to be quicker with the third and final round on road signs,' said Mr Foylan, arranging a stack of pictures. 'I'm giving each team just five seconds to recognise these signs when I hold them up.'

He started with Applesett and held up a red triangular sign with a lightning flash inside it.

'Er, storms ahead?' said Mark Weatherall, hopefully.

'No, it's overhead electrical cable,' said Mr Foylan. 'No mark.' These were going to be hard.

'Cragthwaite next.' Another warning sign was held up, this time showing a gate.

'No gardens,' mumbled Sheena.

'Oh, that's level crossing with barrier,' said Mervyn, without hesitating or consulting his team.

'Correct, one mark.' That brought a small cheer from the weary audience and earned Mervyn a pat on the shoulder from the boy in Class 4. Ingleburn went next and failed to identify an empty white circle with a red border.

'That was no vehicles,' I heard Mervyn utter under his breath. Kettleby struggled with their 'National speed limit applies' sign and I heard their teacher whisper to Emma that these were difficult. The round continued and the three visiting teams were confounded by the obscure symbols that Mr Foylan produced. There were no simple roundabout, keep left or one way signs at all. He held up a loose chippings sign for Cragthwaite, which Mervyn identified instantly, to applause from Joyce. Suddenly there was hope.

Ingleburn got stuck on a no waiting sign and Mervyn notched another point spotting a pedestrian route sign that even I couldn't remember. He was sitting up straight and smiling broadly; his teammates just left him to it and even Vanessa encouraged him on.

'Right, final one for each team,' said Mr Foylan. 'The scores are as follows: Ingleburn have twenty-two, Cragthwaite twenty-one and Applesett and Kettleby both have nineteen. Actually, because we're running late, I'll hold up one sign and the first team to call out the correct answer gets the point. Ready?'

Suddenly a hush enveloped the room and everyone leant forward, even Val. The question master picked up a circular sign and held it to his chest, enjoying the moment. He then spun it round and the children's eyes widened as they stared at an unfamiliar white number on a blue background. Mervyn popped out of his seat and spluttered, 'Spinimum- mimi- minimum speed!'

'Correct!' A cheer burst forth from the assembled Cragthwaite classes.

'Well done, Mervyn!' I heard Joyce call, as I stood up and clapped manically.

The Road Safety Officer raised a hand. 'That means it's a draw and we have joint winners this year: Ingleburn and Cragthwaite. I suggest you share the trophy for six months each.' Another roar erupted and our team stood up waving their arms with joy and smothering the bouncing Mervyn with congratulatory slaps and handshakes.

Val shook her head and looked at me. 'Amazing. Well, I'll withdraw my boot under the circumstances.'

Mr Foylan called the two winning teams over to him and Joyce ushered Mervyn to the front. The generous Ingleburn children held back and I wiped away a tear as Mervyn Sowerby held up the cup to a stirring ovation and was, just for a moment, the most popular boy in the school.

Chapter Five

Lee

Hilda lifted her knees and cackled. It was another after-school staff meeting at Cragthwaite Primary and the teachers were reminiscing about our recently departed vicar, the Reverend Rutherforde, while we waited to meet the new one, who was still chatting to Joyce in her office.

'His leaving speech was a scream,' she said before mimicking the ancient rector's measured warble: '"I am very grateful for all the years I have been invited to this school and it is with a heavy heart that I now must leave . . ." and all the children said, "Aaaa-men"!'

'How old was he?' asked Emma. 'He looked at least a hundred.'

'No, don't be silly,' said Hilda, 'he was much older than that.'

'I can't say I'll miss his assemblies,' I added. 'It was a real battle to stay awake.'

Val concurred. 'Aye, he had a special gift for bringing Bible stories to death.' We all laughed recalling his insistence on singing dirge-like hymns with no musical accompaniment and how fidgeting among the infants reached epidemic proportions.

Sue shook her head. 'I asked him once if we could have "He's Got the Whole World in His Hands" but he said it was too racy.'

'Well now he's retired he can slow down and leave the rock 'n' roll lifestyle behind,' said Hilda, chuckling at her own line as usual.

'I wonder what the new one is like?' said Emma. 'I've heard he's quite young and tasty.'

We didn't have to wait to find out. The door opened and Joyce ushered in our new vicar. The atmosphere in the room changed in an instant, mainly because it was impossible to ignore Emma's jaw bouncing off the floor.

'This is the Reverend Spinks, everyone,' said Joyce.

'Oh no, call me Dave, please.' He smiled and winked. Wearing jeans and a rainbow jumper, he was well built, stylishly coiffured and undeniably handsome. I guessed he was only twenty-five or so.

'Can I get you a cup of tea?' offered Emma, springing up. I looked at Val; Emma never made anyone a cup of tea.

'Hey, that would be great: milk and no sugar, please.' He patted a perfectly flat abdomen. 'Gotta watch this, y'know.' Emma tittered like a schoolgirl while I looked over at Hilda who was struggling not to say something wicked. Sue, practical and efficient as ever, already had the kettle on and signalled Emma to sit down, knowing she'd probably be unable to find the teapot anyway.

Joyce went back into staff meeting mode. 'Er, Dave would like to continue taking the Wednesday morning assembly and he's bravely willing to have all the children on his own.'

There was a buzz of approval from the staff, who immediately sniffed a rare opportunity for a spot of marking or planning time.

The vicar smiled. 'Yes, I'd like to make a few changes in the assembly, if that's all right.'

'What sort of changes?' asked Val bluntly. She evidently hadn't come under the spell of his charm just yet.

'Well, I'm going to bring in my guitar, for a start, so we can have some lively singing, and then I'd like to sit all the kids on benches around the sides of the hall rather than have them on the floor in regimented rows.'

Hilda's eyebrows rose to the top of her head but Joyce spoke first. 'Are you sure about that? Won't you have your back to some of the children?'

'I think it'll work really well: I want the assemblies to be fun and alive so that the kids develop a positive attitude to the faith. I think it'll be cool.'

'So do I!' said Emma, a little too enthusiastically, judging by Joyce's face.

'Right, er, well, I'm sure the staff will be delighted to have an extra fifteen minutes to get things done in their classrooms,' said Joyce. Val, Hilda and I nodded violently. 'So, right, is there anything else you or we need to know?'

'Would it be OK for the kids to call me Dave?'

Joyce shook her head, 'I really don't think that's a good idea – "Reverend Spinks" will do fine.'

'In that case, I'd prefer Mr Spinks – I don't want to appear, y'know, too kind of holy,' he smiled, despite Joyce's reserve, and I could feel Emma simpering next to me.

When he had left, Joyce quickly re-established a business-like atmosphere, even though Hilda and Emma couldn't stop talking about the trendy new vicar. I was surprised at Joyce's apparent lack of warmth, considering how she usually treated visitors.

'He's certainly different from Revd Rutherforde,' said Hilda.

'Yes, well, I've come across his type before,' said Joyce; 'it all sounds wonderful but you know what children are like …'

'Aye, but he clearly doesn't,' said Val.

'Anyway,' said Joyce, flapping through a big file, 'agenda: we need to tie down the details of all the Christmas activities and talk about the HMI visit which is only a fortnight away.'

I arrived home early from work the following day as Barbara had a driving lesson booked for five o'clock and was anxious not to miss the opportunity to practise with her test approaching. The house was reverberating to the sound of rampant toddlers as I stepped inside. Barbara came down the sloping hallway and gave me a kiss. She was wearing old baggy clothes and her hair was full of sawdust.

'I know, I look divine,' she said. 'It's been one of those days.'

I peered through the living room door. 'Has Tom got a friend round, then?'

'It's Stewart,' she said, referring to our friend Iris's three-year-old son. 'Iris has a doctor's appointment in Ingleburn, so I said he could stay here until she gets back.'

'Right, I hope she's not long.'

Just at that moment a little voice shouted, 'Let's sell conkers!'

'Bonkers!' said Tom.

'Yes, we'll sell bonkers conkers!' screeched Stewart.

'They're playing shops,' said Barbara apologetically. 'Well, Stewart is trying to – Tom's dribbling mainly. Anyway, you look tired again – Sheena on form?'

'As always. She introduced my class to the delights of Chinese burns then she ate some Plasticine for a bet. How was your day?'

'Well, despite the extra toddler I made sixty stars and angels for the Christmas Fair at Hauxton this weekend and have created a sensational chicken casserole which is in the oven.' She glanced at her watch. 'Ooh, I'd better get changed, my Allegro GTI will be here in a minute.'

I was glad to hear that Barbara was once more making wooden Christmas decorations to sell, now that Tom was past the baby stage. I wandered into the living room, treading on a sea of plastic fruit and veg scattered over the floor, along with books, Matchbox cars, teddies and wooden bricks. Stewart had also brought a big bag of toys.

'Daddeeee!' said Tom, flinging himself against my legs. I picked him up for a hug and said hello to Stewart who was spinning conkers off a wooden chest on to the carpet. He was wearing one of his trademark fat woolly jumpers with a rabbit's head on the front. He also had fluffy slippers.

'It looks like you two are having fun,' I said, stifling a yawn.

Stewart nodded. 'We made a shop but we've sold everything now.' He was a genial little lad and I was glad that Tom had a friend in the village but on this occasion I did wish they were playing somewhere else. I sat down and put my feet up, then arranged two cushions to lie back. I found myself doing this more and more after work and was just slipping into a snooze when Tom started clambering on top of me, asking for horsey rides. I grunted negatively and kept my eyes shut. He started to prod my face just as Barbara walked in.

'Any sign of Pottsy?' she asked, before spotting my comatose condition. 'Oh dear . . . Tom, you'd better get off Daddy as he's clearly not going to do much playing. I just hope he wakes up if Stewart's mummy arrives.'

Tom scrambled off me and flopped on to the floor with a grizzle.

'Let's be lions,' said Stewart. He crawled on all fours towards Tom, making a growly face and clawing the air. Tom screeched in mock horror while Stewart pursued him sending plastic veg pinging around the room.

'Boys, that's very loud – can you try and be a bit quieter for poor Daddy,' said Barbara, who added very deliberately, 'I do hope that Daddy isn't too tired to get the table ready for tea in the dining room while I'm out.' I pretended to be fast asleep.

There followed about twenty seconds of bliss while the boys did something quiet and Barbara looked out of the window for her driving instructor.

Then it began.

First there was an unfamiliar click of something being switched on, then there was a steady hum before some excruciating keyboard music started and my repose was shattered by the unspeakable saccharine voice of an American woman singing in a ludicrously jovial lilt: *'Oh I love my little Snoofiwoogle, Snoofiwoogle Puppy.'*

I hoped that I really was asleep and that this was just a bad dream but it continued, so cheerful that a wave of nausea began to overwhelm me. I opened my eyes.

'What is *that*?' I saw Stewart next to a small tape recorder bouncing along to the rhythm of the music. Barbara was laughing at the twisted grimace on my face.

'That is Snoofiwoogle Puppy,' she said. 'It's Stewart's favourite song.'

I sat up as a first measure to escape. 'It must be illegal to sound that happy, surely? You know I have a low twee threshold.'

I saw the cassette box and leant over to pick it up. It was entitled *Jolly Songs for Happy Tots*. There was a picture of a smiling woman on the front holding a toy dog. She had big hair and more teeth than a racehorse. Barbara's car arrived. The song got worse. I fled into the dining room.

On Wednesday morning there was a knock on my classroom door before the start of school. It was Lee's mum and even before she opened her mouth I guessed why she wanted to see me.

'Morning Mrs Waggett,' I said, smiling but internally groaning.

'Now then, Mr Seed. Sorry t'bother you when I know you'll be busy but I really can't leave this any longer. It's our Lee, Mr Seed; he's not 'appy. He's not been 'appy all term, really, and it's nothin' to do wi' you as a teacher, Mr Seed – he likes being in your class – but someone's upsettin' 'im and I've never seen 'im like this before.'

'Is it Sheena?' There was no point wasting time.

'That's 'er, aye. Lee's always been a good lad and never gets in trouble 'imself and he's always worked 'ard in school – the other teachers'll tell you that – and he's always been cheerful, too, like, until the last couple of months—'

I put up a hand, fearing that her sentence would go on forever. 'So what has Sheena been doing to him, Mrs Waggett?'

'Well, she 'asn't 'it 'im, as such, although I've 'eard she's 'it plenty.

Lee says he just can't concentrate on 'is work sitting near 'er. He says she just talks and messes about all the time.'

I nodded understandingly, having seen it myself since September. This was also the eighth or ninth complaint from a parent and Sue Bramley had recently told me that she'd overheard a group of mums muttering about Sheena at the school gate.

'All right, Mrs Waggett, I'll move Sheena away from Lee and I'll have words with her.' There was no conviction in my response, not least as I'd sat Sheena next to Lee precisely because he was so quiet and good at concentrating.

'It's same in t'village, you know,' continued Mrs Waggett. 'There's trouble most nights with that girl, and 'er mother doesn't seem to 'ave any control. I don't know . . .'

I looked at my watch as a hint. 'I'll do my best to sort it out right away.' She looked very doubtful but moved towards the door.

I sat down and wrestled with the problem in my mind once again. Should I put Sheena on her own? Would it change anything? Should I try bigger punishments? Or better rewards for good behaviour? None of it seemed to make any difference. Joyce had arranged for the educational psychologist to come and see her but it would probably be December before that happened.

Lee opened the door and came into the room. He was one of the youngest members of the class, a thin, freckled scrap of a boy with large pale eyes. He'd obviously been waiting for his mother outside.

'Hello, Mr Seed.'

'Morning, Lee.' He sat down and took out his reading book. He really was a model pupil: sensible, hard-working and quiet. 'I'm going to move Sheena so that she doesn't disturb you so much.'

'Oh, thank you, Mr Seed, that wud really 'elp me.' I smiled and sighed. If only more children were like him.

After registration, it was the new vicar's first assembly so I marched the class to line up outside the hall, keeping Sheena back for a word and resenting the fact that I was going to lose part of my precious planning time. She stood looking sullen as the other children filed quietly through the doors. I peered into the hall and nodded to the vicar who was standing with his guitar in the middle of a square of benches.

'From today, Sheena, you're going to sit on your own next to my desk.'

She puckered a lip. 'Tharrint fair.'

'I've had another parent coming in to complain about your behaviour; that's why I'm doing it.'

'But others mess aroun', too – 's not jus' me.'

I was going to respond but decided against it; explanation and reasoning seemed pointless. Some instinct also stopped me sending her into the assembly. I took her back to the classroom and set her to work taking down a display. Then I noticed she was pocketing the drawing pins so I gave her a book to read instead. She just pushed it around for a bit then folded her arms and slumped with her chin on the desk.

I'd only managed to mark three English books, when I heard a commotion outside the classroom and saw my class returning. The door jolted open and they tumbled in, shouting, laughing and bumping each other.

'Quieter, please!' I called. Something had clearly wound them up. 'Sit down in your places quickly.' But they weren't quick: they took an age to come in and I could see two boys messing around outside while the rest of the class bubbled with chatter.

'Shhh, come on everyone, quiet now.' Eventually they did calm down and the two latecomers slunk in. 'It sounds like the assembly was fun.'

'The new vicar's really funny,' said Eddie. 'He's good on guitar too.' This opened up a whole flood of responses from children.

'We sat on benches!'

'It were ace.'

'The song he did was dead good.'

'He's called Dave Spinks!'

I spread my palms. 'Whoah, what happened to putting hands up?' They were all jiggling in their chairs, I noticed. 'Anyway, it's Maths now.' There was a collective 'Awww', and they took much longer than usual to get ready. When the lesson started and I began to explain about converting centimetres to metres, the children's concentration was noticeably poor and even Lee was distracted. I put it down to the excitement of a new person coming into school and soldiered on.

There was no one in the staffroom at lunchtime so I dropped into Val's which was also empty. I found everyone in Hilda's classroom, sitting on the scaled-down tables. Entering Mrs Percival's domain was like stepping back in time: there was very little children's work displayed on the wall but instead big old-fashioned charts of times tables, alphabet letters and simple rules of grammar. The room was immaculate.

'Aye up, Red Rose is here,' said Hilda, her tongue in her cheek as ever.

'I keep telling you I'm from Cheshire, not Lancashire,' I retorted.

'What difference does it make, it's the wrong side of the hills, lad – yer foreign.'

Emma changed the subject. 'Did your lot come back from assembly high as kites, Andy?'

'Oh, it wasn't just mine, then? I'm glad I didn't send Sheena in—'

'He wants a bang on the head that bloke,' said Val. 'He's tapped.'

'I think he's sweet, but I won't be able to do anything on Wednesday mornings if my little ones are that excitable.'

'We reckon you think he's a bit more than sweet, young lady . . .' said Hilda.

Val stood up. 'Anyway, I've talked to Joyce. She noticed all the noise in the hall, too, and she had a word with the vicar after the assembly. Apparently he thought it went well and he thinks they'll calm down once they're used to him. Joyce suggested changing the seating plan but he wants to persist. So, there we are, it looks like "Dave" has charmed our head as well. Right, I'm off out for a cig.'

The following Wednesday morning I decided to risk sending Sheena into the vicar's assembly, as she had been a little better having been seated alone for most of the week. I felt sorry for her but the class's work had improved, the number of grumbles had fallen dramatically and, so far this week, no parent had been in to complain either.

As before, the hall had been set up with benches around the sides, and in the middle stood the smiling Revd Spinks with his guitar. He was wearing a white T-shirt displaying a dove.

'Welcome, Class Three!' he cheered, swinging his arm as my children filed into the hall. Once through the door some of them ran to the benches and slid along them, while a couple of others gave a little wave to the vicar. I was tempted to call across not to run but stopped myself, not wanting to compromise his authority. I took one more look: the infants of Class 1 were bouncing on the benches and prattling loudly. I retreated to my room, keen to make the most of the time.

Fifteen minutes later I returned to the hall hoping to avoid a repeat of last week's rumbustiousness as the children walked back to the classroom. Emma was already there looking through the closed door. I could hear a considerable din.

'What is going on?' I asked, approaching the small window.

'Everything, by the look of it,' said Emma, shaking her head. 'Do you think we should go in?'

Inside the hall there were children standing, dancing, shouting, shoving and chatting. The vicar stood in the middle imploring them all to sit down and be quiet. Before Emma and I could make a decision, we were thrust aside by a fast-moving, squat figure and the door burst open. Val had arrived.

'RIGHT, SIT DOWN AND SILENCE THIS MINUTE! This behaviour is an utter disgrace!' Instantly every child froze and dropped to a bench in reflex response. There was total stillness and quiet. Hands on hips and legs wide, she scanned the room for ringleaders. Her hair seemed even redder than usual, as if it had taken on some of her fury. All ninety-six children avoided eye contact for fear of an imagined instant laser death.

'I'll deal with this later,' she said with brooding menace, as she indicated with a thumb for Class 4 to return to their classroom. They tiptoed out with heads down. She spun round, completely ignoring the vicar, and strode out of the hall, stony faced. I glanced at the Revd Spinks as Emma collected her class: strands of hair had fallen across his sweating brow and his cheeks were inflamed. He was breathing heavily.

At the next staff meeting Joyce agreed with us that the new vicar's assemblies were not quite as successful as he'd hoped.

'Not successful? He was one step away from a bloody riot,' said Val, aghast.

'Some of my six-year-olds have more crowd control than that fella,' muttered Hilda. 'It's like he's not there – I call him the missing parson.'

Emma kept quiet but I added my view. 'I think you should see him in, er, action yourself, Joyce, then you'll know what it's like.'

She nodded. 'OK, good idea, Andy. We'll let him do his thing next week and I'll pop in halfway through.'

Val couldn't believe what she was hearing but Joyce was already moving on to talk about the inspector's forthcoming visit.

Every child in the school had been warned about good behaviour and the long line of infants and juniors was hushed as the hall doors were opened for the vicar's next assembly. Under the fearsome eyes of Miss Croker and the other staff in the corridor, the children filed in sensibly and sat down at the now familiar benches. The

Revd Spinks wisely kept a straighter face and restrained himself from arm-waving.

'Well, at least there's a quiet atmosphere at the start,' I whispered to Emma, as she closed the door. The four of us stood there for a moment outside the hall, facing the dilemma of wanting to stay and watch through the window, but also desperate to get things done in our classroom.

'Much as I'd like to see Rome burn, I ain't got time,' said Hilda scuttling off. I looked at Val.

'What time is Joyce coming for a look?'

'Ten minutes.' We all looked at our watches and dispersed.

Nine minutes and thirty seconds later I was back. Emma and Hilda were just behind me but there was no sign of our headteacher.

We heard the cacophony first: adult and child voices yelling, interspersed with unidentified bumps and bangs. I looked through the glass and saw mayhem. Not a single child was sitting on a bench: most were wandering, some were running. Sheena had obtained some PE equipment and was busy lobbing bean bags; a Class 4 boy was attempting to hula hoop. All were ignoring the beleaguered Revd Spinks who had put down his guitar and was bellowing at them to sit down and be quiet. I didn't like to think what was happening in the corner I couldn't see. I turned round. Emma and Hilda had their mouths open but there was no sign of Joyce or Val.

I gulped. 'I'm going in.'

I opened the door quietly and crept into the hall. The vicar had his back to me and wasn't aware I was there but several children noticed and stopped shouting. Others became still as the presence of a teacher became evident. I didn't say anything because I was speechless.

The vicar was still unaware. 'That's better, sit down, thank you,' he said in a voice cracked from hollering. He was also oblivious to someone else who was right behind him. Lee Waggett, little angelic Lee, was on tiptoe, his shoulders bobbing with glee. He was reaching up, two drumsticks from the music trolley in his hands, and pretending to play the back of the vicar's head. The children opposite me sat down quickly and noise dissipated in an instant. But for some reason Lee carried on drumming the pastor's head like a wind-up tin monkey. Then one of the infants from Class 1 laughed and ninety other children followed, pointing. Lee stopped and turned around, mortified. He saw Emma, Hilda and me and gaped. Then he saw Val and Joyce arriving and turned white. The children stopped laughing.

It was Dave Spinks' face that I shall always remember, however. The genial vicar was haggard, purple, dripping with sweat and almost crying. He was defeated, broken and we looked on him with pity.

I was surprised that he came back the following Wednesday but not surprised that all the staff joined him for assembly, sitting next to our classes, who were seated in smart rows along the floor facing the front.

'So, that's it, I had about eighteen minutes of planning time and it's gone,' I said to Barbara, half-yawning as I collapsed on to the settee later that day.

'The poor vicar,' she said, holding a teething Tom and picking up the wooden railway set which was all over the carpet. 'I admire him for coming back.'

I was going to say that Joyce used all her wiles to talk him back into it but my head had found a cushion and the most I could do was grunt.

'Honestly . . .' muttered Barbara, seeing my slumped shape, 'I know you're tired but so am I – Tom's been in a state all day and there's lots that needs doing. Tea's ready in five minutes and I haven't got time to lay the table so make sure you do it.' She walked off and I tried to tell my body to get up but there was no response. Five minutes passed and I was still lying insensible.

Then it started again.

Something jabbed and pierced my consciousness; something loud and repugnant; something unbearable.

'Oh I love my little Snoofiwoogle, Snoofiwoogle Puppy.'

I fell off the settee. 'Arrrghhhh, anything but *that*!'

Barbara was there, smiling, 'Iris thoughtfully asked if I wanted to borrow it. Table?'

Chapter Six

Yvonne

In less than two years, Joyce Berry had radically transformed Cragthwaite Primary School. The previous headteacher, Howard Raven, who had ruled the establishment with dour formality and unbending discipline, had been in residence for over a quarter of a century and, in that time, had established routines which seemed cast in iron. But, piece by piece, Joyce had dismantled the choking strictures of the old regime and, through both force of personality and a genuine care for children and colleagues, she had somehow imbued everyone connected with the school with a positive attitude. For me as a young teacher, the change in the atmosphere was wonderful and liberating.

Joyce constantly communicated with the staff and let each teacher utilise his or her strengths in the classroom. Another refreshing difference was to make parents welcome from the start. Previously, they had been banished to the school gate and it was only a very brave soul who ever dared to come down the path for any reason. At first, Joyce found it difficult to convince mums and dads that they were welcome in school after years of exile, and it was several weeks before finally nervous-looking groups of parents began to venture towards the entrance.

She was sociable, enthusiastic, kind, warm and the most touchy-feely person I'd ever met. She hugged the infants daily, chatted to every visitor and always left her office door open. I was Joyce's biggest fan, and did my best to defend her when Hilda or Val occasionally grumbled that there were too many things going on or that there was only so much gusto they could take.

Joyce was also generally calm and collected in among the apparent chaos of a busy school. She was able to perform five tasks at once and I rarely saw her flustered; that is until a week in early December.

The cause was very simple. His name was Mr Quinn and he was an HMI: one of Her Majesty's Inspectors. We had known that he was on his way for some time: it was a standard visit of a single day, not a full inspection with a team, but just a simple check-up on reading standards in the school. Joyce did not, however, see it that way. Her greatest concern seemed to be that the school would look wonderful: on the Friday before Mr Quinn's visit, she ordered fresh flowers for the entrance hall, arranged new displays on the walls – best work only, double mounted and with handwritten italic labels – and ensured everything was spruce from the PE equipment in the hall to the junior boys' toilet.

'What are you going to do with Sheena on Monday?' asked Joyce as she passed me in the corridor after school, her eyes flicking round at the coat hooks nearby.

'Er, nothing special, but I will keep her close to me, don't worry.' She didn't look convinced.

'And have you chosen your three readers for the HMI to hear?

I know they're supposed to be above average, middle and low but do give him your best one and, er, not, well, you know.'

'Don't worry, Joyce, I'll have it sorted.' She nodded then dashed off to check that everything was ready in the infants. I walked to my room, glad that I wasn't worried about the visit myself. I had plenty of good readers and I'd decided not to get the class anxious about it by telling them an inspector was coming. Only one girl knew anything about the HMI and that was Yvonne Collier. Her father was friends with Pat Rudds' husband and our caretaker had let it slip after complaining she'd had to do extra cleaning.

Yvonne was an interesting character: a bright girl and very good at sports but, for some reason, her family didn't seem to see the value of washing. Not only did Yvonne frequently have a grubby face and black fingernails but she quite often emanated an odour which was far from fragrant. I'd thought once or twice about mentioning it to her but had bottled out, deciding it was just too sensitive a subject.

I gave my classroom a rapid last tidy and then headed home for the weekend, making a mental note to think about my readers for the HMI again, just to make sure that Joyce would be happy.

With December's arrival the temperature in Swinnerdale had plummeted. The archaic oil boiler at Craven Bottoms was struggling to keep the house warm and Barbara, worried about Tom, had persuaded her parents to buy us a wood-burning stove as an early Christmas present. On Saturday morning it was installed and ready to go.

'Right, now we just need some logs – did you ask Mrs Dent?' I said.

'She gets hers from someone in Beckhouses called Stumpy and they cost six pounds a ton.'

'Six pounds! We could buy an electric heater for that. And where will we put them?'

'They'll have to go in the garage.'

'But they'll be in the way in there.'

'In the way of what? We never put the car in it.'

'Well, in the way of my tools and things. They'll take up loads of space.'

'At least they'll be dry.'

'Anyway, we can't afford six pounds each time – I'll go out and pick up some wood from around and about. There's plenty just lying there.'

Barbara gave me a doubtful look. 'Well, go on, then. I want to light my new stove.'

I put on my coat, hat and wellies and headed up Buttergill, the small valley behind our house, trying to think where I'd seen lots of fallen branches. I'd explored most of the footpaths and there were small copses and thickets all over the landscape, but how to carry wood back to the house, that was the problem.

Everything was damp underfoot, the meadows were tired and weighed down with dew. My breath billowed in the sharp air as I trudged up the hill out of the village trying to think which way to go. Around the bend a cluster of familiar vans and pickups stood outside a sagging field barn. The building had been for sale for some time and it looked like someone was having it converted.

Most of the Applesett darts team were there: builders Andy 'Cheesy' Cheeseworth, Dave 'DD' Duggleby, Vince the joiner, Dave 'DW' Whiterow and their leader the wiry John Weatherall, who was wandering around the building poking at the walls with a giant screwdriver. He saw me approaching.

'Aye up, lad. Where are thee off ter, then?' I'd noticed that he always put on a thicker accent when he was with his workmates than, say, when talking to me or Barbara in the pub or on the village green.

'I'm, er, looking for some firewood.' I greeted the others who were busy unloading timber and bags of cement from the vans.

'Is that for yer new log burner, then?' said Cheesy, joining the conversation.

'How did you know about that? It was only fitted yesterday.'

He tapped his nose. 'Me brother-in-law did the job.'

'I 'ope he did it properly,' said John.

'Well, thes a'ways a first time,' laughed the muscular DD, lifting a hefty bag of gravel with one hand. They weren't filling me with confidence.

'It'll be reet, don't worry, lad,' said the affable Cheesy, flicking back his wavy fair hair.

'So yer doing a bit o' scavengin' fer wood; where are yer headed, then?' asked John.

'I dunno, really. I'm just looking around.'

'He wants some o' Vince's offcuts, dost lad,' said the level-headed DW.

'He wants some o' Vince's joinery, more like,' said DD, needling as ever. 'Best place furrit, a fire.'

I heard the deep rasp of Vince from inside his van, 'Careful Duggleby or this four be two might jus' slip in a minute.'

'Oooo-oooh,' replied the hulking DD.

John brought some reason to the exchange. 'Ignore this lot. Tha wants to be ower there. Look, just past them trees.' He pointed to a scrubby patch of bare sycamores and ashes on the edge of a hillside. 'Belongs to Alf Ramskill, does that – he doesn't mind anyone gatherin' on that spot. There's quite a few dead elms 'n' all, so you should find summat.'

I thanked him and started to walk towards the track that led there. I stopped when John called again, 'If yer want to borrow a barrer there's an old one in t'smithy.' I smiled and gave a thumbs up – a wheelbarrow was just what I needed.

An hour later I was in Alf Ramskill's copse with a rusty builders' barrow picked up from the dilapidated old blacksmith's building on the village green which Weatheralls used as a store. I'd called in at home to tell Barbara that I'd found a source of free fuel and she'd excitedly told me to hurry up there so we could get the stove lit. I'd given Tom a quick giggly ride in the wheelbarrow and then pushed it back up Buttergill to the wood ready to do my gathering.

The floor of the small grove was thick with brown and yellow curled leaves and the place was eerily quiet, apart from the scuttle of a panicky pheasant. There were plenty of fallen branches on the floor so I started picking them up, only to find that most were half-rotten and damp. The ones that weren't were no more than thick twigs really and would burn up in an instant. I pushed the barrow over the lumpy ground looking for better material.

As I went, I thought about the forthcoming HMI visit in school.

Joyce really was wound up about it; perhaps I was too relaxed? I wondered whether Yvonne had told any of her friends in Cragthwaite that an inspector was on his way on Monday. Perhaps I should have asked her to keep it to herself, not least because she was a bit of a busybody and one of the more outspoken members of Class 3.

I thought about the readers for the HMI, too. Originally I had decided on Vanessa, as she was the best in the class, Lee because he was a good middle and then burly farmer's lad Guy as the struggler, but I wondered if this was a wise choice, bearing in mind the head's anxiety. I considered Yvonne again: she was a capable reader and I could probably just about get away with calling her average in a bright class. Guy was a risk, so I decided to substitute Mervyn. That should keep Joyce happy.

After forty minutes the barrow was still only half-full so I left it and wandered right through the trees and around the stone walls that bordered them trying to find some good thick branches. It was a waste of time: either someone else had taken all the good stuff or there just wasn't any. But it wasn't like John to distribute duff advice. Perhaps I was approaching it all wrong. I looked up at the trees and saw among the healthy ashes and sycamores a number of pock-marked trunks, denuded of bark, which clearly belonged to dead trees. These were elms that had succumbed to the deadly Dutch elm disease, I realised. They were grey and wretched, with great holes where woodpeckers had drilled in search of insects. I could spot where thick branches had fallen off, too, and no doubt been carried away by someone else searching for free fuel. There were tons of dead wood here but no way of getting it.

In the middle of the copse I found a much smaller skeletal elm, a young sapling with a stem about as thick as a man's arm and about fifteen feet high. Now that was something I could tackle, surely? If only I had an axe. I gave the tree a firm boot with the sole of my welly. It shuddered and drops of grainy water fell on my head. I tried a shoulder barge next but only succeeded in obtaining a bruise and an ugly green smear on my coat. This was useless: I needed tools.

'Is that *it*?' said Barbara, incredulous when she saw the half-load of mouldy sticks I arrived home with fifteen minutes later. 'You've been gone for hours!'

'Well, it wasn't quite as good as I thought . . . but I have a plan.'

'I don't like the sound of this.'

'There is loads of wood there but I can't get to it at the moment.'

'Why not?'

'Well, er, it's still in the trees.'

'What?' Tom was wriggling in her arms, desperate to get at one of the branches in the wheelbarrow. At least he thought my harvest was valuable. I explained about the dead elms and how, if I just had a decent saw and maybe an axe, we could have an endless supply of high-quality lumber.

As usual, she looked more than sceptical. 'You can't just go there and cut down this man's trees!'

'But they're dead.'

'You'll be dead if you start doing stupid things with an axe – you know how accident prone you are. You only touched the kitchen ceiling when we first moved here and it fell on your head. Anyway, you don't know how to cut down a tree.'

'They're only little tiny ones I'm talking about,' I said, understating the diameter with my hands. 'It'll be a doddle.'

'Well, maybe, if they're really that small . . . Won't your saw in the garage do?'

'No, that's for joinery, I need a proper log saw with big teeth.' She gave a groan and put Tom down.

I took off my wellies. 'I'll just pop into town and see how much they are.'

'Wouldn't it be easier if we just bought some coal?'

'No, this'll save us a fortune.'

Half an hour later I was in my favourite shop in Ingleburn: Sedgwick's Ironmongers. This was a treasure trove of tools, farm supplies and much, much more. The walls were stacked with bundles of fence posts and great loops of rope; there were shelves up to the ceiling and countless small rooms, each one full of open boxes. It was great fun to look at the hundreds of varieties of nails, bolts, brass fittings, galvanised gate catches and strange brackets. There were rat traps and mole catchers, bird scarers and electric wire next to brooms, buckets and snow shovels. Further on was a tangle of fly swatters alongside piles of springs, ratchet straps and torches. There were chains, ballcocks, pitchforks and grease guns randomly displayed next to dishcloths and candles.

My favourite section was the tools. This was an Aladdin's cave of everything from giant drills to dainty tweezers. I loved browsing the shiny chisels and meaty hammers, wondering what I could do if I had the budget. I didn't dawdle too long on this occasion, however: Barbara wanted her stove going, and so I headed for the saws. There was a rack of beautiful Austrian log saws, each with a vivid orange frame and a glistening blade. I picked up a small one and imagined myself slicing through fat branches in a flash. The teeth were brutal: each one half an inch long and sharp as a shard of glass. I tried a bigger saw: it felt good to hold, a thing of power and efficiency.

Further along were the axes. There were little hatchets, all-metal log splitters and then the big beasts with hickory handles and blades that exuded danger. I couldn't resist picking one up. It was heavier than I expected and, for some reason, I thought of *Little Red Riding Hood*. I looked around to see if anyone was there. There wasn't, so I lifted it up and gave it a wary swing. Wow, this thing would bring down a house.

And then something peculiar happened. I felt myself moving towards the till gripping the two deadly weapons, unable to let them go. They were simply too fine, too necessary. The price was equal to more than three tons of logs but with these, I told myself, there would be unlimited heat in our home for years. I hurried back through Swinnerdale in the car, blanking out an image of my wife shaking her head.

'You've been out twice and I've had Tom all day – you're supposed to spend time with him on Saturdays,' she said, handing over our thumb-sucking son. 'Anyway, you'll only maim yourself with those chopper things so you may as well hold him while you still can.'

I laughed at Barbara's evaluation, exaggerated as it was. 'OK, I'll stay in for this afternoon but you must let me go up there tomorrow to get some logs. I'm desperate to use the new saw.'

'Hmmm, well, all right but only because I'm desperate to use the new stove.'

* * *

The following day I was back in the wood in Buttergill pushing the ancient barrow containing my shiny new axe and saw. The dead sapling elm was first. I picked up the log saw, grasped the narrow trunk and pulled the blade across its surface. The teeth bit into the wood hungrily and within a moment I was cutting across it with ease, the steel incisors spitting out dust as they ate through the little tree. Within thirty seconds it was done and I pulled the sapling down before stripping off the small branches with the hefty axe and sawing it up into pieces. I chuckled. This was going to be a doddle.

I found a slightly larger dead elm and did the same. The wheelbarrow was now two-thirds full but I really wanted to fill it up with decent logs to justify to Barbara the expense of the tools. I wandered about again and looked through the grove but there didn't seem to be any more small trees. I did find a much larger dead elm, about forty feet high, but this was an entirely different proposition, with a trunk about a foot across and lots of big branches. I stared at it for a while before dismissing the idea as crazy. I had another look around but the only other elms were even larger so I went back: it was this tree or nothing. It was too big and heavy, though, surely? If it fell on me it would be curtains. I looked around. There was nobody in sight so picked up the big axe and decided to have a swing. I took it too straight and the blade bounced off the trunk sending me staggering back with an unforeseen jolt. The next few cuts were better and I took some chunks out of the wood but, at this rate, it would take me hours. I went for the saw.

After fifteen minutes I'd cut a deep V-shape out of the trunk, like I'd seen loggers doing with chainsaws. There was just a small section left holding up the whole tree. I went around the other side, having moved the wheelbarrow well away, and, gulping quietly, I started to saw at the remaining section of the thick stem. The jagged teeth bit into the timber and, within a few seconds, there was a creak followed by an ominous snapping sound. I quickly pulled the saw away and stepped back, expecting the crash of a fall. Nothing happened. I crept forward, wary of a sudden collapse, and pushed the blade back into the slot. My heart was galloping. After just two more strokes of the big log saw there was a loud crack and the trunk started to move – away from me, to my great relief. I stumbled back, anxious to watch the tree come crashing down but instead it stopped. It had tilted just a few degrees and now it just hung there. I looked up and saw the problem: its branches had become entangled in those of a neighbouring tree which was now holding it up.

I just stood and stared. What was I going to do now? Not only did I have no more logs to fill up the barrow but this severed tree could fall over at any time and flatten someone. All it would take was a decent breeze. I could get done for murder . . . There just had to be a way to bring it down. I tried a kung fu kick against the teetering trunk which was balanced on just a tiny section of splintered wood. Nothing happened. Next I thumped it with a hefty piece of branch that had come down. The branch shattered but the tree was unmoved. I would have to go back into the village and ask John Weatherall for help. But the thought of the darts team knowing and the humiliation they would inflict at the next match was just too much – there had to be another way.

That's when I saw that the back of the axe was flat. Maybe that would shift it? Or would it simply break my new purchase? There was only one way to find out. I picked it up, planted my legs well apart and took an outrageous swing aiming just above the cut. There was another crack of splitting wood and the tree shifted half an inch. The axe seemed OK so I swung again. This time there was a ferocious snap and the heavy trunk slid away with a huge clatter and crash of breaking branches. I lurched back, dropping the axe and scuttled away as the tree dropped down almost vertically, thumping into the ground before starting a slow lean with more branches snapping and flying in all directions. It was going! With a great explosion of splinters it bashed through its neighbours and thumped to the ground.

I was covered in mud, wet leaves, twigs and green lichen but smiling. I stood up and looked around. Someone must have heard that. *Everyone* must have heard that. But no one appeared, no one called or drove up for a view.

Two hours later I trundled the wheelbarrow home. It was full of beautiful white split logs. When Barbara saw me she just laughed. I was clarted in sweat, grime and sawdust.

'You look like you've been on a commando camouflage course.'

I just pointed to the barrow, 'Light that stove. And there's more where these came from.'

On Monday morning, Joyce assailed me as soon as I walked through the door of the school. She'd had her blonde hair put into a new style and was wearing an expensive-looking jacket, as well as stupendously bright lipstick. I tried not to stare at her mouth as she spoke but it was difficult.

'All right Andy? There's no sign of him yet. Got your readers all organised? No, don't tell me who they are, my mind's almost full as it is.'

'I'm fine, yes. The school looks great and I'm sure everything'll be fine with the readers in all the classes. I'd better get into my room and make sure it's ready.' I was pleased to be out of the way in my annexe on this occasion.

As soon as children started to arrive I asked Yvonne for a quick word. She bounced into the room with a smile.

'Hello, Mr Seed.'

'Hello, Yvonne, how are you today?'

'Oh, not bad, y'know.'

'Right, well, I'd like you to do something for me. In fact, two things.'

'Ooh, is it summat exciting?'

'No, I'm afraid not.'

She grimaced, 'Awww . . . What is it then?'

'Well, first, please don't say to anyone that an inspector is coming today, will you? I don't want anyone to fret.'

'OK, but am not bothered. It would tek a lot more than a man in a suit to get me worked up, Mr Seed.'

I smiled, 'I know you're not, Yvonne, but there are some worriers in the class.'

'You mean Alvin and—'

'There's no need to name anyone.'

'Oh, sorry. What's the other thing?'

'Right,' I said, trying to make it sound significant. 'The HMI wants to hear three people read and I've chosen you to be one of them.'

'Oh, is that it?' She looked really disappointed.

'Well, it is important, Yvonne. You're a good reader so make sure you do your best. All right?'

She nodded unenthusiastically and explored a nostril, 'OK.'

'Good.'

'But what's an HMI?'

'It stands for Her Majesty's Inspector.'

Her eyes lit up, 'He's from the Queen?'

I suppressed a giggle, 'No, it's just what they're called.'

'But is he coming from Buckingham Palace today, like?'

'No, he's coming from Pontefract.'

'Well, will he be wearing one o' them red jackets with gold on?'

'I don't think so.'

She shrugged and danced off to make the most of the few minutes before the bell. I checked the room again for gloss just in case Joyce called by.

After the first teaching session I was eager to get to the staffroom to find out what the HMI was like. He'd been in the infants all morning so I asked Hilda.

'Delightful chap,' she said. 'All the charm of a corpse.'

'Is he that bad?'

'Reminds me of the Child Catcher in *Chitty Chitty Bang Bang*.'

'Really?'

'No, but you know what they're like these official types . . . Oh, you don't know what they're like, do you? Well, he comes in, dark suit, plastic smile, notebook, fangs . . .'

'Oh, stop it, Hilda,' said Emma shaking her head.

Hilda continued, 'Well, he just sits in a corner and asks for each child to read to him and that's that. No feedback or chat.'

'He reports back to the head at the end, so we will find out what he thinks,' said Val, supping her outsized cup of coffee.

Emma put a finger on her lip. 'I wonder if he'll tell Joyce what happened with little Barry in my room? When I asked him to sit next to the inspector he leant his head over in the poor man's face. Turns out he was expecting a head lice check!' We all laughed just as the door flew open and Joyce thrust her head in.

'Everything all right? Emma? Hilda?' Her eyes flicked between them as they nodded reassuringly. 'Where is he?'

'In my room still, I think,' said Hilda.

Suddenly Joyce's eyes grew huge. 'Onetwothreefour – there's no one on playground duty!'

'Damn, it's me,' said Emma, jumping to her feet and almost spilling her drink. She raced out of the door as Joyce closed her eyes. We heard a call from Emma's voice in the corridor, 'It's OK, Sue's been out there!'

Joyce put her hand on her chest and exhaled in relief. 'Thank God for Sue. I don't know what we'd do without that woman – she's a wonder. Just imagine if anything had happened in the yard with no teacher on duty . . .' She looked at her watch. 'He's with you next, Andy, all right?'

'Yes, I'm all ready,' I smiled to reassure her but she dashed off. 'I've never seen her like this,' I said.

Val shook her head. 'Eee, what a fuss. At my last school in Hubberdale we never went out at break times. Mind you, it was normally snowing there. We just let the kids get on with the job. If they broke a leg, they broke a leg.'

'Times have changed, Valerie, times have changed,' said Hilda rubbing her back as she rose from her chair. 'Bring back slates I say.'

When I returned to my room I received a shock to find Mr Quinn already there, flicking through his notes.

'Er, good morning,' I said, unsure as to whether I should shake hands or not.

'Good morning, Mr Seed.' He held out a hand. 'Gerald Quinn. Now, where shall I sit to hear your readers?' I put two chairs in the book corner and prayed that the class would be well behaved. The bell had rung so I headed outside to intercept Sheena.

Ten minutes later, the class were sitting quietly working through a long comprehension exercise, which I hoped would keep them busy for the duration. Vanessa, my top reader, was with the HMI fluently reading aloud from *The Wolves of Willoughby Chase*. Sitting alone at her desk next to me, I could sense Sheena fidgeting. Ten minutes was about her limit carrying out any task and so I wasn't surprised when a loud burp rent the air.

'Sheena, that really is rude. At least say excuse me.' I gave my best disapproving look but several children were sniggering. I glanced at Mr Quinn who, fortunately, hadn't looked up from making notes on Vanessa's performance.

'I curr'n't hold it in, Mr Seed,' said Sheena, beaming towards those who had laughed.

'Right, well, don't do it again. I'm coming over now to see what work you've done.'

She shuffled and grabbed her paper, which I could see was speckled with blotches and crossings-out. As I moved over to Sheena's desk, Vanessa stood up and came over to me with her book.

'He says can you send the next one now.' Her voice lowered to a whisper, 'He's a bit weird, Mr Seed.'

I put my fingers to my lips and gave her wide eyes. As she slunk away I said, 'Right, Yvonne, please will you go and read to Mr Quinn.' I looked at her, hoping that she understood that I wanted to add the word 'well' to the sentence. She picked up a battered copy of *Charlie and the Chocolate Factory* and headed for the book corner. Meanwhile, I surveyed Sheena's 'work' and tried not to let my shoulders slump too far.

After a couple of minutes I glanced across to see how Yvonne was doing. I could just about make out her reading, which sounded fine. Mr Quinn was still scribbling notes but I was a little concerned by the slight frown on his face.

'Oo is that man?' asked Sheena.

'He's an inspector; he's come to check up on reading.'

'What for?'

'Er, well, I suppose he wants to know if our school is doing its job properly.'

'Nosey, in't 'e?

'He's just doing his job, Sheena, not being nosey.'

'Well, I aren't reading to 'im.'

'No, you're certainly not.' I looked down at her comprehension sheet. It was entitled *Robinson Crusoe* and there was a short printed passage explaining how the hero of the story became stranded on a desert island. There was a black line drawing of Robinson, walking along a beach dressed in goatskins. Underneath were five simple questions with spaces for answers. So far Sheena had drawn a sword through Mr Crusoe's head and added a flying seagull to the scene which was dropping something unpleasant on to the beach. There were scrawls across the other white spaces but she had at least attempted to answer one question:

Q: How did Robinson Crusoe end up on the island?

A: He wos shit recked.

It was the most English she'd done all term.

The afternoon lasted an age but finally the bell for home time rang and the class dispersed. I sat down and had a look through some of the children's work. With Sheena taking up so much time I just wasn't giving the others sufficient attention. There was some good maths, which cheered me a little, although I was dismayed to see the state of Yvonne's exercise book, curled up and grey with finger smears as it was. Her grubby approach unfortunately detracted from the quality of her work, which was generally good, particularly her creative writing which reflected her frothy personality.

I decided to take the maths books home to mark and turned instead to a number of delightful paintings made by the children in the style of the Impressionists. Leaving the numerous other tasks on my list, I chose to put backing paper on some of the pictures, ready for display. I loved the peace of the classroom at this time of the day and the ease of carrying out a simple task like cutting paper and gluing: I didn't have to think, to solve problems, to settle disputes or to explain difficult concepts to unready minds.

An hour and a half had passed when Val tapped on one of the classroom windows and pointed towards the main building. I had no idea what she was on about so I opened the window.

'What's up, Val?'

'Joyce wants us in the staffroom.'

'What, now?'

'No, next bloody millennium . . . Yes, of course, now.'

I left the pile of paintings and hurried through the door, suddenly remembering that Joyce would want to report back the HMI's findings to the staff. I caught up to Val a little nervously and apologised.

In the staffroom Joyce looked her old self again.

'Well, thank you everyone for the big effort made today and leading up to today. Our visitor did mention that the school looked impressive and I must heartily agree, so well done there.'

Hilda shuffled a little and made a big show of looking at her watch; we were all aware that she always left just before five and it was now ten past.

Joyce ignored the gesture and continued, 'Mr Quinn had just two things to report.' She left an annoying pause for effect: 'One, that the standards of reading in the school are generally good.'

'I presume that means above average,' said Val as stony faced as ever.

'It does, and I'm very pleased with that. Give yourselves all a big pat on the back.'

'I'd rather give myself lamb chops and gravy,' said Hilda, visibly concerned about her tea being late.

'What was the other thing?' said Emma. 'You said there were two things to report.'

Joyce raised her eyebrows. 'Very odd this. He said the reading was fine and it was certainly a lot better than the personal hygiene.'

There was a moment's silence then Hilda stood up. 'That's it – I'm not spending a moment longer in a smelly school.'

Arriving at home in the dark, Barbara opened the front door as soon as she heard the car. Tom stood in the doorway, holding her leg and waving. She had a kind of simple grin on her face.

'What's up with you?' I said, giving her a kiss and picking up Tom. 'How's the little lumpy tum?'

'Lumpy tum is tickety-boo. I have a special surprise, though.'

'Ooh, what is it?' I tried to think whether I was supposed to know or not: it didn't appear that I was. We went inside, out of the damp cold.

Barbara continued to grin. 'I can't wait any longer . . . I passed my driving test!'

'Eh?'

'I took it today, in Bilthorpe!'

'What, how? I thought it was next week.'

'Aren't you pleased?'

'Yes, of course, well done, clever you!' In truth I was more confused than pleased.

'Pottsy said I was ready and one of his other clients had booked a test but he was ill so . . . I did it!'

We did a little cheering dance and Tom joined in.

'I need to get you a pressie,' I said.

'Oh no, it's all right – I've got a bottle of wine to celebrate and I thought we could just have a lovely snuggly night in with a meal, some candles and our cosy new stove.'

'Ooh yes, that sounds wonderful,' I said, picturing it as I gave her a squeeze.

'It does, doesn't it?' She pressed me on the nose. 'Oh but we've run out of logs – you just need to nip out and get some more from your special place.'

Chapter Seven

Glyn

It was the Friday before the last week of term and Christmas was just around the corner. This was the day that the County Educational Psychologist turned up to assess Sheena. Miss Woolford was small, bespectacled and serious-looking. She opened a bulky leather satchel and took out a clutch of papers as Joyce and I sat in the school office, waiting for her verdict.

'Sheena's quite a troubled young lady,' she said. Joyce and I already knew that. 'I had a long talk with her this morning.' We knew that, too. 'I used some psychological profiling assessments to evaluate the nature of her difficulties.' That was more the kind of jargon we were expecting.

'We know her problems very well by now, Miss Woolford,' said Joyce, clearly anxious to move things along quickly. 'What's your verdict?'

'Well, she has a complex personality which makes reliability of test results an issue . . .'

'You mean she doesn't always tell the truth,' said Joyce.

'I'm afraid that's right.'

I was getting frustrated, 'But what's causing her behaviour? It's so disruptive in the classroom, and outside it, too.'

Miss Woolford gave her glasses a quick polish and picked up one of the pieces of paper. We were all tired but I had never seen someone who looked so overworked.

'Well, her concentration issues, aggression, dishonesty and learning difficulties point to ADD: Attention Deficit Disorder, in my opinion. There are elements of hyperactivity and possibly even some form of autism, although that would require further tests.'

Joyce was clearly anticipating this finding. 'So what can we expect in terms of support from County for Sheena? At my last school a boy in the infants was given behaviour modification therapy for ADD and some one-to-one which helped a lot.'

Miss Woolford exhaled. 'Your last school was no doubt in a different local authority, Mrs Berry. I'm afraid here in North Yorkshire our budget doesn't stretch to that.'

'So what will happen, then?' I asked, trying not to sound too gloomy.

'Her case will be put forward for consideration by the Special Needs Committee and we'll just have to see what they decide. You'll no doubt be given some kind of help, I just can't say what it'll be at the moment.'

When she left, Joyce shook her head and pursed her lips. 'I'm sorry, Andy. This is dreadful. I'll do everything I can but it doesn't sound hopeful.' I wanted to stay and have a good moan but there was just too much to do: cards had to be made, there was the carol concert to organise and my classroom needed decorating for the end of term brouhaha, the Christmas party. I left the room with shoulders sagging.

The following day was Saturday and Barbara had left early for York to sell her home-made wooden decorations at the Christmas Fair, so I was left in charge of Tom. We started with a late breakfast in bed of sloppy Ready Brek. I parked Tom next to me and fastened on his yellow plastic bib to collect the inevitable overflow.

'Brekky!' he said, leaning forward to reach the tray with his spoon.

'Hang on, I haven't sorted out your pillows yet, Tommy.' He stretched and managed to scoop a blob of cereal from distance, thankfully reaching his mouth rather than the duvet. He was very pleased with himself. I arranged my own bowl and looked at my son, now busy plastering his face with creamy goo. He had big brown eyes with long lashes above a tiny button nose. His wispy strawberry-blond hair was crowned with a tuft where he'd twiddled it for hours and his skin was soft and clear.

'This is fun, isn't it?' I said, smiling.

He nodded vigorously, looking up with those huge round eyes.

An hour later I was squashing Tom's feet into his little red wellies. The sun had peeped out between the clouds and he had gone to the big bay window and pointed to the green.

'Hwing! Hwing!'

'You want to go on the hwings?'

'Yay, hwing.'

'Good boy, that's almost a sentence.' I zipped up his thick furry coat, pressed a cute bobble hat on to his head and we headed for the door. Outside a wintry breeze stung my cheeks but I breathed in the wonderful Dales air and clasped Tom's hand as we made our way down the village green. An erect figure wearing a Barbour jacket and flat cap came striding towards us, a black Labrador with flapping tail at his side. It was Major Asquith, our close neighbour.

'Morning, you two,' he said. 'Well, this young man is walking well, aren't you, Thomas? How old is he now?'

'He's, er, coming up to eighteen months.'

'Splendid. Where are you off to? The waterfall?' Tom just stared at him.

'No, it's the swings today.' The dog walked forward to sniff Tom, who cowered behind my leg.

The Major smiled. 'Oh, don't worry, Jet won't hurt you. Back boy!' he snapped and the Labrador retreated instantly. I smiled, too, because I could never talk to the man without picturing him lying prone and miraculously uninjured in the road after old Sam Burnsall had somehow run him down two years ago.

'Cuggy!' said Tom after the Major had gone.

'Go on, then, you have walked a long way.' I picked him up and gave his now rosy cheek a big kiss, thinking how wonderful it was to be out with my own little son on a morning like this.

After a long session on the swings and fifteen or sixteen goes on the little slide in the middle of the green, Tom moved on to one of his favourite activities: walking on the raised steps around the stone village cross. He climbed the different levels and walked round making little burbling noises before stopping and pointing to the road down the green excitedly. I heard an engine sound and looked up to see the familiar hefty figure of Big Alec Lund racing up the road on his fat quad bike. Tom puffed out his cheeks to make a brumming sound and I waved, surprised when the driver slowed down and trundled on to the grass to have a word. I picked Tom up and went over.

'Now then, Alec.'

'Now.' He stood up and stretched, his blue overalls caked in farm gunge. 'Bit o' recreation is it, fer you lads?'

'Just a go on the swings for Tom,' I said, trying to avoid one of Big Alec's familiar digs about teachers having an easy life just because they didn't work the fifteen-hour manual day that he did. Tom wriggled in my arms.

'Dost youth want a sit on ma Honda, then?' said Alec, winking towards Tom. I hesitated, thinking back to the incident with Adam Metcalfe's tractor. I looked at my son.

'Do you want to sit on the big bike next to Alec?' I was amazed when he nodded. Alec reached over with his shovel-like hands and Tom was wedged on to the front of the seat, dwarfed by the giant farmer. He gave a little smile and once more I wished I had my camera, especially when he leant forward to try and reach the handlebars.

'Go on, you drive, then; I could do wi' a break,' laughed Alec. Tom couldn't quite touch the handles so made do with patting the petrol tank and making engine noises.

'You played well in t'arrers on Tuesday,' said Alec, referring to the darts match where I'd put in a rare winning performance.

'Yes, I was pleased with the double sixteen finish.'

'Aye, berrer than my sorry effort . . . Well, best be gettin' goin',' he said, suddenly picking up Tom and handing him over before blasting up the village flinging little bits of mud off the tyres as he went.

'Well that was fun, wasn't it?' I said, putting Tom down.

'Biiiig bike!' he gurgled, making me smile. His hands were cold so we headed back to Craven Bottoms for a hot drink. Back at the house I lay on the sofa with a good strong cup of tea. Tom sucked juice from his toddler cup before climbing up and lying on my front. He nestled his head on to my chest and I gave him a luscious cuddle.

I closed my eyes and thought about what a wonderful thing it was to be a father. Did other dads feel like this? Most of the time I didn't see many of the fathers at school. About half appeared at parents' evenings but usually it was the mothers who did the talking. Many of the dads were farmers and constantly busy or from traditional Dales families where it was considered not so much of a male role to be involved with school or kids.

And what about Sheena? Joyce had finally coaxed her careworn mother into school for a talk and we'd learnt that her father had walked out two years previously, leaving them in dire financial straits. Mrs Baxter had struggled and slid into depression, while Sheena's behaviour had degenerated to the extent where there now seemed to be no discipline at home. It didn't surprise us to learn that Sheena often started the day with no breakfast and ended it by staying up late to watch TV or even roam the village causing a nuisance.

I wondered how much of this could be explained by her not having a dad. No other child in Class 3 was fatherless and it must have affected her deeply. Had he been a good father anyway? Had she ever experienced a lovely moment like this – a dreamy father and daughter snuggle which washed away all other cares? Perhaps she hadn't. Maybe that was one of the reasons her life was full of trouble?

And then there was the ADD: that wasn't her fault either. If she had a condition then she needed help and, furthermore, help from me as her teacher. Yet I was always telling her off and being negative towards her. Suddenly I felt overwhelmingly sorry for Sheena. No one liked her and that wasn't fair. I resolved to be kinder to her in the final week of school before Christmas.

On Monday afternoon my classroom was a sea of coloured scraps of paper. Unwisely I had planned for the children to make collage Christmas cards using old magazines. I'd asked the class to bring in any unwanted magazines from home so that we could cut out pictures to get lots of colours. I hadn't figured on them bringing mostly women's weeklies, which caused widespread snickering as the class pointed out articles about sex or added dubious pencil amendments to lingerie photos. The theme was supposed to be 'The Three Kings' but most children seemed to have done nothing but make a mess with glue and fragments of Marlboro ads.

'Get off!'

I looked up when I heard the shout across the other side of the room.

'Leave me alone!'

It was Glyn Mudd.

Glyn was, it seemed, often engaged in disputes like this. Despite being a happy-go-lucky character, he was the only child in the class who was visibly overweight and this did make him a target from time to time. He was scowling as I walked over to investigate the problem.

'What's the matter, Glyn?'

'They're calling me names.'

'Who?'

'Well, Mervyn did just now – he called me Bunter.'

Mervyn, looking sheepish, fired back, 'Well, he started it, Mr Seed – he took my scissors.'

'But you're supposed to share scissors, Mervyn,' I said. 'And, anyway, that is not an excuse for name-calling. I won't stand for that.'

He shuffled uneasily, mumbling, 'Sorry.'

I looked at Glyn. 'Was there anyone else?' It was a question I didn't really want to ask.

'Sheena,' he said, sounding tired.

During afternoon break I kept Glyn and Sheena inside while the rest of the class went out to play, once I'd warned them all that name-calling would not be tolerated.

I tried to stay calm. 'Now, Sheena, did you call Glyn names this afternoon?'

'No.' She maintained her familiar stony face.

I turned to Glyn, who gave her an accusing look. 'You did, you called me "blob"!'

'Well, people call me names all t'time.'

I drew in a breath. 'But, Sheena, if you don't like it, why do you do it to others?'

'Doesn't bother me,' she said, picking her nails.

'But Glyn doesn't like it, do you, Glyn?' He shook his head. I strained somehow to bring a positive slant to the exchange.

'Well, Sheena, I'd be really pleased with you if you could make a real effort to stop calling Glyn names. Or calling anybody else names. Do you think you could do that?'

She shrugged. 'Dunno.'

'I am asking you to please try, Sheena.'

'OK, can I go now?' I exhaled and nodded, while Glyn looked at me doubtfully. He spoke as Sheena bumped out through the door.

'Mr Seed, can I ask you about the party?'

'Of course, Glyn, what would you like to know?'

'Well, it's on Friday, isn't it?'

'Yes, that's the last day of term. Er, is that it?'

'Are we going to play games in the hall?'

'Yes, fun in the hall then back to the classroom for our party tea.'

His face lit up. 'That's what I wanted to ask about, Mr Seed. Are we bringing food like we did in Class One and Two?'

'Yes – sandwiches, crisps and cakes and things as usual. I'm sending out a reminder letter about it tomorrow.'

'Are we allowed to bring sausage rolls?'

I smiled. 'Of course you can.'

'And chocolate fingers?'

'Glyn, you can bring anything like that within reason.'

'What about marshmallows?'

I got up. 'Listen, you talk to your mum and dad about it when they've read the letter and I'm sure they'll send you with lots of nice things, OK?' I could tell that he wanted to ask more but I ushered him to the door for the last couple of minutes of playtime, hoping that I might still have time for a drink to save my parched throat.

I opened the door and smelt something unpleasant. I'd just arrived home on Wednesday evening and could immediately tell from Barbara's face that all was not well. She'd been on a high for the last few days, having sold nearly all of her decorations and successfully driven all the way to York and back at the weekend. Since then she'd been enjoying the stove and getting the house ready for Christmas, but now she looked grim.

'It's the drains,' she said.

'Oh dear, I thought the smell couldn't just have been Tom.'

'They're blocked somewhere and water's come into the utility room and passage.' She opened the door along the hall to show me. There was a two-inch flood of grimy water right across the concrete floor. At least it was on a level lower than the rest of the house.

'Have you called John?'

'I've tried four or five times and just got his wife, Christine, the last time. She said he's out doing a big job in Chapelgarth and won't be back till late. She suggested trying Mal the plumber but his phone's engaged.'

'So, where's the water coming from?'

'I don't know but I've mopped it up three times and it just keeps coming back.'

'We'll have the frogs back in at this rate,' I said, recalling when we first moved in to find a family of amphibians in the back yard who kept hopping in to the house because it was damper in than out. At that moment Tom came over and gave me a hug.

'Daddee home!'

Barbara stroked his head. 'Poor mite's been left in front of the telly most of the afternoon.'

I went to get changed and put my boots on so I could search around and try and find the cause of the drainage problem. It was cold and dark in the utility room and the odour made it thoroughly unpleasant. The last thing I wanted to do after a hard day at work was wade through effluent with a torch. After fifteen minutes I gave up, not least as my knowledge of drains was almost zero.

At eight o'clock there was a knock on the door and there stood the familiar plaster-haired figure of John Weatherall, Applesett's resident builder, and, at that moment, my personal hero.

'Heard yer experiencin' a spotta bother.'

'Come in, John,' I said. 'I hope you've had something to eat since work.'

'Not really,' he said, twitching his nose. 'Christine said you 'ad water in t'back so I thought I'd best come straight over. Smells like drains all right.'

I showed him the utility room, then he stepped through the back door into the yard. 'Where's yer kitchen waste pipe, then?'

'Er, erm, I don't know.'

Barbara appeared and greeted John. 'Well the sink's in that corner,' she said, looking at the kitchen window.

John went over to the stone wall that ran out from next to the window. It was a good seven feet high but he grabbed the top and scraped for a foothold before scrambling up so he could peep over.

'Can't see from 'ere, it's too dark.' He went back through the house and grabbed a torch from his pickup before walking through the gate next to our house and into the small garden of the cottage at the rear. Barbara and I waited in our back yard where we heard him poking about with a stick the other side of the wall.

'I found yer pipe,' he said. 'Drain's next door, which is unusual . . . And there's yer problem: the grate's full o' leaves.' We heard some scraping and rattling, then the sound of water gurgling. A minute later, John was back with us, wiping his hands on his oily jumper.

'Sorted. You'll just 'ave to mek sure that the drain next door is clear when they're away.'

Barbara and I looked at each other and shuddered. The 'they' he referred to were our part-time next-door neighbours, Wanda and Ralph Holt. They were the wealthy owners of the second-home cottage at the back of our house and our relationship with them had not started well, our having accidentally destroyed their brand new luxury bathroom suite before they'd even used it when an apprentice damp-proofer drilled through the wall with rather too much gusto.

John seemed to be reading our minds. 'Oh, don't worry about them – they're never 'ere and you can just 'op round from time to time and check on the drain.'

'Will the water in here disperse now?' asked Barbara, pointing to the still-flooded utility room.

'Aye, will do eventually,' said John. 'It seeped up because it's on such a low level, but now the drain's flowing it should seep back down again. No plastic membranes these old places, yer see.'

'Thanks so much for coming straight out, John,' I said, feeling inadequate after I hadn't been able to fix such a straightforward problem. 'How much do we owe you?'

'Nothing,' he said, walking back to his truck. 'Just win again at arrers next match.'

When Friday arrived I drove to school with a sense of relief that the Christmas break was just around the corner, but there was also a feeling of trepidation at the thought of facing the traditional class party with Sheena likely to be in overdrive.

After a morning of carols, a retelling of the nativity story by the vicar and a futile attempt at some quiet reading, the afternoon arrived and a gaggle of mums bustled into my classroom to move the furniture and set out the food as Class 3 bounced into the hall for some party games. Mrs Towler, Bernadette's mum, was struggling with a huge box full of bowls, plastic containers and bags.

'There's enough biscuits and jelly here to see out a siege,' she quipped, pressing her back against the door. I had no time to reply, however, knowing that there would be mayhem in the hall if I didn't get there soon. Fortunately, sensible Nina was at the head of the line of children and made them wait outside the door. Half of the class had dressed up for the occasion, the girls wearing cotton frocks and the boys smart shirts, while the rest were attired in regulation school scruff, not least Sheena, whose jumper featured a number of holes. They were all incredibly excited.

Glyn gave me a broad beam, 'I can't wait for the party food.'

'I hope we're playing musical statues so I can laugh at everyone's dancing,' said the effervescent Eddie.

'Aren't Class Four coming in 'ere wi' us?' asked Yvonne.

'No, Miss Croker is going to have the hall after we've finished.'

There was a brief 'Awww', which soon subsided when I told everyone to find a space for the first game – musical bumps. Although the game started well, I soon remembered the profound disadvantage of an activity where most of the children were out and therefore sitting bored around the sides of the room. First they started fidgeting, then messing around, before moving on to bickering. I tried hard to keep Sheena in the game but she wasn't the quickest and I was soon assailed by complaints from those who were called out despite sitting down more quickly than Sheena. Everyone knew the precise moment she touched the floor each time – we could feel it. My mood wasn't improved by the music from Wham!

Next we played Captain's Coming, an old favourite with lots of nautical actions. It had the advantage of lacking music and nor was anyone out. The game still irked a number of children, however, because it was meant to get faster and faster but I could see that poor rotund Glyn was struggling to keep up, so I maintained a rather pedestrian pace.

Next we had pass the parcel, which necessitated more ghastly pop from the tinny cassette player and an extraordinary number of spats. The first time I stopped the music, the parcel was halfway between Vanessa and Chris. Neither would let go and a mini tug-of-war ensued with the girls all crying for justice for Vanessa and the boys screaming about unfairness. I simply put the music back on, which caused more uproar as no paper had been removed.

'Carry on!' I shouted and the poor battered package slowly moved round the circle. Next time I made sure it was in just one child's hands: Yvonne's. She began manically ripping off sheets of newspaper the moment I pressed pause. This caused pandemonium.

'You can't do *that*!'

'She's cheating!'

'Oi, one piece only!'

'MR SEED!'

I hit play just as Sheena slid across with the clear intention of mutilating Yvonne. The parcel landed in Lee's lap and I stopped the music. I wasn't supposed to be watching but the window reflection was proving very useful. Surely Lee would play by the rules. He did, carefully removing just one sheet of paper, while twenty-two pairs of boiling eyes watched him ready to lurch for even the tiniest infringement. A smaller parcel wrapped in gift paper was revealed. Lee didn't know what to do.

'Have I won?' he said.

I tried to explain that he hadn't but no one could hear me for the howls of adjudication.

'Course he ain't won!'

'He musta!'

'He can't see the present!'

'Just cos he's a boy!'

'It's gotta be fully unwrapped, you dope!'

Sheena reached across, swiping the package from Lee's hands and giving it to the child next to him. I started the music, head in hands. The tension rose, everyone knowing that the prize was near: they could feel it as they passed the crumpled thing along, each child holding on to it for as long as they dared before the air of fermenting violence broke their nerve. I decided not to look, then stopped the music. I turned round to see Glyn holding the little parcel, his mouth wide in triumph, amid a ragged circle of slumped disappointment. Sheena was right next to him, her face seething with envy.

Glyn ripped off the wrapping paper to reveal a small packet of felt pens. There was a moment of silence before someone muttered.

'Is that *it*?'

At least Glyn looked pleased and he gave me another smile and a thank you. I was considering stopping the games there, especially as Sheena was now shoving several of the boys as they stood up, but Nina begged if we could play 'Greetings Your Majesty'. It was a game that I'd mentioned to the class the day before and an old favourite of mine. It also had the advantage of being quiet, so I acceded.

I sent Nina to get a chair and a scarf, before threatening everyone that we wouldn't play any more games unless they were quiet. Calm eventually prevailed but Sheena was at breaking point.

I explained the game: 'Right, I'll choose one person each time to be the king or queen. He or she sits on the throne there.' I pointed to the chair in the middle of the room. 'We blindfold the king or queen then I point to a very quiet person and he or she must tiptoe up to the chair and say, "Greetings your majesty" in a disguised voice. The king or queen then guesses who it is and we keep going until they get one right – then someone else has a go on the throne.'

Half the class looked confused but I'd long ago learnt that lengthy explanations were pointless with young children: you just started playing and clarified as you went along. I made sure everyone took their plimsolls off then chose Nina to be queen, since she had asked for the game.

'Not fair,' said Sheena as I blindfolded the ginger monarch with the scarf.

'Shhh!' went the children who had understood the rules.

When Nina was ready I put my finger to my lips and surveyed the class. Everyone wanted to go first and several sat up pillarbox straight with folded arms. Others had their arms in the air and more gave me pleading looks. I was worn out just deciding. Then I saw Glyn and decided to reward his politeness in the previous game. I pointed to him and he responded with an enquiring finger in the chest. I nodded and the hands went down. With a little difficulty he stood up and crept towards Nina. Unfortunately there was a ripple of sniggering as the floorboards creaked slightly under his weight. Unfazed, he approached the plastic throne and mangled his voice into a peculiar high-pitched squeal.

'Grreeeetings your majesteeee.'

There was a muffled cackle and all eyes were on Nina.

'Er, Vanessa?' she said. The class erupted into mirth. This was going to be a good game. I pointed to Bernadette next and she kicked several people in her eagerness to reach the queen.

'Oops, sorry,' she whispered.

'Bernadette!' said Nina with glee. Again, everyone laughed and clapped.

Mervyn was next as king and took several goes before recognising a subject. Class 3 were really enjoying this but I was aware that Sheena wanted a go. She was still shoving people and had managed to obtain Glyn's felt pens from his pocket.

'Right, come on Sheena, you can be queen now,' I said, trying to ignore the grumbles from the well-behaved children who'd been waiting patiently.

''Bout time, too,' she muttered, standing up huffily and managing to tread on Eddie's fingers on her way to the front, which brought from him a volley of protest.

I tied the blindfold tight and pointed to dark-haired Rachel who crept forward in cat-like silence and spoke the greeting in a deep alien growl.

'That's Chris,' said Sheena, sounding confident. The class cheered and I chose someone else to make the salutation. Once more she was wrong and it occurred to me that she didn't know her classmates as well as the other children, most of whom had been together since starting at Cragthwaite Primary. She got five more wrong before I realised that everyone had now had a turn. Sheena sat there quietly as if her temporary blindness had somehow subdued her.

At this point a very mischievous idea entered my head and I was just about to dismiss it, because Sheena might flip, when I realised that it would be better to go ahead and do it – to treat her like any other member of the class. I mumbled a few 'Errs, as if deciding who to choose, then crept towards the door and opened it very slowly. I put my finger to my lips and signalled for everyone else to stand up. I then beckoned them towards the door and the plan began to dawn. The children snuck out of the hall like thieves, and Glyn had the sense to slide rather than walk. We left Sheena sitting there in regal isolation and I closed the door.

Most of Class 3 were grinning wildly and whispering about the immense fun of the situation but I shushed them and made sure that everyone could see through the glass doors. How long would she last? The children around me started shaking with silent glee as we watched the blind sovereign wait in agitation. I felt sure that she would lift the blindfold any second but she just sat there. I was beginning to feel that we'd left her long enough when the opposite door of the hall opened and in walked Joyce, her mouth agape.

I pushed our door and sprang forward.

Joyce gave me a puzzled look, realising that it was a game, and whispered, 'Mr Seed, your party food's ready.'

Sheena shot upwards, 'Mrs Berry!'

The rest of the class burst through the door like a popped balloon, shouting and roaring with laughter, as Sheena pulled off the blindfold looking dazed.

'I thought summat were going on!' yelled Sheena, unsure whether to laugh or not. With delight I noticed that the children cheered her acceptance of the jest.

Glyn ran up to me gushing with elation. 'Mr Seed that was brilliant fun, and now we can have our *food*!' I thought for a moment that he was going to hug me. Joyce shook her head and left the hall chortling.

The classroom looked magnificent. It had been decorated with balloons and streamers and all the desks had been pushed together and covered with paper tablecloths to make one long, wondrous feast table. It was sagging under the weight of sandwiches, sausage rolls, crisps, slices of pie, cheese on sticks, buns, jellies, cakes and chocolate biscuits. The children claimed to have washed their hands in under five seconds and each grabbed a chair. I made my usual plea for everyone to consume at least one savoury item before gorging on cakes but I knew it would be in vain.

Five minutes later there was relative calm: the class were forcing so much food into their mouths that they had no capacity to communicate other than by pointing. The mums and I trundled round, refilling plastic beakers with economy squash, while each child explored the limits of what a paper plate could hold. It was grotesque. After another five minutes, the sausage rolls had all gone and the pace began to slacken. One or two green-looking individuals ceased eating and Sheena began flicking Hula Hoops.

'Right, just stop there please, everyone. I think we need to have a little tidy up: there's more food on the table than on your plates and I do not want to see any more on the floor. Clear?'

There was a mumble of agreement as the children slowly moved around picking up half-chewed Scotch eggs and gathering hairy lumps of pastry from the floor. I went over to thank the mums for all their efforts but had to return swiftly when the noise level began to rise. Nina had her hand in the air.

'Right, that's enough, quiet everyone!' It subsided only a little.

'Mr Seed,' said Nina.

'Hand down, Nina, you can ask me later.' Still the hubbub continued. 'Come on, Class Three, don't spoil the party.'

Then I saw the cause. A lump of plastic vomit on the table. Someone had been to the joke shop. The children screeched with delight when I saw it, but there was worse, and a number of individuals couldn't stop themselves from pointing further down the table where, nestling in among the crumpled mini-rolls was a shiny fake dog turd. I pulled a suitably disgusted face and the class roared. I laughed, too, shaking my head and making the calamitous error of not checking my chair as I sat down.

It took a full ten minutes for the class to calm down after the whoopee cushion erupted and even the mums were beside themselves with glee. Sheena danced with delight and I didn't need to be told who the culprit was. I just had to laugh along: it was the end of term after all.

'Well, you paid me back for the trick in the hall, fair enough,' I said to Sheena. Then I felt a tap on the shoulder and there was Nina, the only child in the room who wasn't in raptures.

'Mr Seed, Glyn isn't here.'

I found him in the toilets, sitting in the corner. His face was streaked with tears and his breathing jumpy between sobs. Judging by the amount of crumpled toilet roll by his side, he had been there for some time.

'Glyn, whatever's the matter?' I said in a soft voice. He didn't reply; in the distance we could hear the hubbub from the classroom. At least the mums were there.

I tried again, 'Glyn, come on, you can't stay here.' He looked down and started to cry again, blowing snot on to his sleeves. I passed him some more tissue but didn't know what else to do. I waited. After a minute he spoke.

'She was calling me names again.'

'Who was?' It was a pointless question.

'Sheena.'

'Was it just her?'

He nodded. 'Really horrible things, saying I'm too fat and shouldn't eat any of the food or I'll die.'

'You know that's not true, Glyn.'

He continued to sob, 'I was *so* looking forward to the party, Mr Seed.'

'I know you were, Glyn, I know you were,' I said.

It felt like I was back to square one. But I had to do something for this poor crumpled boy, so I helped him up, gave him another tissue and said, 'Now, look at me, Glyn. I am going to do something about this situation, you can be sure of that. And do you know what? I'm really, really pleased with you today: in the whole party, you were the *only* one who remembered to say thank you, and that's very important. I'm going to tell Mrs Berry about that, too. You are a good boy, just you remember that.'

He stared up gravely, gave an enormous sniff and nodded slowly. I gave a nod in return and we walked back to the classroom together.

Chapter Eight

Jess

We spent Christmas away from the Dales, driving between our parents in Cheshire and Essex who were desperate to spend time with Tom. It was wonderful to have not only babysitting but a chance to lie in and enjoy good food and drink. Barbara and I felt thoroughly refreshed as we drove back to Yorkshire and the high hills which had become our home.

'I'm sure I just heard somebody cough,' said Barbara as we carried our bags upstairs to the bedroom on our return to Craven Bottoms.

'Maybe squatters have moved in while we were away.'

'Don't joke, I definitely heard something.'

'Perhaps the mice have pneumonia.'

'Wanda and Ralph aren't here for New Year, are they?'

'I didn't see their car or any lights on. Anyway, last time they were here we couldn't hear them at all: the walls are too thick. Are you sure it wasn't Tom?'

'He's still asleep in his car seat.'

'Oh well, a puzzle then.'

After we'd had a cup of tea and unpacked, I did have a good look round upstairs, including in the mysterious pink cupboard at the end of the landing. This had been an access point from the cottage joined on to the back of our house, and was where the ancient Miss Tiplady, a previous tenant of the cottage, once had 'bathroom rights', enabling her to use this tiny room in our property. Apart from dust, cobwebs, junk and mice droppings, there was nothing there. I went to tell Barbara that the house was clear.

'I heard something again when I was on the loo,' she said. 'It sounded like it was coming from next door. Like something creaking.'

'You mean from the flat?'

'I think so.'

'But it's been empty for two years – you'd have thought Mr Crockett would've told us if someone had moved in.'

'Maybe he's sold it.'

'But there's not been any "for sale" board or anything.'

'Just go and look, would you?'

'Look at what?'

'At the flat outside – see if there's a light on or anything.'

I dutifully put my shoes back on and tramped out on to the road outside to look up at the strange building adjoining our house. It was a kind of large two-storey extension built on to the side in brick and painted to look like stone. The bottom half belonged to us, consisting of our garage, utility room and the peculiar L-shaped passage joining the two, but the upper part was a self-contained flat which still belonged to the previous owner, Mr Crockett, and had been unoccupied ever since we'd moved in. He had tried to sell it to us but we couldn't afford it and found it a most depressing, uncared-for place anyway. Since then it had fallen into further disrepair with paint peeling off the walls and the window frames showing signs of damp rot.

Looking up there didn't seem to be any signs of life. The same greying net curtains filled the large window at the front and the small window at the side was dark. Just to make sure, I went round the side, climbed the ugly concrete stairs and knocked on the door. There was no answer so I returned home to tell Barbara that Boo Radley was playing hard to get.

'Hmmm, well, I definitely heard something next door and it wasn't just a mouse.'

'It's a mystery . . .' I said in a stupid eerie voice.

Barbara gave me a withering look. 'Anyway, what have you got lined up for the rest of the holiday?'

'Well, er, I've got to plan next term's work . . . er, tidy up the study a bit . . . maybe go for a climb up Spout Fell to work off some of this turkey blubber – why?'

Her tone changed distinctly at this point. 'Well . . . when I was in the bathroom hearing the strange noise, I was also looking at those awful tiles on the wall.'

I knew where this was heading. 'But we only decorated the bathroom just over a year ago.'

'We did the wallpaper, yes, but not those horrid brown tiles.'

'That's because we couldn't afford to replace them and we can't now – especially after an expensive Christmas.'

'Well, I was thinking about that and there's still some of the two hundred pounds left that I made from selling the decorations in York.'

There seemed no escape. 'But even if we found some tiles we

could afford, it's still a big job to take off the old ones and there isn't that much of the holiday left.'

Then she played her trump card. 'I know, I know, but I think we should at least go to Hauxton and look at the price of tiles and, anyway, it would be much better to do this now while I'm still just a little pregnant rather than when I'm enormous or we have wailing babies again.' I couldn't win.

Annoyingly we found a warehouse in Hauxton that sold very cheap tiles which were a tasteful off-white and so that was that. I resigned myself to spending New Year pasted in grout.

When we returned to Applesett and Tom was having his nap I did manage to sneak out of the house for a quick walk before the DIY began: I was desperate to stretch my legs after all the inert overindulgence of Christmas.

Rather than go down to the waterfall or behind our house to Buttergill, I decided to walk to the top of the village and along the path from Hill Top Farm. A late December greyness had settled on the buildings under thick cloud and even the grass on the green looked tired and worn. I passed the lofty village hall, which had once been a non-conformist chapel, then two tiny squat cottages until I reached old Sam Burnsall's grand eighteenth-century villa which looked down over the length of the green. I passed nobody – the population of the village being tucked up in front of cosy log fires on a bleak day like this, no doubt.

Hill Top Farm was awash with mud so I decided to abandon walking over the field and instead take the stony lane which ran across to the Buttergill road. The clouds scudded low overhead, driven by a wind that seemed to be in a hurry to reach the end of the year. I soon arrived home again and spent a moment outside, kicking my boots against the garden wall to get some of the mud off. A movement above caught my eye and I looked up to catch the most fleeting glimpse of a face in the window of the flat before it was hidden by the net curtains. My heart jumped. It was ghostly and pale – had I really seen someone? Could it have been a reflection? There still seemed to be no lights on but it appeared that Barbara was right – I hurried indoors to tell her.

'Was it a man or a woman?'

'I think it was a nun.'

'Don't be silly – was it a woman?'

'Yes, er, I think so. But I barely saw her – it was a nanosecond, honest.'

'Well, do you think we should go and say hello?'

'No! I mean, not yet. She did look kind of, well, strange.'

'That's not very neighbourly.'

'I know. Perhaps we should. Or you go and I'll start taking off those tiles.'

'Wimp.'

The tiles didn't want to come off. They seemed to be welded to the wall and I had to resort to chiselling away the mortar between them and then levering them off with a screwdriver. After an hour of futile effort, Barbara brought some coffee.

'Is that all you've done?'

'It's hard work, this. Anyway, have you been to see Mrs Boo yet?'

'I went and knocked on the door but she didn't answer. You're right – it's really odd that there don't seem to be any lights on.'

After a sit-down and a drink I decided to change my plan of attack and belt the tiles with a hammer to break them up. I heard Tom downstairs pleading to go and see what exciting noisy thing Daddy was doing. There were two hammers in my toolbox: a small metal-handled claw hammer and a big, hefty club-type. I put on some goggles and went for the big one. The first tile smashed with a satisfying crunch, splintering into cracked pieces which would prise off more easily, no doubt. I whacked the next one and felt the whole wall shudder. In fact, it seemed to be moving rather a lot. Then I realised that the tiles were on plasterboard. Perhaps it would be easier just to take the whole board off? I thumped another one and heard a strange wailing sound.

'Barbara?' She didn't answer so I stepped out of the bathroom and on to the stairs. I could see that she'd shut herself in the kitchen with Tom; the radio was on in there, too. I went back and put my ear to the wall. Nothing. I crunched another tile and heard the sound again: a definite wail – a human voice.

I stopped again and considered exactly where I was in the peculiar old stone building that was Craven Bottoms. For some reason, the bathroom was built halfway up the twisting stairs, between the ground and first floors. This had always struck us as very odd but now I realised the reason. There was nowhere in the house to have a bathroom, apart from the tiny cramped cupboard in the eaves, so a previous owner must have knocked through the outside wall at this point and taken some of the space from the flat next door. No wonder the walls were so thin and no wonder there was moaning from the other side – I was belting the sides of a hollow box right next to Mrs Boo's living room. I put down the hammer and went next door.

It was dark outside now and, looking up, I could see a faint light from the flat window. She was definitely in. I climbed the steps and knocked.

'Hello?' There was no answer. 'It's Andy from next door!' I shouted. 'I want to say sorry for all the noise!'

Across the green a curtain twitched and a light came on. Someone had heard me. I knocked again and waited.

After an age I heard movement and the click of bolts and chains. The door groaned open a fraction and I saw a milky female eye regarding me with deep suspicion. No wonder: I still had the goggles on my head and was coated with dust.

'Hello, er, I'm your neighbour from next door and I just want to apologise for all the noise – I'm doing some DIY and I can't really do it quietly,' I gabbled.

The door was open barely an inch but I could detect the strong smell of cigarettes and could just make out a strip of an ashen, middle-aged face.

''Ow long will yer be?' she said in a nervous croak.

'Erm, a couple of hours or maybe three. Would you like me to wait until you've gone out?' It was clear that she was the kind of person who avoided going out.

'No, best just gerrit over with.' She shut the door and I scuttled home to tell Barbara that I'd met Mrs Boo.

A week later I was back at school with the spring term having just started. Sheena was away and the atmosphere in my room was unquestionably different as I settled the class down to talk about our new English project.

'Right, who knows what an autobiography is?' I wrote the word on the scratchy blackboard. Just two hands up.

'Yes, Lee?'

'Is it something to do with cars?'

'Ah, I see your thinking – good try but it's nothing to do with cars.' I turned to Vanessa.

'It's a book where someone writes about another person's life.'

'Excellent, although actually that's a *bio*graphy. So what do you think an *auto*biography is?' Vanessa put up her hand again. 'Let's have somebody else. What do you think, Mervyn?'

His face creased in thought. 'Is it a book about someone written by a machine?'

'Not quite, but that's a clever answer.' Suddenly four hands shot up. 'Yes, Bernadette?'

She was bobbing in her seat. 'A book about machines written by a person!'

'No, forget machines and cars and think about people.'

Hazel offered an answer. 'A book about people written by a person?'

I realised that we could be here forever so I turned to Vanessa who gave me a 'Why didn't you just let me say so before' look before explaining that it's a book someone has written about themselves.

'Well done, Vanessa. That's our new project for this half-term: you're each going to write your autobiography.'

Jess Iveson looked aghast. 'We 'ave to write a book? I can 'ardly read one!'

I chuckled, 'No, you don't have to write a whole book, just a few pages about your life.'

'But am only eight – I've 'ardly done owt.' Her mouth was open and she was looking at her friends as if I was nuts. Jess was short with tightly curled dark hair and a polkadot freckled face. She lived in the small village of Pikebergh, which clung high up on the valley side in mid-Swinnerdale.

'That's actually a very good point, Jess, and I do realise that you're all still young and very few of you have had an interesting job or travelled the world.'

'You're dead right there; the furthest I've been is Bridlington.'

'Don't worry, I'm going to give you all a help sheet with ideas for the sort of things you can write. It'll be about your home and family and your pets, and then you can also write about your hobbies and your possessions, too.'

She didn't look convinced. 'But my house is really boring. I don't want ter write about my brother either – he's a berk.' Several children laughed and I had to calm them down before continuing.

'Autobiographies often start with a section about grandparents and parents – if they've had interesting lives you've got a good start. So, the first thing you're all going to do is some research at home.'

I could hear Jess muttering to Yvonne, 'What a rubbish idea for a project—'

I cleared my throat. 'Did you have something to say, Jessica?'

'Can we do pictures as well?'

I had to hand it to her – she was sharp. 'Yes, the writing will be illustrated.'

I was just about to give out the help sheets when there was a knock at the door and two diminutive infants from Class 1 entered looking very pleased with themselves. They were holding a plastic box.

'Yes, girls, what can I do for you?' I said, putting on an extra-friendly face.

They answered in unison, 'Would you like a piece of shortbread?'

'Did you make it?' They nodded with big grins. I looked in the box. 'So you've been baking with Mrs Bramley this morning, have you?' They nodded again. The shortbread smelt good but looked strangely grey. I picked up a small piece with every eye in the room following me.

'Awww, can we have a bit?' said Eddie, who already knew the answer. 'It's not fair.'

The two infants looked interested in my verdict so I took a bite. 'Mmm, delicious, girls – well done.' They lifted their little shoulders and skipped out, giggling. It was actually very tasty so I quickly scoffed the rest while the children pulled faces.

At lunchtime I went in search of Val to see if she had any treasury tags for the booklets my class were going to make. Despite her gruff manner she was always a great help and I liked her immensely as a colleague. She was standing on a desk taking down a mobile.

'Keeps setting the bloody alarm off.'

'I didn't know we had an alarm.'

'That's because they didn't bother to wire up your saggy old outhouse.'

I noticed a square of the infants' shortbread on her desk. 'You've not had your shortbread, Val. And why is it grey, by the way?'

She turned round. 'You didn't eat it, did you?'

I gulped. 'Yes, why?'

'Why do you think it's grey? They've been playing on the muddy field and then they're told they're going to do baking. Emma sends them to wash their hands but they're too excited to do it properly. She doesn't check them – Sue told me.'

I held my stomach. 'Ugh.'

'Best keep a basin by your bed tonight,' she laughed.

Val found me some treasury tags and asked what they were for.

'My class are doing autobiographies. I want to make them loose-leaf so they can add bits and pieces from home like a kind of scrapbook.'

She looked doubtful. 'Idea from college is it? Sounds like one.'

'Er, no, it's one of mine actually. I just thought it might get some of them doing some research at home and perhaps involve a few parents. It might just inspire a few to write a bit more if they have an interesting family.'

'Oh, right, I see. Well, I hope it works.' Her indifference didn't instil me with confidence.

On the way back to my room I passed Joyce who seemed to be talking to herself before she noticed me.

'Oh, Andy, sorry, I was miles away. Don't forget Sheena's mother is coming to see us at four tomorrow in my office.' She dashed off before I could reply.

At home that evening I surveyed the new tiles in the bathroom, while we gave Tom a bath. They looked good and I was just about to admit to Barbara that she was right about changing them when Tom went into a manic splashing routine, spraying water in all directions while singing, 'Bish, bish, bosh!' By the time we stopped him both of us were soaked.

'Tommy, you are a fruitcake!' said Barbara.

'Froopcake,' said Tom.

Just as I reached for a towel, we heard the now familiar cough from next door.

'Mrs Boo is in, for a change,' I said.

'You really shouldn't call her that, she might hear you.'

'But we don't know her real name.'

'I still can't believe you didn't ask when you spoke to her last week.'

'I don't think she would have told me; she's very spooky.'

'You still should've asked.'

'But somebody in the village must know who she is – what about Mrs Dent? She knows everything.'

'I asked when I was in the shop. She knew a woman had moved in but had no idea who she was and hoped I could tell her.'

'Perhaps she's a recluse run away from a guilty past . . .'

'What I don't understand is where she gets all her fags from when she never goes out.'

'Maybe she has a secret tunnel.'

'Oh no!'

'What's up, you worried about the tunnel?'

'No, Tom's just peed in the bath.'

After he was rinsed and dried I put him in his elephant pyjamas and read him a few nursery rhymes from the book he referred to as 'Manna Goose'. His eyelids drooped and I rapidly scooped him into his cot. Barbara came in to give him a final kiss and we crept out of his room together. I looked at her as we closed the door.

'Do you think asking eight-year-olds to write autobiographies is stupid?'

She didn't hesitate, 'Yes.'

After school the next day, I found myself sitting in Joyce's office waiting for Mrs Baxter, Sheena's mum. It was quarter past four and she was late.

'I'll give her a call,' said Joyce. 'This is wasting our time.'

Just as she reached into her drawer for the contacts file, there was a faint knock at the door. I stood up and opened it. On the other side was a large woman with dyed blonde hair and an air of resignation.

'Come in, Mrs Baxter.'

Joyce proffered a chair. 'Do sit down; we're glad you've made it.'

She looked anxious. 'I'm everso sorry am late; I jus' lost track o' time.'

'Not to worry,' said Joyce smiling. 'You're here now.'

Mrs Baxter turned to me, 'Sheena's 'ad a temperature last couple o' days. Well, she says she 'as, so I've let her stop at 'ome, like.'

'OK, thanks for letting me know,' I said, hopeful that Joyce would do most of the talking.

'What is Sheena like at home, Mrs Baxter?' asked Joyce.

She shuffled in her chair. 'Well, a 'andful'd prob'ly be best way to describe it.'

'You have problems with her, then?'

'Well, she's out of 'ouse most of time, 'anging round the village but, aye, she can't stay away from trouble, that lass. She's aged me, she 'as.' I wondered how old she was. Thirty-five? Forty? Her face was drawn and she sat on the edge of her chair in a frayed coat squeezing the handles of a shopping bag.

Joyce continued, keen to get to the nub. 'I'm sorry to hear that. And are you aware of the number of problems we've had with her at school, as well?'

'Well, Sheena don't tell me nowt, but a couple of the other mothers 'ave made it plain to me, aye. I'm sorry, but it's a real struggle for me wi'out 'er dad on t'scene, I can tell yer.'

I couldn't help but feel deeply sorry for this woman who clearly had no control over a daughter who was only nine.

Joyce continued to sound businesslike, 'And is her father still absent?'

'Aye, and I don't even know if I want 'im back either.'

'I'm sorry this is all a bit personal, Mrs Baxter, but we've got to be aware of the situation so that we can all work together to help Sheena stay out of trouble.'

After a few more questions Mrs Baxter began to relax a little, perhaps realising that any relevant information might make a difference to her daughter and ultimately herself. She told us that there had been more problems at her previous school than their report suggested and that the family had moved partly for the pub job she now had at Chapelgarth and partly to try and start over. She regretted that Sheena was an only child and wished that she knew where everything had gone wrong.

'The doctor's put me on tablets fer me depression, too. That doesn't 'elp.'

I was moved by her sad speech but Joyce, who had clearly heard many such tales before, continued making efficient notes and went on to explain about the educational psychologist's visit and how there would be a meeting to decide on the best way for County to support the school in dealing with Sheena. Mrs Baxter seemed to be only half-listening, her hands once more twitchy, perhaps at the mention of official intervention.

'It's really vital that you come to the next meeting here at school so we all know what's going on and can all sing off the same songsheet,' said Joyce, her eyes fixing the agitated parent hard.

I felt the need to say something. 'How do you think we can best help Sheena, Mrs Baxter?'

She turned but barely looked at me, instead shaking her head. 'I 'aven't a clue; I 'aven't a clue.'

Jess bounded up to me with a fat cardboard folder. It was Wednesday morning just before the start of school and she'd come straight off the minibus which delivered the children from Pikebergh and surrounding farms to Cragthwaite.

'Look at this, Mr Seed, I've got loads!'

'I can see that, but loads of what?'

Her eyes were sparkling. 'Research stuff, you know, fer the author biographies.'

'Autobiographies.'

'Yes, whatever, look!'

She opened up the dog-eared folder and out slid piles of crusty photos, all black and white, letters, newspaper cuttings, receipts and old handwritten lists in beautiful tilted script.

'Is all this about your family, then?' I asked.

'Aye, it's mainly about me dad – 'e we were famous in Swin'dale when 'e was a lad. They never told me before.'

I looked at the numerous old newspaper articles and photos from the 1950s. The pictures all showed the same thing: a small boy on a donkey.

'Why was he famous then, Jess?'

She straightened out one of the larger press photos. 'Well, this is me dad when 'e was about five. Ma grandparents 'ad a farm back then at the bottom of the big 'ill below the village.'

'In Pikebergh, you mean?'

'Aye, and they didn't 'ave a car so me dad 'ad to walk to the old school in the village up that massive 'ill.'

'Oh, I see, so they put him on a donkey to climb the hill.'

'Yeah, the donkey were used to it cos it carried milk cans from the fields usually.'

'So how come the story made all these newspapers?'

At this point, Yvonne came into the classroom to see what was going on, but Jess ignored her, comically placing her hands on her hips.

'Well, what happened was, after a while me grandad got fed up wi' walking up the big 'ill every day wi' me dad and 'e reckoned that after a few weeks the donkey knew the way to the school so he just sent 'im out on 'is own.'

I was speechless and Yvonne saw her chance. 'Really? Is that true, Jess?'

She nodded. 'Look at the newspapers 'ere.'

I tried to picture the scene. 'So, your dad's parents put him on a donkey at the farm at the bottom of the hill, what, about half a mile from the village, and just let the donkey walk up to the school along the road unsupervised? And he was just five?'

'Aye, it's funny in't it?'

'It's unbelievable.' But there was the evidence right in front of me. 'This is fantastic, Jess . . . How did the press find out?'

'You mean the newspapers? Well, a man went past the donkey in a car and stopped to take a photo, then he sent the picture to the newspapers and then loads o' reporters started turnin' up at the farm, me dad says.'

Yvonne was rifling through the pictures. 'Ha! Your dad looks just like you.'

'But what happened to the donkey when it got to school?' I asked.

Jess looked at me with surprise. 'Hey, I asked that 'n' all, Mr Seed. Well, the teacher – Miss Thorner I think she were called – got me dad off the donkey then put it in a meadow at the back o' the school yard. Me grandad gave them some 'ay for the winter.'

'What, then the teacher put 'im back on the donkey at 'ome time?' asked Yvonne, while Jess nodded. 'Ace!'

'I think we should enact this for an assembly,' I said, nudging Jess. 'We'll put you on a donkey and send you back to Pikebergh.'

'No way!' she blurted, unsure whether I was serious. 'I'll fall off in front o' everyone.'

'Exactly,' said Yvonne. 'Let's do it!'

'I was only kidding, girls . . .'

Jess started to gather all of the cuttings back into the folder.

'Anyway, Mr Seed, when can we start writing our aut- our au-to-bi-ographies? I can't wait.'

Three weeks later I was at home marking books on the dining room table. Barbara came down the stairs after putting Tom to bed and walked over to massage my shoulders as I worked.

'I saw Mrs Boo at the window today. She is creepy, isn't she?'

I looked up. 'I thought we weren't allowed to call her Mrs Boo?'

'Well, it *is* a good name. Anyway, Tom's started saying Mrs Boo now so that's that.'

'Have you spoken to her yet?'

'No. I keep thinking of popping round, though, or inviting her in here. She must be so lonely. Maybe she'd like to have a toddler to play with.'

'But what if Tom starts calling her Mrs Boo?'

'Oh, that's a point.'

'And the cigarette smell in that flat is horrendous.'

She pulled a face. 'Hmmm, I wouldn't like that.'

'Erm, it's nice to have a chat right now but I really must finish marking these autobiographies – I told the kids they could have them back tomorrow.'

'Sorry, I'll leave you in peace . . . Are they any good, by the way?'

'Any good?' I handed her a smart red booklet entitled *Jess Iveson: My Life*. 'Read that.'

She took it off to the living room, then returned twenty minutes later.

'Andy, this is brilliant! That story about the donkey is just amazing; I can't believe it. It's so interesting, with all the press cuttings and everything. I take back what I said before – clever boy – you must be thrilled.'

There was a smug grin on my face as I slid the remaining pile of autobiographies into my bag. I didn't tell her that they were rubbish.

Chapter Nine

Eddie

'Why didn't we do a pantomime last term, Mr Seed?'

I turned round, knowing that it would be Eddie. We stood shivering on the rimy tarmac waiting for the bell. My tea had gone instantly cold and all I could think of was getting back inside to a warm classroom: this was not the best day to do playground duty.

'I'm sure you've asked me that before, Eddie.'

'I know but I'm desperate to be in a show – I love panto.'

'Maybe next Christmas we'll do one.' I knew which part Eddie would want: he would make a wonderful dame. His family were incomers and he was nothing like a typical Dales child: he was exuberant, witty and loved to show off. Right now, however, he looked miserable: running round a damp school yard on a bitter January morning was not his idea of fun. He much preferred the company of adults.

'I loved the *Jack and the Beanstalk* you did two years ago. I was in the infants then but I was desperate to be on the stage. If we perform that again can I be Jack's mother?'

I thought back to the various disasters which had befallen that show, not least the tragi-comic moment when poor Daisy the Cow had split asunder after her back end failed to negotiate the steps up to the stage.

'If we do *Jack and the Beanstalk* again, I'll make sure you have a suitable part, Eddie.'

'Oh goodie!' He clapped his hands together and jumped up and down. He'd probably go around telling everyone that we were going to do a panto now.

'Ah, Eddie, I want to ask you a favour while you're here.'

'Of course, Mr Seed, anything,' he said, smiling.

'Well, tomorrow I'm out for the morning, visiting another school, and Mrs Forrest the supply teacher will be taking you.'

'Ooh yes, I like Mrs Forrest, she always tells us about her puppies.'

'Yes but Mrs Forrest is going to be busy because she'll want to mark all the work the class does before she leaves at lunchtime.'

He looked slightly perplexed. 'Er, OK.'

'Now, if she's busy marking, she'll need to have some peace – to be left alone.'

'Why are you telling me, Mr Seed?'

I fixed him with a mock-stern stare. 'Eddie Sykes, you know exactly why I am telling you this.'

'You mean I like to talk a lot?'

'You like to talk a very lot and, although I'm sure Mrs Forrest would be delighted to have your company normally and to discuss puppies or kittens, I think it might be best if you left her alone.'

He nodded reluctantly, then changed the subject. 'Which school are you visiting tomorrow, then, Mr Seed?'

'Ingleburn RC.'

'The little Catholic school? I used to go there!'

'I didn't know that.'

'Yes, just in Reception – that's where I started before we moved to Cragthwaite.'

'Oh right, was it a nice school?'

'It was nice in some ways but very different from here. Sister Mary Brendan used to lock naughty boys in the stock cupboard.'

'Eddie, you're making that up.'

'Well, that's what the older kids used to tell us. Anyway, it's worth going just to see the wimples.'

I laughed hard then looked at my watch. There was still a minute to go but I sent for the bell anyway.

The following morning at half past eight I climbed into the Alfasud and mumbled my usual prayer for the car to start. It was fine in the warmer months but maintained a special resentment towards these damp winter days and often refused to cooperate at all. I turned the key and felt the familiar throb of the starter motor trying to coax the engine into life. At least the battery was OK. On the fourth attempt there was a splutter, then a rumble from the exhaust as the noisy flat-four engine finally awoke.

I turned right towards Doddthorpe, instead of left towards Cragthwaite, and looked forward to spending a few hours in another school for the first time since I was at college.

My visit to Ingleburn was an indirect result of the government of the day's drastic reforms of education. Concerned that some schools were not covering all the necessary subjects in a balanced way, they introduced a new curriculum written by panels of 'experts'. The result was thousands of pages of unrealistic expectations because no one had thought to take a holistic view: each author of every one of the ten subject folders crammed his or her document to the brim, insisting it was the most important.

The Swinnerdale headteachers had met together to discuss this new curriculum and the numerous problems of initiating it in small rural schools where there were several age groups in each class and limited specialist expertise among the staff. Design and Technology had been identified as one of the new subjects which struck particular fear into older teachers who found change difficult. At this point, Joyce had helpfully suggested that I was now virtually an expert in D&T, as it was known, and that perhaps the cluster of schools could use some of their in-service training money to pay for a supply teacher so that I could be released to visit other schools and offer advice.

At first I was doubtful about the whole scheme, especially when I thought back to the early disasters I'd overseen when first trying to instigate the subject at Cragthwaite. There had been my infamous 'Inventions for the Blind' project, in which the children, in their misguided enthusiasm, had produced a number of highly dangerous and inappropriate aids for unsighted people, some of them illicitly dismembering PE equipment to obtain components. Then there was the replica sewage farm, which had nearly poisoned a child in my first class. Was I really the right person to advise others? But Joyce had talked me into it, saying it would be good for my career, and heaped praise on my later work. And so it was that I headed towards Ingleburn Roman Catholic Primary, after its head, the legendary nun Sister Mary Brendan, had pleaded with the other schools to be given help first.

I had no idea what to expect as I parked my car next to the large Catholic church in the town and made my way to the tiny stone school adjoining it. There were a few boys running round the enclosed yard at the front of the building chasing a mangy tennis ball as I opened the gate. I recalled two of them from the last time we had played the school at football. They clearly recognised me, too.

'Hey, it's Cragthwaite's manager!' said one, nudging his friend. 'Hello.'

'Morning, boys,' I said. 'Where's the main entrance?'

'It's just there. It's the only entrance,' he said, pointing to a door that looked like it led into a house. Inside there was a narrow, gloomy corridor with a door to one side, which led to a cramped infant classroom. The only other way was up a flight of stairs so I ventured on to the upper floor. There I found another small teaching space and a large cupboard, which appeared to act as an office. Inside, licking a brown envelope was the figure of a petite, shrivelled nun facing away from me. I was surprised to see her head uncovered.

I cleared my throat, 'Ahem, hello.'

'Weeuurrpp!' She jumped in fright before composing herself. 'I'm sorry, we're not used to men in here. You must be Mr Seed.'

'That's right, please called me Andy.'

'Alfie? You don't get many of those these days.'

'No, *Andy*.'

'I'm sorry, Andy, as in Andrew, I see. I'm Sister Mary Brendan. I've heard a lot about you, young man.'

'Ah, some of it good, I hope,' I said, smiling.

'No, all of it was good, actually.'

I decided not to waste any more time. 'So, I'm here to help you with Design and Technology – how would you like me to start?'

'Hold your horses, I've a few things to do first, then I need to get the children in and call the register, and then set them off to work. You can wait in here, if you like, or, well, there's nowhere else really.'

'Oh, right. Er, is there anything I can be doing in the meantime? Looking at children's work or seeing what kind of resources you have, maybe?'

She stood up, which didn't seem to make her any taller. 'Well, not really: we don't have any resources for CDT, or whatever it's called, and the children haven't done any work – that's why you're here. I was hoping you'd get us started.'

I was just about to say that D&T couldn't be done without tools and materials when I recalled my early days at Cragthwaite with Howard Raven, the first head, who had landed me in just such a situation and yet somehow I'd made a start.

I looked around. 'Well, I'm sure you have paper and scissors and card and glue – there are quite a few things you can do with those.' But Sister Mary Brendan had gone. A moment later I heard a handbell ring, so I used the opportunity to peek inside the junior classroom. I thought Hilda Percival's room was old-fashioned but this was Stone Age: the walls were bare and the old, wooden desks were lined up in rows facing a blackboard and a large framed embroidery of The Lord's Prayer next to a crucifix. This was not going to be easy.

There was a rush of stomping feet as the older children came up the stairs with their teacher trailing behind howling at them not to run. I retreated into the poky office and scanned the room. There were overloaded shelves everywhere containing a jumble of books, folders and dusty boxes. A battered filing cabinet was topped with a stuffed owl, and half of the space was taken up by a solitary desk crowded with papers, beneath which seemed to be an antique typewriter. There was no evidence of tea- or coffee-making facilities. Opposite me was a door I considered might lead to a kitchen area or toilet. Or perhaps this was the infamous stock cupboard?

I twiddled my thumbs for a few minutes, then made a few meaningless notes in the exercise book I'd brought along. I could hear the register being called in the echoey classroom next door. A moment later there was a click and Sister Mary Brendan bustled in to pick up a pile of papers from the office desk.

'Of course I'm retiring in a few years; I'm very tempted just to leave all this new curriculum nonsense.' She disappeared again and I heard her issuing instructions for the children to get on with a handwriting exercise. She reappeared. 'I only get part-time administrative help here, too. There's no hall, no staffroom, no kitchen or dining area, the toilets are outside . . . We don't have a field and there's not enough space to do anything and yet I'm expected to teach drama, techno-whatsit, science, and all this other hogwash, just like the big schools.'

'What's in there?' I said, pointing to the unmarked door.

'Oh, just a cupboard, nothing exciting.'

'Do you remember Eddie Sykes?'

The change of subject threw her slightly. 'Edward Sykes, verbose little boy?'

'Yes, that'll be him.'

'He was here for a year in the infants but I didn't teach him. He's at your school now, I believe.'

'Yes, he told me he used to come here. He, er, said it was a nice school,' I added quickly.

'Did he? Well, I wish I thought it was a nice school, Mr Steed.'

Ignoring the mental picture of *The Avengers* that the nun had just conjured, I decided to be brave. 'I hope you don't mind me asking, but, you don't really shut naughty children in that cupboard, do you?'

She didn't bat an eyelid. 'On occasion, yes. But aren't we here to discuss design and things?'

'Sorry, yes.' I could hardly believe what I'd just heard; it was like stepping into the pages of Dickens. 'Right, well, I could either look through the curriculum document with you and, erm, explain what it actually means in plain English, or I could give you some ideas for easy activities to do in the classroom—'

She stood up, said, 'Excuse me,' and then disappeared into the classroom. I heard a few shouted threats, then she returned. 'Right, where were we? Oh, yes, ideas. I think I need ideas.'

I thought she needed a lot more than ideas, but I began to sift mentally through some simple activities. 'Here's a good one: paper towers.'

Her eyes widened. 'Paper towers? Isn't technology all about using tools and machines?'

'No, it's just about solving practical problems, really. You give them a question or task and they come up with ideas or designs, make them and test them.' I could see her eyes glazing over.

'Right . . . Well, how do we make paper towers? The trouble is,

I haven't a clue so how on earth will I teach the children anything?'

'It's like that with all teachers some of the time. I think we just need to be brave, let the children experiment and do our best. Sometimes I have to tell my class I don't know the answer.'

She looked at me aghast. I also felt very peculiar, a twenty-four-year-old teacher with barely two years' experience telling a mature headteacher how to do her job.

She sighed. 'Right, well, come on, then; how *do* you make paper towers?'

I took out a piece of A4 paper from the folder I'd brought. 'Right, OK, it couldn't be much simpler – you give each child a piece of paper and a pair of scissors and you challenge them to make the tallest tower they can.'

Sister Mary Brendan scratched her head. 'What, no glue or tape or anything else?'

'No.'

'Well, how does it stand up?'

'That's one of the problems they have to solve.'

'Well, shouldn't you show them first?'

'If you did that, they wouldn't go through the process of trying out ideas and thinking the task through.'

'But, won't they just cut up the paper and waste it?'

'Some will, so you need to have a few spare sheets handy.'

'That's an awful waste of paper.'

'Paper is cheap, though, compared with wood or construction kits.'

She shook her head. 'I don't know; this is all far removed from the things I've been doing in the profession for years . . .'

'The children will enjoy it, I guarantee.'

She gave me a blank look. 'Do you have any other, erm, ideas?'

It was half past twelve when I arrived back at Cragthwaite, exasperated and desperate to talk to someone about Sister Mary Brendan. She possessed an uncompromising dignity and no doubt taught certain things very well but surely someone needed to tell her that she couldn't go around imprisoning children in the 1980s.

Joyce's door was open but there was no sign of her inside and no one in the office, so I popped my head into the staffroom, only to find that empty, too. Where was everyone? I tried the hall next where the clash and babble of school dinners was in full swing, and Mrs Hyde, the mountainous, formidable dinner lady was in her usual full-shouting mode.

'Err-I-aren't-standing-for-this-dreadful-racket. Pipe-down-now!'

As ever, they took no notice.

'I-SAID-BE-QUIET! CLIVE-LAMBERT-PICK-UP-THAT-RISSOLE-THIS-INSTANT!'

Behind her Eddie was trying to explain something, 'It wasn't Clive, Mrs Hyde, it just slipped off my fork when I sneezed.'

She was oblivious, as ever, 'NO-ONE-IS-GOING-OUT-UNTIL-THERE-IS-SILENCE-IN-HERE!'

I closed the door and fled. My next stop was Val's room but that was empty so I returned to the office where Eileen had appeared. She was wearing a lace collar, lambs' wool cardigan and tartan skirt, as always the very picture of primness.

'Hello, Andy – how was your morning in Ingleburn? Fruitful, I hope.'

'I think "interesting" would be the best way to describe it.'

'She's a sweet lady, though, Sister Mary Brendan, don't you think?'

Good old Eileen, she always saw the best in everyone. 'Er, well, yes, but I hardly got to know her in such a short visit – I spent most of my time making paper towers with her class.'

'Well, I'm sure you did a super job.'

'Erm, Eileen, do you know where Joyce and Val are?'

'Yes, part of the fence around the back field has fallen down so they've just gone to have a look at it.'

I headed towards the back door and noticed Hilda in her room as I passed. Should I mention it to her? I opened the door marked Class 2.

'Hilda, can you help me out?'

'Certainly, which way did you come in?'

Did this woman ever stop? 'Hilda, that's older than the Bible.'

'Well, "even as Christ forgave you, so also do ye".'

'Yes, well, er, do you know Sister Mary Brendan?'

'Of course, she's been teaching nearly as long as I have. How did you get on with her this morning?'

'Sort of OK, but did you know that she locks kids in the stock cupboard as a punishment? Eddie Sykes told me this morning and I didn't believe him but it's true.'

Hilda chuckled, 'Ha, everyone knows that. She used to do much worse things, I can tell you . . .'

'But, don't the parents complain?'

'Are you kidding? She's a nun! The parents are terrified of her anyway.'

'But in this day and age . . . And those poor children in the tiny, cramped classrooms.'

'Well, what did you expect, *The Sound of Music*? All the schools in the dale used to be like that. Rather than bemoaning them, just be grateful we have this wondrous place.'

I had no answer to that so skulked out and decided not to mention the morning to Joyce or Val after all.

My classroom looked strangely big when I returned to it for Maths that afternoon. I stopped and pondered how I would manage stuck in a nineteenth-century stone building the size of a garden shed.

'Are you daydreaming, Mr Seed?' It was Eddie.

'Oh, sorry, Eddie. What's up, are you stuck?'

'Yes, I just can't get this algebra nonsense – it may as well be in Chinese.'

I explained it to him slowly and he nodded. 'I think I get it now.'

'Good, off you go, then.'

'And you enjoyed your visit to Ingleburn RC this morning?'

'Yes, Eddie, now go and do your Maths.'

'Liked the wimples, did you?'

'You know as well as I do there were no wimples.'

'I'm glad I don't go to that school any more.'

'Maths.'

'Everyone's much nicer here. Well, apart from Mrs Hyde and Sheena and tha—'

'Eddie?'

'Yes, Mr Seed?'

'You did leave Mrs Forrest alone at dinner break, like I asked?'

'I'd better get on with my Maths.'

On Sunday, Adam and Ruth Metcalfe and their four children came round for lunch. I made a monster shepherd's pie and Barbara produced a wonderful lentil soup for starters. Ruth brought a glorious-looking apple crumble.

'Do you mind if I say grace?' asked Adam, his red face glowing like a traffic light in the warmth of our new stove.

'Grace,' whispered Beth, which set Hannah and Robert snickering. Their father raised his eyebrows for a moment, then bowed his head.

'Father God, we thank you for everything you do for us and for the blessing of friends, fellowship and good food, amen.'

I glanced sideways at Barbara as we echoed 'amen' but she still had her eyes closed. Tom thought it was very odd.

'This smells lovely,' said the soft-faced Ruth, who was struggling to hold a writhing baby on her lap. 'Is it all right to give David a lump of bread?'

'Of course, everyone just help yourselves to bread.' The children jumped at it and smothered their pieces thickly with butter, as Barbara ladled out soup and passed the bowls round.

Robert pulled a face. 'Euurrgghh, my soup's got grass on it!'

We all smiled. 'Those are chives,' said Adam. 'At least, I think they're chives.'

'Yes they are,' said Barbara. 'Sorry, I should have asked before sprinkling them on top.'

'Oh, don't worry, they'll eat anything,' said Ruth. 'I've tried to grow herbs before in my garden but Reddle's not very conducive to Mediterranean plants.'

'It's not very conducive to growing any plants,' murmured Adam, 'especially grass.'

'So how is the farm?' I asked.

Adam breathed in. 'Things are a bit of a struggle at the moment but, you know, we just get on wi' job.' Barbara and I both knew that times must be very tough indeed.

'I'm doing some baking to help us make ends meet,' said Ruth. 'It'll be a lot easier when these three are at school.'

'Speaking of school, how are you getting on at Cragthwaite?' said Adam. 'I hear there's been a few changes there since old Raven left.'

I half laughed. 'You could say that. The head is great, though – really supportive and the kids love her. Most of the parents do, too.'

'Andy's got a very challenging girl in the class at the moment, though,' said Barbara.

'Oh aye?' said Adam. 'What does she get up to, then?'

I sighed, 'What doesn't she get up to would be quicker to explain. Fights, messing about in class, stealing, just disrupting everyone basically. She never does any work either.'

'Nothing new there – just the stuff I recall when I was in the juniors.'

'So how did the teachers deal with it then?' said Barbara.

'Easy,' said Adam, miming a whacking action. 'A couple of belts wi' the slipper and the trouble was over. For a while, anyhow. It worked on me.' He pretended to rub his bottom which made Hannah giggle.

'Well, I wouldn't want to do that anyway. I've tried talking to her and keeping her apart from the class and sending her to the head. I've had a go at being extra kind, too, and made sure she's included in things but it all just seems to backfire.'

Ruth shook her head. 'It must be really difficult for you.'

'Most of the kids are no problem at all – they're fantastic. But this girl . . .' I opened my palms not knowing what else to say.

Adam put down his spoon. 'Have you tried praying for her?'

I wasn't sure if he was serious or not. 'What do you mean?'

'Well, if it were me in your position, I'd pray for her every day – ask God to bring peace to the situation.'

'You don't mean in school?' said Barbara.

'No, just when you get up of a mornin': bring her before the big man upstairs in your prayers and say, well, help.'

I looked a bit nonplussed but Adam smiled at my reaction and suggested I give it a try, since it certainly wouldn't do any harm. 'Yer can let me know how it goes next time I see you. I'll pray for 'er, too.'

Barbara thought it was a great idea and, with the children calling for pudding having wolfed the shepherds' pie, we finished off the meal as Ruth explained how she made an apple crumble taste like heaven.

A week later I called Ingleburn RC School to see how they were getting on with their Design and Technology.

'Sister Mary Brendan? It's Andy Seed from Cragthwaite Primary.'

'Ah yes, the young man who visited.'

'How did the paper towers go?'

'The what?'

'The paper towers – remember, the activity I showed you?'

'Ah yes, well they haven't done it yet.'

'But I thought you were going to try it this week while it was, er, fresh in your mind.'

'I was, I was, but I told the children they couldn't do it, as a punishment for talking too much in class.'

'Oh, right.' So much for the new curriculum, I thought. It was just as well Eddie Sykes had moved here after all.

'Mr Seed, while you're on the telephone.'

'Yes?'

'Father Tim the priest was speaking to me and he thinks we should get a computer for the school. Do you think we're ready for one?'

'Err, I'll think about that.'

Chapter Ten

Victor

I opened the curtains and was dazzled. Applesett was white. I shouldn't have been surprised: the temperature had been dropping for days and, as January shivered into February, the wind picked up and we saw the first few light flurries of snow. I'd spent hours sawing and chopping up the last of the hefty elm logs which I'd dragged into the garage a few weeks before so that we had a good supply of fuel.

Despite the cold spell, the overnight fall of snow had caught everyone out: it hadn't been forecast and it was clear as I looked down from our bedroom window that several inches had fallen. The swells and dips of the long village green were accentuated by a faint early morning sun and each rooftop was cake-icing white with only the dark stone fronts of the houses and the black silhouettes of the trees breaking up the flawless mantle of snow.

Barbara was usually up well before me but it looked like she was still dreaming, so I crept downstairs and made a cup of tea before peeping outside to see how deep the fall really was. A shock of chilled air hit me as I opened the front door and I knelt down to feel the snow. It was round about eight inches deep – an exquisite, soft powder. Tom was going to love this, and I wondered whether it would last until the weekend. There might even be a chance to go sledging, something I loved, but a more pressing question needed to be answered first: how on earth would I get to school today? Would it be open? The Alfasud would be on strike for sure. I looked at the road and saw one set of tyre tracks: no doubt the milk delivery Land Rover.

I took Barbara some tea and gave Joyce a call. She lived near Bilthorpe, nearly twenty miles away, and I wondered if she'd be able to make it in.

'Do you have much snow?' I asked.

'Just a light dusting, really, what about there?'

'Quite a lot and it'll be roughly the same in Cragthwaite. The roads will be dodgy so—'

'Well, in that case, I'm going to set off now – go carefully, won't you?'

'Erm, yes, but do you really think enough children will be able to make it in, Joyce?'

'Course – most of them live in the village so they can walk, and all these farmers have four-wheel drive, don't they?'

I gulped silently. 'Right, OK, well, I did just wonder if you might be closing the school.'

There was a moment's silence. 'We can't do that, Andy; imagine how much bother it will cause the parents. Right, I'd better get going. Bye.'

Barbara came down the stairs with her hair in a comical frizz.

'It snew!' she said.

'It certainly did snew. I thought Joyce might be closing the school but I just rang her and she's not.'

Barbara jiggled her face as if she wasn't hearing right. 'What! That's ridiculous – there must be a foot of snow out there – it's far too dangerous.'

'Well, there's not much where she lives and I did try to explain—'

'You can't go out in the car in this!'

'I'll go slowly, don't worry.'

'You won't go at all in our rust bucket – it'll never start and, even if it did, you'd have to dig it out.' She shook her head. 'This is mental.'

I put on my boots and gloves and stepped out knowing that I had to at least try. The door of the Alfa was frozen but I heaved it open, managing to knock a small avalanche on to the driver's seat. I didn't bother to clear the windscreen but instead stepped into the gloomy car and turned the key. There was a feeble, dying whine and the lights on the dashboard barely flickered. I tried again but it was comatose. Well, that was that; I went inside to tell Barbara.

'Oh good,' she said. 'Well, that's sorted that problem, then.'

'What about Iris's jeep?'

'What about it?'

'Well, don't you remember? She said we could use it if we ever needed to.'

'Don will be out in that, surely.'

'But he's in Belgium with work.'

Barbara didn't hide her irritation. 'Oh yes, but it'll still be dangerous on these hilly roads.'

'It's four-wheel drive, much safer than a car.'

She looked at me, knowing what I was thinking. Namely, that

I'd been waiting for an excuse to drive the big Toyota. 'Oh, *boys* . . . well, as long as you light the stove first.'

But I was already on the phone to our neighbours.

The jeep's huge diesel engine growled and throbbed as I ploughed through the narrow lanes on the way to Cragthwaite. Although it felt wonderfully sure-footed, I was wary of the unforgiving dry-stone walls on either side of the road, so kept my speed right down, following the wide tracks of the early morning milk lorry through the sparkling snow and ice. There was nothing on the road except the odd Land Rover and I saw more than one abandoned car on a verge.

I arrived at the school at twenty to nine. Only Val's Hillman was in the car park: Joyce obviously hadn't made it. A few children were whooping and sliding on the playground at the back of the building. Inside, Val was on the phone in the office; she didn't look happy.

'Yes, right, right, bye.' She clattered the phone down. 'Flamin' 'eck.'

'Hi, Val,' I said, smiling.

'I don't know what you're so happy about. That was Joyce – there's a jack-knifed lorry blocking the Ingleburn road so she can't get through. She's going to try again later.'

'So the school's not closed, then?'

'No, the school is blinkin' well not closed. It should be – Hilda's not coming and I can't imagine Emma will make it, she's a nervous driver at the best of times. It took me twenty minutes just from Millscar and that's only cos a farmer cleared the track.' She shook her head and dug in her bag for some cigarettes. 'How did you get here, anyway?'

'Four-wheel drive. I borrowed a neighbour's jeep. Wish I could afford one of those things, they're great.'

'Well, at least one of us'll get home, then . . . I don't think half the kids'll make it, though – the buses won't run in this.'

We heard the door open behind us and were amazed to see Emma walk in, wearing a giant sheepskin coat and about nine scarves.

She stamped her boots on the mat. 'I'm sure I've got frostbite. What a morning!'

'Don't tell me you drove?' said Val, her mouth hanging agape.

'No, my next-door neighbour took me in his Range Rover. The heating wasn't working, though.'

Val gathered her composure. 'Right, well, we'll just have to see how many kids show up now. At least there's one very good bit of news.'

'What's that?' I said.

She fixed my eye. 'You and I won't have to take the infants.'

At ten past nine there were fourteen children in my classroom, with no sign of any more. I was looking forward to having a small group to work with but the rumbles of discontent among those present were growing by the minute and they were led by an olive-skinned, fractious boy called Victor Wood. Victor was an offcomer, his family having moved to one of Cragthwaite's larger houses two years ago from Darlington. He was also a complainer. His list of on-going grievances was long and wearisome:

'The room's too hot.'

'It's not fair that Class Four go into dinners first.'

'When can we play dodgeball?'

'Why do we always do singing?'

'My pencil's too short.'

'Do I have to sit next to Bernadette? She's picking her nose again.'

But now Victor was not alone: he had a consensus, a rabble behind him who, for once, agreed with his strident protests.

'You can't make us work, Mr Seed. That's *really* not fair. Half the class are getting the day off and playing in the snow but we have to do stupid English and Geography and stuff.'

'English is not stupid, Victor,' I said. 'And I do not like you speaking to me in that way.'

Yvonne joined in. 'I 'ate to say this, Mr Seed, but fer once 'e's right. Why should we 'ave to work when they don't?'

'Well, you still have to work if someone is off sick, don't you?'

Victor took over again. 'Yes, but that's different – it's snowing today! I want to go sledging and have snowball fights like the others'll be doing.'

'But you can go out at playtime.'

The whole group was now standing up, yelling their dissent; I was glad they didn't have pitchforks.

I folded my arms and tried to look stern. 'Class Three, sit down, now!' Reluctantly, they dropped to their seats, although Victor continued to grumble.

I lowered my voice, 'Listen, I understand that you think this isn't fair—'

'But it's not!'

'Victor, that's enough!' I stared him down and he sulked with a protruding lip. I continued, 'I know you want to be outside playing, and I love sledging and making snowmen, too, but this is a school day and it is my job to make sure you learn something. If you're good, I'll give you a longer playtime, maybe. Now, reading books out.'

I filled in the register but, looking up, noted that not a single child was reading. Everyone was staring out of the window, glassy-eyed, marvelling at the pristine snow and longing to be in it. I wasn't surprised to see Bernadette and Chris distracted but even Vanessa and Lee were gazing. I tried teaching some Maths but their concentration was zero, so I relented and let everyone go out: perhaps they just needed to get it out of their system. They gave a huge cheer and scurried to fetch their hats and gloves.

Outside, the low sun was beaming between distant clouds and illuminating the landscape into outrageously beautiful vistas. Grey dots of sheep on the far hills huddled and there was an eerie peace in the dale as the wind vanished. The quiet lasted only a moment, however, as it was shattered by the high whoops of the remnants of my class pouring on to the blanketed field and scooping up handfuls of snow. It was good to see such uncontained joy.

I wandered round to the front of the building but there was no sign of Joyce. No headteacher: we could do anything we liked. I felt like a kid myself and contemplated lobbing a snowball at Victor when the rotund figure of Glyn came trekking over to me. I smiled, glad to see that he had put the painful Sheena episode behind him.

'Mr Seed, Lee and me are gunna build a igloo!' He skidded off again before I could answer.

I watched the two rosy-cheeked lads: they clearly had no idea how to build an igloo and failed even to push the snow together to make a solid lump. I wandered over to give advice.

'You need blocks, boys.' I picked up a handful of snow. 'This is too dry and powdery. Try some of that under the tree where it's melting a bit.' I noticed the warming sun was causing the ice on the branches to melt and drip on to the snow below.

'How do we make a block?' said Lee.

'Good question. I think the best way will be to roll a big ball, about two feet high – its weight will compact the snow together. Then you'll need to scrape the sides to make it square like a giant brick.'

'OK, we'll try it,' said Glyn, with great enthusiasm.

'What shall we use to shape it?' asked Lee.

'I think there's a plastic shovel in the caretaker's room,' I said, feeling a bit of excitement myself. 'I'll go and look for it.' As I moved off I saw the two boys squashing the wet snow together and trying to roll a big snowball.

The shovel was in Pat's open cupboard so I helped myself and was amazed to see that Glyn and Lee had already rolled a good sized lump of snow when I returned. I was about to congratulate them when Vanessa ran up to me with a snarl.

'Mr Seed, Mervyn's just shoved some snow down my neck!' It appeared that he was on a mission to make himself unpopular again.

I called everyone over and laid down what was and was not

allowed, threatening that we would go back in to do Maths if the rules were broken. The fourteen then scattered into friendship groups and I watched them at play. Vanessa and Jess were making a snowman while most of the boys were trying to organise some kind of snowball war involving shelters to hide behind. Alvin stayed well away from this group, cowering near the school building in case any flying snow should come near him. Yvonne and Nina were looking at animal tracks and, behind me, Lee and Glyn were now on their fifth big block and using the shovel to sculpt each piece carefully.

It was a wonderful scene, with the sun shining and the children, Alvin apart, enjoying themselves so freely. It brought back happy memories of my own childhood, of joyous days in the snow and of whizzing down big hills on a sledge. I couldn't wait to take Tom sledging at home and there was certainly no shortage of slopes around Applesett.

'Mr Seed!' called Glyn. ''Ow do we join the blocks together?'

I went over and offered more advice, 'Right, well, I think you just push them together and smooth over the join with more sticky snow like this.' I moved the blocks into a semi-circle and helped fill in the seams. Nina and Yvonne wandered across.

'What are yer makin'?' asked Yvonne.

'An igloo,' said Lee, his red nose dripping as he lifted his head.

'Ooh, can we help?' asked Nina.

I looked at Glyn, who nodded a little reluctantly, and soon there were two teams making giant ice bricks. When the first layer was complete we left a gap for the door and I watched as the two boys lifted the first block of the second layer with a struggle.

'These are heavy!' said Lee, almost dropping it. They plonked the block on top and I saw that this wasn't going to work.

'I've just realised something, everyone.' They gathered round. 'The sides have to lean inwards or the walls of the igloo won't meet at the top. We need to shape the blocks so that they are angled.'

'Oh, I see,' said Nina.

'I don't get it,' said Glyn.

I lifted up the new block then tipped it on its end and used the shovel to angle the top and bottom. I then carefully lifted it back on to the first course, ensuring that it bridged a join underneath.

'You see how it leans in slightly now?' I said.

'Oh yeah,' said Yvonne.

Lee looked a little troubled. 'That what you just did, Mr Seed, looks quite hard. If we bring the big snowballs over, will you shape them into blocks?'

Glyn nodded. 'Oh, yes, pleeeease, Mr Seed – then it'll be really good.'

I agreed, not least as I was delighted to see boys and girls working together so well in a team. They scampered away to roll some more lumps of snow and I opened my jacket, having heated up considerably in the sun's warming rays. Three more boys came over to see what was happening and soon the whole group was joining in, even Victor.

'How big is it gonna be?' he asked.

'Well, not very big, or it'll never get finished,' I said.

Glyn overheard. 'Awww, we must finish it, we must.'

I glanced at the car park but there was no sign of Joyce's car.

'Well, let's just carry on and see how it goes. If everyone works together, we might do it.'

Victor stood up and bellowed, 'Right, everyone has to work together – Mr Seed says so!' I chuckled and carried on scraping the blocks.

After half an hour, my gloves were soaking wet and I was in desperate need of a cup of tea. Igloo block production had slowed right down as the pairs of children tired and had further and further to walk to find fresh snow to use. They then had to roll the heavy snowballs back to the construction site.

'Perhaps we should have a break now, children,' I called.

'No, no! We need to carry on or we'll never finish,' said Glyn, his face like a beetroot. Several others agreed.

'Right, well, you carry on and I'll go and get a cup of tea,' I said.

Chris picked up the shovel and stood erect by the half-finished dome. 'I'll stand here and guard it in case Class Four come out.' I shook my head, laughed and trudged to the staffroom. Val was in the office on the phone.

'Most of the schools in the dale are closed,' she said, joining me in the staffroom. 'I might've known we'd be one of the daft ones.'

'Who's with your class?' I said.

'Class? I've only got eight! Anyway, who's supervising your lot?'

I told her about the igloo. 'Aren't you sending your kids out, Val? It's beautiful out there.'

'I will when they've finished their spellings, cruel woman that I am.'

When I returned to the field, the infants were out but Emma

had them walking round the playground holding hands rather than running free. Chris watched them warily from the side of the igloo, the shovel in his hand like some kind of cartoon spear. There were three big snowballs waiting for me to shape.

'Right, let's get these made into blocks,' I said.

'Can I help?' asked Chris. 'I could use a plastic ruler.'

'Good idea.' He raced off and the building programme continued as lunchtime approached. Constructing the igloo proved to be much harder than envisaged and, at one point, we had a collapse where we had leant the blocks inwards too much. Victor dived inside to rescue as many of the pieces as he could.

'I think we need to reinforce it inside,' he said. 'Mr Seed, shall I stay here and pack some of this snow against the insides to make it stronger?'

'Excellent suggestion, Victor.' Like most of the other children he had a runny nose and I could hear him sniffing continuously as he worked. The igloo now began to get taller as we made the sides less steep and I realised that this meant it would take even longer to finish, but the fourteen children worked relentlessly in their excitement so I didn't mention it.

At midday I called a halt and the children hurried inside, suddenly aware of how desperately hungry and thirsty they were. I wolfed my own cheese sandwiches in no time and downed three huge mugs of tea. Half an hour later, the remnants of Class 3 were outside again and rolling yet more snowballs, determined to see their project finished. I didn't tell them but I was almost as excited. By this time, the sun was melting the snow apace and everyone was dripping wet as everything turned slushy, but the ice compacted much better than the powdery drifts we started with and so we were able to bolster the walls of the igloo despite our fingers losing all feeling.

By two o'clock I had given up all pretence that the children would do any more work in the classroom that day; Joyce clearly wasn't going to make it into school and, anyway, it would have been the height of cruelty to stop now with the round ice house so near to completion. The children worked feverishly, with Victor maintaining his role of interior plasterer. He also encouraged each person who brought another block until he could no longer see over the sides.

'Brilliant, we only need a few more, Chris,' he said. 'We'll be finished soon. Come on, everyone, keep them coming: the Cragthwaite igloo is almost there.'

But by half past everyone was tiring. It was now a long trek to find virgin snow and the wet snowballs were so hefty that moving them took an age. Unable to help me reach the top of the construction any longer, Chris joined Victor inside. I used the shovel to scoop up chunks of ice that had been scraped off the blocks and wedged them into the top. A few moments later there was just a small hole at the apex of the dome. Yvonne and Nina lolloped over with a sorry-looking snowball plastered with mud and bits of twig.

'Is it done, Mr Seed, because we can't manage any more – am about jiggered.'

'Your piece might just do it girls.' Their faces lit up and they called for everyone to come over. I lifted up the lump of dirty snow and gently pressed it on to the gap. It fell through.

'Euurrgghh!' Came the cry from inside. 'That went right in my face.' It was Victor. I also heard Chris trying not to laugh.

'Sorry, boys, my fault,' I said. 'We obviously need a bigger block and you'll need to reach up to support it inside.'

'OK,' said Chris.

'And warn us when it's ready!' groused Victor.

I looked around at the children. No one wanted to go back and get any more snow. They were shattered. I had an idea and vaulted the fence nearby: there was fresh material in the field just yards away. I quickly rolled a lumpy ball of slushy ice and carefully lifted it over the fence. I warned Chris and Victor that it was coming, then lifted it up, not bothering to trim it with the shovel at all: time was running out.

Gingerly I lifted it on to the apex of the dome. I could just see the glowing pink hands of the boys underneath. It stayed in place and I heard the sound of ice being urgently pressed against it underneath. I reached up with a ruler and gently scraped the top so it didn't look like a cherry on a cake.

'Careful, Mr Seed,' said Yvonne. The rest watched, holding their breath. Then Chris and Victor shuffled out into the light, their eyes ablaze.

'It's finished.'

There was a whoop of delight. Some clapped, some danced a little jig and some just stared: we'd made an igloo. I stepped back to have a proper look. It was lumpen, wonky, strangely tall, muddy and nothing like the ones in books but it was an igloo.

'Can we go in it now?' cried Mervyn, rushing round towards the entrance.

'Yes but wait!' I called. It was too late – he was inside and we all heard him.

'It's ACE! There's loads of room in here, too – it's really big.'

That did it: all fourteen of them dived round to the little opening and fought with each other to squeeze inside. After about five were in I shouted for them to stop, which brought howls of protest from those left out in the cold, especially as they could all hear the children inside having fun.

'It's not fair!' cried Glyn by my side. 'It was my idea and I haven't even gone in yet.' He had a point.

Yvonne called from the interior, 'There's loads more room – just let 'em all in, Mr Seed.' I severely doubted her wisdom and peeped in to look. It was genuinely Tardis-like, I had to admit.

'Go on, then, the rest of you,' I said. 'It's not every day we build an igloo.' They cheered and rammed themselves through the doorway until there were squeals of complaint from inside that Nina was being squashed and somebody's backside was dangerously close to someone else's nose. But within a few seconds they'd all wriggled into better positions and began to giggle. There were fourteen children inside.

'Come on, Mr Seed, you come in, too,' said Lee.

I looked again, doubtful that I could even make it through the poky entrance, but the group reassured me that there was room. I knelt down and poked my head inside. There was just enough space, so I wedged my tall frame through the slushy opening, anxious not to brush the walls and cause a collapse. Once more the children spontaneously hurrahed. My legs were a problem but I somehow slithered in and folded them against my body.

Inside, the children's steaming bodies added an unexpected warmth and it was surprisingly light with the thinner parts of the ice walls letting in the sun's rays. The children beamed, too, their faces glowing with the peculiar thrill of having built a shelter from nothing and climbed inside en masse. I couldn't help smiling either: it was simply marvellous.

Amid the hubbub of delight, it entered my mind that I needed a photo. The igloo could collapse or melt at any moment. I ordered everyone to be really careful, then wriggled out and charged into school: someone must have a camera. Val did, of course. I ran outside with it, praying that the building was intact. It was. I took a shot with everyone inside, then realised that no one could be seen, so told them all to vacate and stand around our creation for a better shot.

This they did: fourteen filthy, frozen, exhausted, dripping-wet children, each with a glorious smile from ear to ear.

When I put the camera down, Victor rushed up to me. Would there be a late complaint to sour the occasion? 'This has been the best school day ever, Mr Seed! Those kids who didn't come in are going to be so sorry.'

The temperature dropped that night and the melted snow turned to ice, making the roads even more dangerous. Sense prevailed and the school was closed the following morning, giving me the joy of a day off. The children of Applesett were freed likewise and most of them headed to the top of the village, where Big Alec had a small field that sloped quite prodigiously in one corner: this was evidently the village's preferred tobogganing venue.

'I think it's time for Tom to have his first taste of sledging,' I announced after breakfast.

'Andy, don't be silly, he's nineteen months – hardly old enough to go hurtling down the side of Spout Fell into some barbed wire,' said Barbara, who was under the impression that school closure was some sort of signal for me to carry out unfeasible quantities of household chores. I chose to ignore her rather jaundiced view of sledging.

'I just mean, I'll take him along to watch.' That wasn't what I meant but it seemed to do the trick.

'Oh, that's all right, then, as long as you stand well away from where they are.'

'Aren't you going to come out, too, then?'

'No, it's too icy and I don't want to fall over. I don't think the luge is ideal for the pregnant woman, in any case.'

Tom was desperate to be out in the snow and I jammed him into a ridiculously thick quilted jumpsuit, having already mummified his body in babygrows, vests, tights and jumpers. He looked like a giant stuffed toy; I daren't think what would happen if he pooed.

'Hnow,' he babbled, as I wedged an arctic-grade bobble hat on to his head and wrestled with some gloves which seemed to have been knitted from dockyard rope.

'Yes, ssssnow,' I said, wondering how he managed to conjure an h sound.

'Do you think he'll be warm enough?' said Barbara, nudging me aside and adjusting various straps and zips and then forcing his swathed feet into little wellies.

'He's lagged like a hot water tank,' I said. 'If anything he'll combust.'

She ignored my remarks as usual and gave our son a kiss as I togged myself up and went to look for our sledge. It was at the back of the garage under a pile of newspapers: the old, red, wooden one that my dad had made fifteen years ago.

'Who needs those stupid plastic things when you've got *this*,' I said to myself. I gave the rusty runners a quick wipe and attached some cord to the front.

Outside, I could hear the shrieks from the children who were racing down Big Alec's field. I held Tom's hand and steered him up the village but with his stiff-legged gait he could hardly move.

'Come on, it'll be spring by the time we get there,' I said, lifting him up. He squealed and pointed to the sledge. I waited until Barbara was no longer looking from the bay window and sat him down on it. He gave a little gurgle of delight, so I gently pulled the string. He immediately fell backwards, his boots popping into the air.

'Oh, dear,' he said. At least there was no chance of injury with that much padding.

We tried again and this time Tom stayed on. I pulled him over the bobbly grass of the green, across the snow which had turned to ice and was now thawing again. When we reached the field I was surprised to see Iris Falconer there, sedately descending one of the milder slopes on what looked like a giant yellow tea tray. Stewart was at the top of the slope looking nervous. I propped Tom on the wall at the bottom and waved.

'Yoo-hoo!'

Stewart noticed and waved back, pointing us out to Iris. 'Hello!' she screeched. 'Look at gorgeous little Tommy!' He smiled and tried to waggle his fingers through the bulky mittens.

We watched the sledgers for a few minutes but it was obvious that Tom wanted to join in, or at least get closer to the action, so I pushed open the gate and tugged him through on the sledge. I was surprised to see a small flock of sheep in one corner, cowering together as far as possible from the revellers. I picked Tom up and, with difficulty, carried him around the edge of the field over to where the Falconers were stationed.

'Thanks so much for lending me the jeep yesterday,' I said. 'Are you sure I can't give you anything for fuel?'

'No, it's our pleasure,' said Iris, who was wrapped in some kind of brown fur coat. 'Now, is little Tom going to go sledging?'

'He'd love to but his mum isn't so keen on the idea,' I said. 'Are you having fun, Stewart?' He shook his head and pulled a face.

'He doesn't like sledging, do you chuck?' said Iris.

'That's a shame,' I said, revelling in the knowledge that at least out here he had no access to Snoofiwoogle Puppy.

'This slope is really gentle here,' said Iris. 'I'm sure that Tom would be all right if he sat on your lap, don't you think? Or he can come with me.' Now I liked that idea – Barbara held Iris in the highest regard and she had suggested it, so . . .

'Tom, would you like to go on the sled with Iris?' He went into a kind of manic rapid breathing and pointing mode that I took to be assent, so I gave her the nod and passed him over once she'd sat down. Iris locked him into her considerable bosom, lifted her feet off the ground and gave the plastic sled a shove with her hand. It crept forward and picked up pace off the glassy slope.

'Wheeee!' said Iris, and I could tell that Tom loved it. She offered to stay with him for a while so that I could have a few runs on the main slope with my sledge. I thanked her and went up to the steep section of the field that was now criss-crossed with tracks. There were numerous village children there and three adults, including Big Alec himself.

'Aye up, Seedy,' he said, holding out an outsized hand. 'That'll be five bob.' Alec's young daughter tugged at his trouser leg and he scooped her up swiftly, plonked her down on a feed bag full of hay and then shot down the slope with the girl screaming as they spun round. It was a classic farm 'sledge'.

I waited for a clear run, then lay on the sledge on my front and pushed off, expecting to rocket down. It slid forward feebly, however, despite the gradient, and I regretted not waxing the rusted runners. At the bottom I found a lump of hard ice and rubbed it rapidly against the metal, trying to get some shine: sledging was only real fun if you went fast. The second run was better and the third good too when I gave myself a running start.

The whole scene brought back happy memories again, with that delicious sense of being a child once more that snow seems to conjure more than anything else. I thought about the igloo and how, even life's natural moaners, like Victor, couldn't help but have fun on days like this.

Hearing voices from the other side of the field I looked across and saw Tom sitting in the snow next to Stewart while Iris cleaned some ice off her sled. I decided I'd better go back.

'Tom's really enjoying this!' said Iris, loading him on to her lap again as I approached. 'Daddy's going to watch us, Tommy,' she said. I noticed that she'd started from slightly higher up the slope this time. Iris gave the plastic sled a start by digging her heels into the snow and they were off. I cheered as the beaming Tom slid past then watched as they hit a lump which caused Iris to fall backwards. She held on to Tom but couldn't see where they were going now and she was unable to prevent the bob from shunting sideways as they veered downhill on to a steeper incline. They hit another bump and, to my horror, my toddler son flew out of Iris's grasp and into the air. But worse was to come as she followed him. He landed first in a thankfully soft patch of snow but poor Iris was powerless to prevent herself from taking the same trajectory and Tom disappeared with a dull 'ummmp', as she landed directly on top of him, rear first. She swivelled off with surprising dexterity as I tumbled down the slope to see if he was still alive.

The poor boy was neatly pressed into the ice, his arms and legs sticking out like a woollen starfish. But, unbelievably, he was laughing. Iris stared down, convinced that she had flattened the poor mite but I distinctly heard him chuckle and say, '*Big* bottom.'

I think he would have pointed and asked to go again if he could have moved. I assured Iris that all was well as I propped him up, and she almost burst into tears with apology, begging me not to tell Barbara. I assured her that there was zero chance of that, although both of us turned to glance at Stewart, in whom the evil glint of blackmail was surely absent. Surely?

Iris scuttled off home, still mortified, and I thought that it was probably time for us to do the same. Then I looked across and saw the last of the children leaving the steep run in the far corner of the field, too. We could have it all to ourselves.

'Come on, trouble,' I said, lifting Tom on to my arm. 'Let's have one go on the fast bit.'

The next minute or so was memorable.

With great difficulty I carried Tom up the slippery hill, dragging the wooden sledge behind. This was not the time to lose one's footing. At the top I sat down and plonked my little son in front, folding my legs around him protectively.

'Let's go.'

As soon as I took my other foot off the ground we began to move. I held Tom tight, realising that we now had no braking. The sledge rapidly picked up speed as we dipped down the steepest part of the slope, bumping along with cold air and flecks of snow spitting up at us. I gave the traditional whoop but cut it short as we started veering to the right instead of going straight down the hill. The ground was rougher here and we jolted brutally as the little toboggan raced down. I felt Tom slipping and wrapped my knees round him tightly, wishing that I could brake, but it was hopeless. We careered on, racing for the far corner at speed.

The sheep saw us coming but were slow to react. The edge of the little flock split in two but the ewes in the middle were unable to escape and they pinged off us to the left and the right in a clamour of panicky bleating as we ploughed straight through, greasy wool blinding us.

The stop was instant, caused by the sudden appearance of the stone wall at the bottom of the field. Fortunately the sheep had buffered us almost to a halt and so I was able to catch Tom as he catapulted forward on impact. There was a three-second shock delay before he started crying. I stood up quickly to cuddle him properly, although he probably couldn't feel me through the four inches of clothing that coated his body. He sobbed for a moment, then quickly calmed. He was all right and so was I. No sheep seemed to be dead or unconscious. Then I looked down. The old, red sledge had not fared so well: it was split in two.

I left the pieces in the field, cleaned the frozen snot off Tom's face and headed home.

'Was it good?' asked Barbara.

'It was great,' I said, pulling Tom's hat off and releasing a billow of sweaty heat.

'Did you enjoy it, cherub?' she said, kissing his fat, ruby cheek. His eyes were huge and I wondered how he'd respond, silently thanking God that he couldn't speak properly yet. 'Mummeeee,' he chirruped, nuzzling into her.

'Oh what a good boy you are,' she said. 'You're so precious. I'm sure Daddy took extra, extra good care of you out there.'

Chapter Eleven

Fay

'Do you play snooker, Andy?' Don Falconer was bored. He'd finished his cup of tea and evidently didn't want to spend the rest of the morning sitting down and making small talk with Iris, Barbara and myself, or playing wooden railways with Tom and Stewart.

'I've only ever played about three times, on one of those little six-foot tables,' I said, recalling a friend who had a cheap and wonky set-up at home. 'I enjoyed it, though.'

'Did you know that there's a full-sized table down at the reading rooms?'

'Yes, John Weatherall told me about it, but I've never been.'

'Do you fancy going down there for a look?'

'Yeah, OK, if Barbara and Iris don't mind.'

It was the first Saturday after the snowfall and Applesett was still in the grip of the freeze with icy roads and temperatures only just above zero. Don, the small, balding and hyperactive husband of Iris Falconer, had somehow made it home from his work trip to Belgium and had come round for coffee with his family. With Tom and Stewart playing happily, Barbara and Iris didn't mind us going out, so we put on hefty coats and headed down the village.

'Who has the key for the reading rooms, then, Don?' I asked.

'Ah, that's one of those local mysteries. You've got to have lived here for at least five years before anyone tells you that.' He tapped the side of his nose and smiled.

'Well, we've only been here two, so are you going to break the rule?'

'Yeah, Dennis at the pub told me.'

'And . . .?'

'The old lady who lives opposite has it. Mrs Hammond, I think she's called. Anyway, apparently her front door's never locked – you just reach in and the key's hanging on a hook just inside.'

I smiled to myself: that was typical Dales security. 'Have you played on the table much, then, Don?'

'No, never,' he said. 'In fact, I've never played snooker in my life.'

We reached the reading rooms along one of the narrow winding roads towards the bottom of the village where the buildings were tightly packed together. It looked much like an ordinary house except for the words *Village Institute* carved in stone above the door lintel. There was darkness inside, so at least no one seemed to be in there before us. Don stepped across the narrow road and approached the tiny cottage opposite. Looking around first, he turned the handle of the door, which opened, then peered inside. He reached in then turned round, a Yale key swinging from his finger.

The reading rooms felt colder inside than out. The front room was empty except for a rickety table and chairs but the larger space at the back was filled up by a most magnificent and ancient snooker table, in chestnut wood with great fat turned legs.

Don lifted off the large sheet of fabric covering it. 'Wow, look at that.'

I found a light switch which illuminated its full glory: the green baize was worn in places but still bright. All the balls were there and there was a rack of cues on the wall next to a brass and mahogany scoreboard, which must have been from the last century.

'This is wonderful, but we need some heating in here or we'll die,' I said, shivering. He disappeared down the passage next to the room and I heard his voice echoing.

'There's an old oil boiler here – looks like something from the *Titanic*.' The room had no radiators but rather great, fat pipes circumnavigated the peeling walls. The place seemed to be in a time warp and I felt sure that it hadn't altered since Edwardian days. I followed the clanking sounds from the back and found Don kneeling beside a monster furnace which was black with dirt and oil. It was creaking and groaning with zeal.

'Well, I'm amazed, but I think I've got the bugger lit,' said Don, brushing his hands together.

'How long do you reckon it'll take to heat this place up?' I said.

'About three days in this weather. Come on, we'll give it half an hour – let's go to the pub.'

I'd never been in The Crown on a Saturday lunchtime before and Dennis Helliwell, the jovial landlord, was pleased to have some unexpected custom.

'Now then Don, Andy, what can I get you on this delightful day? Cocoa?'

'Anything, so long as we can sit by the fire,' said Don.

I stepped across to the notice-board to have a look at the darts results.

Dennis noticed me. 'We're still top by one point: The Black Bull only beat The Swinner by two so we're still there.'

I moved over to the huge crackling log fire. 'Do you really think we can win it then, Dennis?'

'Course I do, we've got the best team, haven't we?'

'Yeah, but you said that last season.'

'And the season before.' It was old Sam Burnsall, parked on his corner stool, as always.

'Don't you play darts, Don?' said Dennis.

He laughed. 'Me? No, I'm away too often working. I'd be useless anyway.'

'That doesn't stop Andy,' said Sam.

'Byyy, you're on form today,' laughed Dennis.

Twenty minutes later we were back at the reading rooms where the temperature was just about tolerable. The giant iron pipes along the walls were red hot but the cold dampness of the building's aged stones was putting up stout resistance.

'Do we have to pay someone for using this?' I said, arranging the heavy, coloured balls on to the table.

'Yeah, we need to put 50p next to the key when we've locked up,' said Don, picking up a blackened cue and peering down its length.

I rolled another of the antique cues on the baize to see how straight it was. The tip wiggled comically.

'This one's like a banana,' said Don. 'Is that any better?'

'Nope, I think they're all the same. Anyway, shall I break?' He nodded and, unable to find any chalk, I lined up the white ball and tried to remember what to do. At least, with Don not having played before, I hopefully wouldn't be thrashed. I aimed for the edge of the cluster of reds and pinged the white forward. It missed the pack and bounced back up, kissing the brown.

'Good start,' I moaned. 'Four points to you.'

'Can you do the scoring?' said Don. 'I'm not really sure how it goes. In fact, you'll have to tell me what to do as we go along.'

'OK, no problem. Basically, you've got to hit a red now.'

'I know that – I'm not daft,' he chuckled. 'I do watch it on TV.'

He lined up the white ball, looking very unsteady, sliding his bowed cue back and forward unconvincingly. He then jabbed it forward and missed the white altogether going for too much power. It was a struggle not to laugh.

'Do I take that again, since I didn't touch it?' he said, looking rather serious.

'Er, I'm not sure. Well, go on, then.'

Once more he poked hard with the cue, this time connecting sharply. The white smashed into the pack of reds, knocking them in all directions. One crawled towards a pocket and dropped in.

'Yesss!' said Don, punching the air. I marked him another point, then quickly moved the brass slider for myself as he missed the black. I moved round the huge table to line up a straightforward red, taking my time to slide the cue smoothly. I made good contact but the ball rattled in the jaws and rolled along the cushion. Don sprung forward and surveyed the balls: he had plenty of choice, there being at least six he could go for. Once more my opponent jabbed at the ball, rather than sliding the cue on to it gently, and once more he missed. This was going to be a long game and, what's more, I feared for the table's threadbare baize.

Fifteen minutes later, I was 28–21 ahead, having potted just one red: all the other points on the board except one were from fouls. What's more, almost every ball was now positioned along the sides of the table, making them even trickier to pot. I was about to blast the white at a couple of safe reds when the front door creaked and two large chilled bodies entered the room: the giant Daves Duggleby and Whiterow from the darts team.

'Aye up, Andrew,' said DD. 'I didn't know thee were a snookist.'

'He's not, by t'look o' them balls,' laughed DW, dropping his colossal frame on to a chair.

'Now then,' said DW, nodding at Don, who clearly didn't know the two mischievous builders as well as I did. 'Good men f'getting heatin' on.'

I tried to compose myself for the shot but ended up hitting the first red too straight. The cue ball rebounded back and dribbled into the middle pocket for yet another foul.

'Shot,' said DD. 'Wish I could do that.'

Don didn't seem to appreciate the friendly banter of the two watchers and he proceeded to play even worse than before, if that were possible. I tried rolling a red up to the corner pocket slowly so at least Don stood a chance of potting it.

'Aye up, they're playin' pool,' whispered DW audibly.

I willed Don to pocket the easy red but could see the tension in his arm as he took the shot, once more slamming the white far too hard. The red dropped in but the cue ball followed it to the amusement of the Daves.

Fifteen minutes passed before the next red was potted and our audience were getting fed up.

DD rubbed his eyes. 'Come on, lads, the oil'll be running out soon.'

I began a new policy of blasting the balls hard, hoping to at least move some of them into the middle but it was not a success. Don didn't look like he was enjoying it at all but when I accidentally potted the pink and gave him six bonus points he perked up, thinking there was still a chance to win. At this moment, the door creaked again and in walked John Weatherall, Big Alec, Billy Iveson and Andy Cheeseworth.

'Byyy, it's like Whitby on a bank 'oliday in 'ere,' said John.

'I didn't know you played snooker, Seedy,' said Alec.

'He doesn't,' quipped DD. 'This match 'as been goin' for two days already.'

'Well, at least it's warm in 'ere,' said Billy. 'Am about paggered gerrin' about in this ice.'

'Shhh you lot,' said DW, 'let 'em concentrate or we'll never get a game.'

I attempted an ambitious long pot with my next shot and, by some miracle, it went in, bringing a smatter of admiration from Billy at least.

'Get 'im signed up fer t'team,' said John as I lined up an easy blue. I missed it by a mile, sending the white in off.

'Scrub that,' he said.

The next quarter of an hour was agony as Don and I continued to miss even the easiest shots and the spectators grew restless.

'What about next ball potted wins?' grouched Alec, who was

sitting on two chairs, one per buttock. 'Or it'll be ma bedtime before I getta game.'

We all admitted it was a good idea. 'Anyway, you should be out there farmin', Lund, not in 'ere,' said John.

'I've fed the sheep and thes nowt else I can do wi' ground solid like this.'

DD looked across. '*Shut up,* and let these buggers finish!' He had been waiting over an hour.

Don was still desperately trying to win and lined up an unlikely looking cut into a corner pocket. He smashed the white hard and it rebounded off several cushions before missing the red then clipping the yellow which rebounded off two more balls and slowly rolled into a pocket. A huge cheer went up from the builders and Don held up his cue in triumph.

'But he can't win with that!' I protested. 'It was a foul.'

'Next ball potted wins,' said DW, already resetting the scoreboard. 'You agreed.' Big Alec laughed at my open mouth.

'Come on, let's go,' said Don. 'You lost.'

'Andy – just who I've been looking for.' Joyce put her arm on my shoulder as I walked into the school office with a pile of early morning photocopying. I knew that she was going to ask me to do something I probably wouldn't want to do, but her warmth and charm always made resistance seem churlish. 'I've just fixed a heads' meeting for Friday next week and it's in the afternoon, I'm afraid, so I won't be here to do the assembly.' She extended her fingers and moved her hand to press gently against the top of her chest as she delivered the blow. 'How would you like to take the assembly?'

Her perfume was overpowering and all my mind could register was, 'She's standing very close – what will Eileen be thinking?' She continued, 'I think you'll do a fabulous job of it, love; I would normally ask Val but she's doing an assembly Wednesday.'

'OK,' I mumbled.

'You're wonderful,' she said, and moved towards her office. 'I don't mind what it's about, Andy – I'm sure you'll come up with something creative for the parents.'

So that was it: my first school assembly.

One of the ways that Joyce had changed the direction of Cragthwaite Primary School was by introducing a Sharing Assembly last thing on Friday afternoons, with visitors welcome to attend. These events quickly became established and soon the hall was full of mums, toddlers and grannies, all eager to see the children presenting a piece of work from that week.

I had contributed to assemblies before, with just the children and staff present, but the thought of having to host the end of week celebration in front of a group of expectant parents filled me with trepidation. There was one thing to ease the burden of this unexpected situation, however: my class had some excellent work going on and it took me a remarkably brief time to decide that the children themselves could present most of it.

The topic on Ancient Egypt was hugely popular: we had seen videos about the pyramids; heard the wonderful story of the discovery of Tutankhamen's tomb; looked at pictures of beautiful golden artefacts; found out how the Nile kept the desert land fertile; made clay jewellery; written on modern papyrus; drawn hieroglyphics; and carried out interesting research about Egyptian children, slaves, homes and food. But there was one subject that fascinated every child in the class with an engrossing fervour – mummification. There is something strangely captivating about dead bodies which have been wrapped up for thousands of years and placed in eerily decorated wooden sarcophagi, and the class were enthralled to learn all the gory details of brains and other organs being removed with monstrous-looking hooks. Yvonne, never short of ideas or a willingness to express them, came over at the end of one particular lesson.

'Can we mek some model Egyptian coffins, Mr Seed?'

'That's a good idea, Yvonne – we're a bit short of materials, but I'll have a look.'

While I was searching the stockroom shelves, I found some large sheets of corrugated card, used for packaging deliveries of art paper. With a rare jolt of inspiration, it occurred to me that these could be used to make a life-sized Egyptian coffin – now that *would* be exciting. The same evening I sketched out some plans and the following day I announced to the children that I would be splitting them into groups and they would each help to make different parts of a large sarcophagus, while the rest of the class were carrying out quiet research.

Eddie, being just about the tallest member of the class, was chosen to draw around. He lay on top of three pieces of the card with his legs tight together, trying to look dead, while Hazel, in fits of giggles, pencilled an extremely wobbly outline of his body in the manner of a police murder scene. Chris and Victor then cut out this shape while Jess and Rachel fixed together several more pieces of the card with brown paper tape for the sides. The next group cut flaps in these and bent the card to follow the outline of Eddie's frame. The children worked purposefully, and there was a growing sense of excitement as the curved sides were fixed to the base and the construction began to take the recognisable appearance of a coffin. Yards of brown paper tape were ripped off the big roll and dipped in trays of water to secure the joins on both the inside and outside. Even before this was dry, requests to lie in the coffin began.

'I asked first, Mr Seed.'

'Go on, Mr Seed – you never choose me for anything.'

'I'll be really careful.'

'I'll give you the Kit Kat in ma packed lunch.'

I resisted.

The next group started work on the coffin lid: this was the most difficult part, because the children and I agreed that we should try to make it curve outwards in the manner of a real Egyptian sarcophagus, rather than settle for a flat lid, and we also decided to add the shapes of protruding feet and a proper face mask. It was becoming a major project but was taking shape beautifully and the class were enthralled to be making something so large and challenging. Chris and Bill were put in charge of the face mask, the hardest part of all: Chris was fairly practical so long as you kept reminding him what to do and Bill was a genius at solving problems of this kind. The coffin was going so well that I decided to let the two boys have a go at an adventurous art technique that I had tried in college a few years previously.

The mask began with Bill smearing Vaseline all over Chris's face with his leathery farmer's son's hands.

'Ey, the vet does this when he sticks his arm up a cow's bum,' said Bill in a matter-of-fact way, but Chris just held his usual indomitable grin, even when Bill accidentally forced copious measures of petroleum jelly up his nostrils. Next, a piece of blue tissue paper was laid across Chris's face and pressed down to match the contours of his features. While the boys were busy with this, I produced a box of plaster-impregnated bandage of the type used to set broken limbs. This was wetted and carefully laid in strips across Chris's face – even Bill could appreciate the need to be careful at this stage. I could hear whispers from the rest of the class behind me – they had long ago given up working and were watching this delicate operation with quiet fascination. The plaster began to set right away and, very soon, a forbidding deathly white face mask took shape, although it was an unmistakably English one, bearing Chris's slightly pointed nose. I was, along with Bill, unreasonably proud of its success, until an interruption came from behind; it was Yvonne.

'Mr Seed, why is Chris kicking his legs about?'

'Is he all right?' added Vanessa. He did seem very agitated.

'Mebbe it's because we 'aven't left 'im any breathing 'oles,' said Bill, as matter of fact as ever. I lunged forward and snatched the death mask off his face, the irony escaping me in this moment of panic. Chris's body spasmed as he sucked in several minutes worth of air in a giant gulp. He looked as ill as any human being I had ever seen in my life and my heart thundered for a brief moment as I thought he was about to pass out, until I realised that the horrific blue colour of his skin was actually caused by the dye leaking out of the tissue paper. He sat up and shook his head like a dog drying itself.

'Sorry, Mr Seed – I couldn't hold my breath much longer. I haven't spoiled the mask have I?' The boy was a treasure.

As the rest of the week passed and the remaining groups took their turn, the coffin became a thing of wonder: the feet were taped to the coffin lid and the whole thing was painted with a mixture of earthy brown colours mixed with glue. Nina, Kirsty and Libby, all artistically inclined, decorated the top of the lid in magnificently detailed hieroglyphs based on several real archaeological finds that they had come across in their research. And then the final touch was added – the face mask was trimmed and eye and mouth holes were cut in it before it was sprayed gold and fitted to the lid. It looked resplendent and would be the perfect centrepiece for my Ancient Egypt assembly on Friday.

Rachel Sunter, usually one of the quietest members of the class, spoke for everyone. 'I'm real proud o' that, Mr Seed. I think it's dead good.'

When the children had gone home, I couldn't resist nipping next door and inviting Val to come and see the finished coffin.

'Byyy, that is impressive.' Compliments from Val were real compliments; I fought hard to stop grinning proudly like an oaf. She leant towards the hieroglyphs and ran a finger over them.

'They've worked really hard, Val – I was amazed – even Sheena took an interest in this.' She raised an eyebrow and reached into her handbag for a cigarette.

'How's Sheena's behaviour been recently, anyway?'

'Well, apart from today, just the same: mostly awful. She responds well enough to lots of attention but, if I do that, none of the others get a look-in. It isn't fair on them.'

'Aye, she's a troubled lass, all right, that one.'

'She is, but no one seems to know the answer.' Val noticed that my previously high spirits had ebbed so she turned back to the coffin.

'Who's going to be the mummy, then?' I didn't answer; I just kicked myself mentally for not having thought of this earlier. Val could see that she had just given me a brilliant idea, but she didn't rub it in. 'Come with me.' She led me to the caretaker's cupboard and unlocked the door, using a key from a huge bunch in her bag. 'Pat'll be sweeping the hall – don't tell her I gave you these.'

I was mystified by what Val was doing, until, that is, she produced a pack of four white toilet rolls.

'There, wrap your mummy in those – but choose someone sensible, won't you?'

'Val, you're a wonder,' I said, taking the rolls and making a series of fiendish plans as I returned to my room.

Fay Lambert was a tall, poplar-shaped girl with a crown of crinkly ginger hair. She was a quiet, thoughtful child who never upset anyone in the class and who often arrived at answers after others had given up; the kind of person that, as a teacher, it is truly hard not to favour. Her many qualities were modestly deployed to good effect whatever task she was given and, as I watched her now, I could see that she was giving careful consideration to something that everyone else had dived into.

I had just told my class the plans for the Friday Sharing Assembly: how we would take in lots of our work on Ancient Egypt and how volunteers would be needed to explain it all to the other classes and the parents. Then a huge rumpus broke out when I suggested that someone might like to dress up as a mummy and hide in the coffin: it was like offering free sweets for life. Hands shot into the air and shoulder sockets almost popped with the strain, among longing looks and cries of 'Pleeeease!' Even when I explained that the person would have to be very sensible and that he or she would need to be in there for some time, keeping still, and that it would probably be dark, hot and stuffy, not a single hand descended from its stretch.

There was Eddie, bouncing up and down in his chair; Bernadette looked in pain, she was waggling her hand so hard; and Yvonne tried to smile in between dagger looks at the neighbours who were trying to steal her part. There were only a few hands not raised: Alvin, who was too nervous; Chris, who had forgotten what I'd said; and Fay, who was still thinking. Then, without a sound, and still sitting in her chair, Fay slowly raised her hand. She had decided and I couldn't resist choosing her.

Sheena, who had been remarkably good up to that point, spluttered in disgust.

'Yer always choose 'er fer things like this.'

I was tempted to wrap her in toilet roll just to shut her up. The groans subsided but I knew, and everyone knew, that Fay would do a great job.

When the day of the assembly finally arrived, my nerves had disappeared in the rush of organisation to get everything ready. Half-past two was suddenly upon us and the hall was full of rows of squirming infants, parents and pushchairs. We had sneaked the coffin into the room fifteen minutes earlier, along with all the other pieces of work, ready to show off. Two Egyptian guards, Vanessa and Bill, holding cobbled-together spears, stood either side of the upright coffin, which was placed against the back wall as the centrepiece of our impressive display. The teachers sat next to their classes at the sides. Val gave me a wink.

The members of the class who explained their written work and pictures spoke well, giving the assembly a good start and, after a short, tuneless hymn, it was my turn to speak.

'Well, children, Class Three have done some wonderful work on the Ancient Egyptians, haven't they?' A few of the infants gave exaggerated nods near the front, with replies of 'Yasssss'.

'Well, there is one more piece of work to show you which we haven't mentioned. Has anyone spotted it?' I made the error of looking at the back row of older children where Val's class were splayed. A top junior girl rolled her eyes upwards. I battled on, concentrating on the younger customers, several of whom were pointing at the sarcophagus.

'Yes, that's right, it's over there. But what is it?'

'A cofffffffffiiiiin', came the chorus from the slightly older infants. For the next two minutes I described, in suitably vivid detail, what the sarcophagus was for and how it was used three thousand years ago. Even Val's class perked up at this stage.

'Does anyone want to see what's inside?'

'Yesssss!'

'Even if it's something scary?'

'Yesssss!'

'Are you sure?' I glanced at Val, who gave me a 'don't overdo it' look.

'Yesssss!'

'Right, then: guards, open the coffin . . .' Vanessa and Bill put down their spears and carefully prised the lid off the cardboard sarcophagus, as if it were made of solid gold. There was an audible gasp from the watching children as a half-sized toilet-roll-clad mummy was revealed, neatly tucked into the coffin and standing as still as a post box.

'It's a mummy,' I explained. They knew. At this point I was expecting questions, but the children simply stared at Fay's tattered figure in complete awe. I was just about to elucidate a little more about mummies when behind me Fay twitched and slowly began to raise both arms out towards the children. The whispering stopped and the hall was gripped by total silence, although I spotted a few parents at the back stifling titters. My fear that some of the Reception children might scream and race for the doors was unfounded, even when, with arms now fully extended, the Andrex zombie edged a foot forward and stepped out of its tomb with shuddering stiffness. Fay could act, in addition to all her other abilities, and she took a few Karloff-inspired paces towards the watching audience, leaving a trail of torn white tissue.

Val was now openly guffawing and I moved attention away from her by giving a commentary on the mummy's movements. Fay gave a rusty swivel and veered to the left, skirting the children and heading towards the rear of the hall.

'Where's it going, I wonder?' The children just stared, still unsure whether to laugh or not. Fay spotted a chair among the parents and plonked herself down for a much-deserved rest.

'Oh look, she's gone to sit with the other mummies . . .' It was a shocking line, but raised an appreciative groan from the older children, who spun round to watch as Fay tore away the loo paper from her head. Her face was as red as a traffic light, but smiling, and I could tell she was quietly pleased with her performance. I was pleased, too, not least for having remembered to leave her breathing holes.

On Monday morning Joyce called into my room.

'Well, I've heard all about your amazing assembly with the mummy and everything.'

'It did go much better than expected – my class did really well.'

'Hmmm, perhaps you should be doing the Friday assemblies regularly—'

'No, it didn't go that well.'

She laughed, 'Don't worry; I've actually come to talk about something else. There's going to be a meeting about Sheena on Thursday at Bilthorpe. I'm afraid we can't both be there but I'd better go, I think.'

'Good, it's about time we found out about getting some help.'

'I wouldn't get your hopes up too high, Andy.'

Chapter Twelve

Libby

Everyone in Swinnerdale was glad to see March arrive and with it the end of the cold snap which had lasted several weeks. Barbara, now seven-and-a-half months pregnant, was particularly glad to feel the temperature rise. She wasn't happy, however, that I was going to be away for two nights on a residential training course.

'Where is it you're going again?' she said, sounding weary.

'Shreeve Hall, near Ripon. It's a big old house owned by the LEA.'

'And what are you going to be doing, exactly?'

'I told you last week – it's a PE course.'

'I know you told me but Tom was whining and I wasn't listening. Anyway, why are you going on a PE course?'

'Well, to get some good ideas for lessons and to, er, find out what other schools do.'

'But why do you have to go away just when the baby's nearly due? You did this with Tom.'

'Hang on, there's still two months to go.'

'Seven weeks – it could easily arrive early.'

'Well, just call the Hall – I'll leave you the number. It's only about thirty miles away.'

'Only?'

'It's just two nights, Barb, I'll be back on Thursday. Iris'll be here and I'll call you each night.'

'You'd better,' she said in mock misery.

At school I was eager to hear the latest news from Joyce about Sheena. Following the first meeting in Bilthorpe, there had been fundamental disagreement on the way forward, with a psychiatrist suggesting the behaviour-modifying drug Ritalin. Joyce had been against this radical step but it depended on Sheena's mother, who had failed to turn up.

Joyce had just returned from another meeting and didn't look happy.

'Her mother thinks the Ritalin is a great idea,' she said, pressing her long fingers into her cheeks.

'But you obviously don't. What does it do?'

'Well, it does help kids to concentrate, no doubt about that, but it also makes some drowsy and one little lad I used to teach had terrible insomnia with it.'

'I must admit, I don't like the idea of children being, well, drugged.'

'They say there aren't any harmful long-term effects but you never know.'

'Perhaps we should give it a try – I can't go on with Sheena the way she is. She's just about all right some days but impossible others.'

Joyce sighed, 'It's a done deal, Andy, now that her mother's said yes.'

I was taken aback. 'Oh, right . . . Er, what about other help?'

'Well, we're not getting as much as we would've if she wasn't on tablets but it's going to be two hours a week one-to-one out of the classroom with a special needs tutor.'

'Two hours? Is that all?'

'That's more than some kids get, but I know what you mean. At least it'll be intensive and give you a bit of breathing space with the class. Let's hope we get someone good to do it.'

She scrabbled through the papers on her desk. 'Oh, speaking of people coming in, Jenny Forrest's broken her ankle so can't do your supply for the PE course. There's a lady from Crackby called, er, Mrs Palmer coming instead. Has she been before?'

The name was new to me. 'I don't think so, not while I've been here.'

'Well, leave her plenty to do, won't you? I'll be on Sheena alert.'

The following day, I was sitting in the staffroom at morning break listening to Hilda tell a joke.

'Ooh, you'll love this one: there's an old Yorkshire couple who are dedicated chapel goers. They're both in their nineties and the husband is devastated when his wife dies suddenly in the night. He manages to pull himself together enough to make the funeral arrangements and he decides he wants to give her a really lovely marble gravestone. So, he goes to see the mason and they talk it over.

'"What wording would you like, sir?" says the mason.

'"Well, I've thought long and hard about this. She was a simple Yorkshire woman of great faith and God was really the centre of her life. So I just want the stone to say *She were thine.*"

'"Right, I've got that," said the mason. "I'll get right on the job – you come back on Friday to check it over."

'So, a few days later the old gentleman walks back to the stone-mason's yard and opens the door.

'"Hello, sir," says the mason. "I've got your headstone right here." And he pulls away the cloth on top of the stone. The old gentleman's face falls immediately.

'"Oh, no, no, no, that's not right," he goes, quite upset. "It says, *She were thin*. You've missed the e."

'"I'm terribly sorry, sir, I really am. I'll put that right this afternoon. Please come back tomorrow and it'll be sorted."

'So, the old gent goes off, shaking his head and he returns the next day. The mason greets him.

'"Here you are, sir, all right now?" He pulls back the cloth and the gravestone says, *Eee she were thin.*'

Val nearly spurted her coffee across the table and Sue doubled over. Emma and I laughed, too, but it was Hilda herself who enjoyed it the most, slapping her knee and howling with delight at our reaction. The door opened and Eileen popped her head in.

'Whatever's going on? I could hear you all from the office.'

'Go on, Hilda, tell it again,' said Val, wiping her eyes, but before she could reply there was a loud rap and a bulky figure pushed Eileen aside. It was Sheena.

'Mr Seed, Libby's just called me a git!'

The small blonde head of Hazel then appeared. 'It's true, she did.'

I stood up, tried to get Sheena to apologise to Eileen, then said goodbye to the rest of the break. I listened to Sheena's gabbled version of events, then went out and called Libby Westholme over. She was a stocky girl with long, fair hair; she was bright but noted for being somewhat moody.

'Libby, why did you call Sheena a git? That's not a nice word.'

Her arms were folded: she hated being told off. 'She called me dogbreath.'

'Well that was wrong but calling her a name back was only going to lead to more trouble, wasn't it?'

'But she started it; I get fed up wi' bein' called names by that girl.'

'I've told Sheena to stop but—' I nearly said, 'You know what she's like.'

'I'll stop if she stops.' Libby's mouth was set tight.

'Libby, that won't work. If she calls you a name, I want you to come and tell me, don't retaliate.' I hated saying this: I didn't want her to tell me at all. 'Now, off you go.'

She gave me a dark look, then stomped away.

It was English after break and I began the lesson by reading a poem, the wonderful 'Flannan Isle', about a mysterious deserted lighthouse. A movement distracted me: Libby was fiddling with a small Rubik's cube.

'Libby, leave that alone, please,' I said. 'Why have you got a toy on your desk, anyway?'

'It's not a toy, it's a key ring,' she said with a slight air of impudence.

'Well, anyway, put it away now, please.' She crinkled her nose and pushed the cube into her pencil case while the whole class watched.

Fifteen minutes later the children were writing their own mystery poems, except that one table seemed to be chatting instead. Unfortunately, when I looked up it was Libby.

'Quiet, please, over there – this is writing time, not discussion.'

Libby protested, 'But Bernadette asked me fer help; I was only telling 'er what to do. It in't fair that I were told off.' She glowered again.

'Bernadette, please ask *me* if you need help with anything, not Libby.'

I toured the room and was pleased with the results. Arriving at Libby's table I stopped, hoping to say something positive. She had, however, only written two lines and the handwriting was almost illegible.

'Libby, you can do better than this.'

She just sat and said nothing. I'd had a few minor contretemps with Libby over the first half of the school year: she was a strong character and someone inclined to speak her mind, but I'd never experienced intransigence like this. Whatever had caused it, I felt strongly that I needed to show it wasn't acceptable. She was quite capable academically, too, so it was unlikely that she was struggling with the work.

I pointed to her book. 'You've changed your writing. Why have you done the letter A like that?'

'That's how my sister does her As.'

'But it's not how we do them here, Libby, you know that. We should be doing joined handwriting in Class Three.'

'I think it looks better like this.' By now, most of the class were staring.

'Now, come on, I want you to write properly and do as much as you usually manage: you can do much better than this,' I said again. I stood up and turned around, my sombre face giving a clear signal for everyone to concentrate. As I walked to another table I heard Libby whisper to Bernadette.

'I've gone right off Mr Seed, have you?'

I tried to ignore the sinking feeling I felt inside but found it impossible. Was it Sheena who had brought out the worst in Libby or had she just got out of bed on the wrong side? Perhaps I should have a word with her mother? Or was I being unfair? My mind veered between thinking that this could be the start of a really unwelcome trend and then dismissing it as just another everyday episode in the primary classroom.

At the end of the afternoon I reminded the class that I'd be away for the next three days. From the corner of my eye I saw Libby furtively clenching her fist in mock celebration.

'There's going to be a new supply teacher with you: Mrs Palmer. I've left her a list of work to do and I expect the very best behaviour from you all. I shall be checking up with her when I'm back.' I paused for a moment as I heard myself. 'Ugh, I sound just like all my worst old teachers,' I thought.

It was a great relief to have a few days away on the PE course. I'd always enjoyed teaching the subject but, after two years of doing the same activities with the children, I felt the need for some new ideas. I'd heard from a teacher in Hauxton that the County PE Adviser was very good so I begged Joyce if I could go on one of his residential training events. She was not a fan of sports or games herself, indeed notorious for getting herself out deliberately in the annual staff versus children rounders match, so was glad that someone in the school was willing to enthuse the children and she readily agreed to my participation.

I turned the Alfasud through a pair of large gates, having already taken the wrong turning twice, and meandered up a long, tree-lined drive towards a grand eighteenth-century mansion of considerable size. I passed the pillared entrance and followed the signs to the car park. Shreeve Hall was impressive, indeed, with acres of immaculate grounds, the historic house itself and a large modern annex around the back which housed dormitories.

After signing in, a cup of tea and a chance to meet the other participants from primary schools across North Yorkshire, we were told to get changed and assemble in the Hall's elegant dining room for the first practical session. An immaculately presented, upright but surprisingly portly figure addressed the twenty or so teachers as we gathered in the beautiful Georgian room with its polished wooden floor.

'Good morning, ladies and gentlemen. My name is Jeff Osbourn and I'm Senior County Adviser for PE. Welcome to this course, which I hope will inspire and equip you to do great things when you return to your own schools.'

In his mid-fifties with slicked-back, grey hair, he was wearing an old-fashioned tracksuit with startlingly white plimsolls. There was definitely an air of the sergeant major about him.

'At some point, I hope we'll get outside to run a few games sessions but today we're going to start with a range of warm-up exercises and activities that you can use with children at the beginning of lessons. The course will be very practical and there's no need to stop and make notes as everything is detailed on hand-outs which I'll give you at the end of each session. Right, then, any questions?'

There weren't. I was going to enjoy this.

Half an hour later, I was lying on my back, breathing hard, along with the other teachers. One or two were on their feet but bent over with hands on knees. Only Jeff stood up straight, barely a glistening of sweat on his brow, even though he'd demonstrated all the exercises himself.

The woman next to me, a slim figure in her forties, was groaning as she mopped her face with a tissue.

'I'll never keep this up for three days,' she gasped. 'I'm jiggered after twenty minutes. My first-year juniors would die if I had them doing this.'

'Right, everyone, on your feet!' called Jeff with a breezy clap. 'Balances next.'

This session was much less tiring and produced rounds of clandestine giggling as a number of people discovered that their sense of balance was some measure short of their own assessment. Others baulked at the realisation that they couldn't do half the movements or body shapes that they'd routinely ask the children to perform in lessons. There were twisted, collapsed and quivering figures strewn across the floor.

'Dearie me,' said the PE adviser, 'it's like a Friday night in Bradford.'

I was doing fine until the forward rolls. I felt confident that the manoeuvre was straightforward but when I tried it, all the blood rushed to my head and a wave of bleary dizziness caused me to stagger comically as I stood up.

I hoped no one had noticed but the woman next to me gave a snicker and commented, 'Stay here, you make me look good.'

After more embarrassing gymnastic routines we were given a hearty lunch and a rest period, then returned to the hall for a session with bats and balls which was tremendous fun and a lot easier than the morning's workouts. I looked with envy at the baskets of brand-new, top-quality equipment that we used, thinking back to Cragthwaite's battered and sorry-looking gear. How on earth could I persuade Joyce to spend money on a subject that she didn't value highly?

After calling Barbara in the early evening, I wandered through to the oak-panelled bar where the course members had congregated, along with a group of secondary teachers, who were attending an exciting-sounding school management seminar. It was good to meet other people in the same position as me: there were teachers from every corner of the county, from the bigger towns like Harrogate and Scarborough, and from tiny villages I'd never heard of. Several people were envious when they heard I worked in a beautiful place like Cragthwaite.

'Ooh, I'd love to teach in the Dales,' said one woman. 'It would make a nice change from Selby.'

'It is wonderful, I have to say,' I beamed.

'I bet all the kids are really good, too.'

I thought of Sheena and, at this moment, Libby as well. 'Most of them are, but I do have the odd little, er, problem.'

'It's the odd one that isn't a problem at my place,' chipped in an older man. 'The school's on a tough council estate near Scurragh Garrison.'

'Are any of the children there on Ritalin?' I asked.

'There's three or four in the school, aye. One lad in my class, who's a right tearaway, and a couple in the top juniors. It's good stuff, if you ask me.'

'It works, you mean?'

'Well, it's made a difference with this lad Gary in my class, for sure. He needed something, too, I can tell you . . .'

I was just about to ask if he'd noticed any drawbacks to using the drug when the teacher from Selby launched in with a tale about difficult children at her school and the conversation quickly turned into a swap shop of behaviour problems. Hearing the various grim stories made me think that perhaps Libby wasn't so bad, after all, but that we were right to think Sheena did need professional help and perhaps medical intervention, too.

The following day was bright and clear so we went outside to learn about ways to teach team games. We split into pairs to practise skills, then small groups to have mini-games. We did hockey, football, rounders, netball, cricket, benchball and tag rugby. The amount of cheating was scandalous but it was enormously enjoyable.

After lunch we shared ideas for indoor games, then discussed some of the common organisational problems with PE and tackled issues such as how to approach the subject in a school with no hall: a common problem among North Yorkshire's numerous smaller villages. We finished off with a long and frantic game of dodgeball, exploring different variations until people began to fade. Like the others, I went to bed early that night.

For the final day of the course we visited a local primary school in the morning and watched Jeff give a demonstration lesson using the large apparatus – climbing frame, ropes, benches, vaulting box and mats. He used his years of experience to work with an unfamiliar class and had the ten-year-olds moving round purposefully – jumping, rolling, crawling, running, stretching and climbing. He used praise sparingly but effectively and regularly stopped the class so that capable individuals could give demonstrations of different movements and sequences. The watching teachers sat impressed.

For the last session after lunch the adviser announced that we had a special treat: none other than Reg Finley, the Olympic athletics coach, would be leading us. A very small muscular man stepped forward and we duly applauded. None of us had heard of Reg but he made his credentials very clear by reeling off a list of familiar medal-winning athletes he'd trained, including our country's world champion female javelin thrower. At that point, I was impressed.

Reg told us that he had planned all sorts of exciting outdoor activities, such as running, jumping, relay and throwing events, using special new primary schools' equipment but, as we looked through the hall's tall windows at fat raindrops falling on the glass, it soon became clear that an indoor session would have to suffice. This didn't appear to perturb Reg, however, and he was soon organising some jumping activities using small individual mats.

'Right, put your mat down and when I say "Go" move around without touching the floor, jumping from mat to mat: go!'

After one or two entertaining collisions, we soon got the hang of leaping round the hall, before Reg told us to speed up, which caused much hilarity.

'Right, from now on if you touch the floor you're out!' boomed Reg.

Two or three of the less fit participants were glad of the rest and 'accidentally' missed a mat, while the younger male teachers, myself included, were all the more keen to stay in.

'Faster!' he called, and a few missed their footing as they started to tire. With my long legs I was having no problem, although I was running out of breath.

'OK, stop and sit on a mat.'

He allowed those who were out to rejoin the game but he then took away six mats causing large gaps to open up.

'Heck, I couldn't jump that on a horse,' said the slim woman I'd been next to on the first day.

'Off you go, same rules,' called Reg, watching us eagerly. Several people were out quickly and more when he ordered us to speed up. This left a group of eight, the younger and more athletic ones, myself included, who could jump the spaces. Reg stopped us, took two more mats away and then gave two of our number a coloured band to wear.

'These two are now chasing: if they touch you, you're out. Keep off the floor or you're out. Go!'

Now it was tasty, as we had to keep an eye out for the hunters who came bounding after us. I dodged and weaved for a while and was in the last three before being caught. The winner held up his hands and received a round of applause plus a word of congratulation from Reg. I looked on with a hint of envy.

Next we worked on standing jumps from the floor to our mats, taking a step backwards each time. Again, Reg made it into a competition by telling us to sit down when we missed. As before, I kept going strongly but was just pipped by a rangy young teacher called Phil.

'Right, who knows how to do the triple jump?' called Reg, slapping his hands together. I put up a finger, as did a few others.

'OK, you, young man, would you give us a demonstration?' He pointed to me. I stood up, confident that I would remember how to do what used to be my best athletics event at secondary school.

'Do you mean with a run-up?' I asked.

'No, there's not enough room for that: standing start again.'

I wobbled on my left foot for a moment then hopped forward before taking a step and finishing with a small jump and landing on two feet.

'That's it, well done,' said Reg. 'It's hop, skip and jump. Have a go, just taking it easy.' We all tried it out, some more successfully than others.

Reg halted us. 'Right, I know from experience that many children find this hard, so just think how you'd explain it or demonstrate it to, say, a seven-year-old. Get together in twos and discuss.'

I avoided the slim woman, who didn't show much interest, and moved towards Phil. We talked enthusiastically about breaking the movement down or starting with three hops and working on the transition. Reg interrupted us and looked at his watch.

'Right, I've been told we need to stop at four and we've just ten minutes left so let's finish the session with one last competition

– standing triple jump. It's just as before: start a metre back from your mat, put down a marker cone, do your triple jump to the mat then start a pace further back and repeat. Sit down when you're out.'

This was it, my last chance to shine in front of an Olympic coach: I was determined to win. Phil looked across at me and winked. I found a good space in which to work then stepped back, reaching the mat with just a hop the first time. I went two paces back to save time, then hopscotched forward with ease. The movement brought back memories of tough inter-school athletics competitions from the late 1970s.

I moved back again several times, trying not to rush, and occasionally glancing across at Phil, who was managing the task with ease but didn't have quite as smooth an action as I expected.

'Keep going, push yourselves!' shouted Reg, as a number of people sat down, all jumped out. Three minutes later we were down to four, three males and a very sporty young woman who'd had plenty of attention in the bar each evening. Phil was still going and I was now having to put some real effort in.

'OK, let's watch these four carefully now,' said Reg as quiet descended on the high-ceilinged room.

I sprang forward, really getting into the rhythm of the event, and remembering how to generate power from the step and use my arms in the jump. The mat was a long way off but I made it with a bit to spare. I wandered back to the small yellow cone slowly and watched Phil straining through his jump. He fell an inch short of the mat and collapsed in a weary heap. I silently cheered and watched the other two. The girl fell well short but the other young man just made his jump, producing a swell of applause.

I moved my marker back carefully and bounded for the small green mat once more. I was tiring now and only just made it, my heels catching the edge. There was more clapping and admiration then all eyes turned to my competitor. He was fading, too, and feigned a comedy collapse before setting himself for another effort. He gave a mighty hop but stumbled on the jump and landed nowhere near the mat. There was a disappointed 'Awww' from the spectators and I allowed myself a brief smile of triumph before wandering across towards the chairs.

'Right,' said Reg, 'we have a winner.' He then saw me wandering away. 'Whoah there, young man, we haven't finished yet; you've still to go for the last jump.' Phil and the others laughed as, this time, I mimicked fainting behind the coach's back. I wandered back to the cone, which was now set another pace back, and shook my head. The mat was now a preposterous distance away.

Reg went over to the cone and reached up to put an arm on my shoulder. 'You know, it never ceases to amaze me the talent I uncover on these courses when I go around the country.' My head was in danger of popping right there and then. Reg put his heel against the cone and started to work out the measurement to the mat, heel to toe. I assumed my starting position, left foot first, my right leg extending back and arms swinging to gain momentum.

Reg reached the mat and put up his hand. 'That's a twenty-six-foot standing triple jump, ladies and gents.' He turned to look at me. 'Over to you now, what's your name?'

'Andy.'

'Right, Andy.'

Reg moved away and I swayed back and forth, swinging my

arms in rhythm. I felt good now after the short rest. I launched into a mighty hop, kicking hard with my left foot before touching it down again and pushing off fiercely to generate a fast step, and straining forward with my right foot. The room was silent. The mat was nearer but surely still out of reach. I put everything into the jump, straining each sinew to its fullest extent, bouncing high and thrusting my arms forward, as I recall my games teacher showing me. I brought my feet together and willed them to land on the scuffed mat, which was almost, almost there. My toes touched it and, somehow, with manic exertion I hurled my body forward so I didn't drop back on to the floor. There was a whoop from the assembled teachers then a tumult of clapping. I had done it.

'Great jump, lad, well done,' said Reg, patting me on the back as I tried not to let my face split with a stupid grin of delight.

I raced home to tell Barbara, almost spinning the car at one point as I took a bend too fast.

Mrs Boo's curtain twitched when I switched the Alfa's engine off and I was tempted to give her a little wave. Tom sprang at my legs as I opened the door and Barbara wobbled through to give me a kiss. Her bump looked like it had grown just in the last few days.

'You look tired,' I said.

'Well, it's hardly a surprise, having Thomas the toddler here all to myself.'

I picked him up for a huge squeeze.

'I hope the course was worth it,' said Barbara.

'It was great; especially today.'

'Why, what happened? Did you win at team tiddlywinks?'

'No but an Olympic coach said I was amazingly talented.'

'Yeah, sure. Did they have Daley Thompson there to give out pole-vault tips for infants as well?'

'No, really, there was a guy called Reg something who coaches the GB athletics team and we did this kind of jumping contest with mats and cones and it was kind of me against this big guy Phil and two others but I lasted the longest and then Reg made everyone stop and watch and I did this twenty-six-foot triple jump then—'

'Andy.'

'What?'

My wife flopped into a chair, her face blotchy. 'Can you make me a coffee?'

The following day was Friday and I was looking forward to being with my class again at school and trying out some of the new ideas I'd learnt in PE. At quarter to nine in the morning my classroom door flew open and in marched Jess and Yvonne.

'Mr Seed, that supply teacher was 'orrible!'

'Shhh!' I said. 'You mustn't say things like that.'

Yvonne looked at her friend. 'But she was, wan't she, Jess?'

'Yeah, we 'ad to work in silence all the time.'

'And we got told off fer nothin'.'

'She kept us all in at playtime cos Sheena drew a willy on Fay's spelling book.'

'And she said lots of us needed to speak properly and she sent Eddie to Mrs Berry when he 'adn't really done anythin' and—'

'OK, I get the message, girls.'

'She gave us extra homework, too, the mean, old—'

'Yvonne!'

'Sorry, Mr Seed.'

Jess giggled and the door opened again. It was Libby.

She waited until Yvonne and Jess moved away, then sidled up to my desk, looking down and back up at me.

'I'm really glad you're back.'

I smiled, genuinely touched. 'It's good to be back, Libby.'

She walked away, stopped, then skipped back.

'Yes?' I said.

'Sorry.'

Chapter Thirteen

Guy

Guy Calvert pushed his bag through the wooden fence at the edge of the school field, then clambered between the horizontal rails, squeezing his stout frame through the gap. He probably could have pushed the fence down, he was so strong. This was how Guy came to school every morning, living on the farm next door as he did. He was a jovial character who enjoyed life, despite struggling with the written word, and someone who was fun to have around. But as I watched him trudge towards the playground I felt a shiver pass down my back. The reason was simple. Guy wasn't alone: he had his little brother with him.

During my first two years at Cragthwaite School, I had encountered many emotions: joy, anxiety, laughter, disappointment, confusion and a great deal of embarrassment, but I had never actually known outright fear. That was all to change in mid-March, and Guy's little brother would play his part in it.

It all began, strangely enough, with a wedding invitation received by Emma, the young, bead-wearing, straggly haired Reception teacher at Cragthwaite. She bounded into the staffroom during a Monday morning break looking unusually excited.

'I've just opened my mail and my best friend Carol's getting married this summer!' she beamed. 'It's so exciting.'

'Lovely,' said Val, not looking up from the pile of books on her lap. 'When is it?'

'July ninth.'

'That's a Tuesday,' I added, scanning the enormous year planner on the notice-board.

Val looked up from her books. Emma's face dropped into a twist of anguish and she left the room quickly.

'What's up?' I said.

'Officially, you can't have days off for weddings in term time,' said Val.

'Oh, I see.'

It soon became obvious that Emma Torrington was of a crafty disposition and was not for a moment going to let a minor Local Education Authority rule spoil her chances of dressing up and going to church for her friend's big day. I couldn't quite picture her in smart wedding garb, as she typically wore baggy, exotic clothes in loud colours and patterns along with curious accessories but Emma surprised us by revealing a new side to her personality as the term went on.

She mounted a campaign to win over Joyce, who, as headteacher, had the power to give her permission to miss a day's work, officially or not. It seemed very odd to me: I felt sure that Joyce wouldn't hesitate to let Emma go down with a severe twenty-four-hour virus, but Emma was taking no chances.

Val noticed that things were different just a few days later. 'I see

Emma's caught a nasty dose of helpfulitis,' she murmured as we passed in the hall.

It was true – Emma seemed to have acquired an unnatural desire to lend a hand every time Joyce was about. She suddenly took a new interest in making the coffee at break times and tidying the music trolley. There also seemed to be an awful lot of pressing issues which she needed to discuss with Joyce in her office, and we couldn't help notice that a large number of these seemed to involve raucous laughter.

Not only was Emma's behaviour strange, but her classroom underwent a radical, almost magical, transformation in that period, too. New displays of work appeared daily – huge vivid creations of splendour, with cascades of colour and imagination, adorned every wall and the surfaces were arrayed with interesting objects: stuffed animals, rare stones and large fossils, Victorian toys, curved mirrors and strange African carvings. Everything was beautifully labelled and there were printed questions everywhere to stimulate thought and promote learning. I had never seen anything like it.

A couple of days later Val wandered into my room. 'Know anything about sprogs?'

'About what?' I said. She rolled her eyes.

'Sprogs – four- and five-year-olds.'

'Not a lot – I'm barely getting to grips with my own class.'

'Well, you will soon enough.' She produced a rare smile.

'Val, what are you on about?'

'I've just been to see Joyce and it turns out that Emma's been even busier than we thought. She's made lots of suggestions for "interesting" activities, apparently, and as art coordinator for the school she wants to visit every class and do some creative stuff with all the different age groups. Joyce was dead keen.' I looked blank, but responded anyway.

'That'll be nice – my class love art.'

Val simulated slapping her head. 'And who's going to take her class of evil midgets while she's faffing about with tissue paper and Redimix in yours, Seedy?'

My mind finally caught up. 'When?' I asked.

'You're first, lucky boy – next week.'

Things happened very quickly after that. I panicked and went to see Emma in her classroom right away after school. She had already prepared several lists for me – she was out to impress, all right. I glimpsed that she was even wearing smart shoes instead of her usual floppy boots.

'Don't worry, Andy, the little ones'll be fine. And, anyway, you'll have Sue to take care of things all afternoon.' That was one thing that did ease my terror a little; Reception children were bundles of never-fading energy and never-ending demands but Sue Bramley, the classroom assistant who worked part-time with Emma, was widely recognised as a human marvel – at least I could turn to her.

'Now, you'd better sit down so you can take all this in.' She produced several sheets of paper while I descended about five and a half feet on to what I was convinced was a chair from a doll's house. I felt like Gulliver. Emma just about managed to keep a straight face as she started going through the lists. 'They'll be in groups – they're named after flowers this term – Daisies, Bluebells, Buttercups, Primroses and Violets.'

'No pansies, then?' She ignored me.

'There are five activities planned and Sue will set out all the resources. Here's the chart showing the rotation of groups with all the timings. Remember, playtime is at two fifteen for infants, not two thirty like juniors, and make sure they all wear a coat. Story is at three – you can carry on reading *Burglar Bill* if you like – on the carpet, book's on the top shelf behind the globe. It's Buttercups' turn to sharpen the pencils and make sure that no one puts their finger in the electric pencil sharpener. Watch out for Hayley's asthma and don't let Michael go near Luke. You won't understand Vicky with the ginger hair (Sue will translate) and Claire needs to go to the toilet every fifteen minutes – it's fairly obvious when she's ready. Russell usually cries when men come near him and Ivan is sick a lot. Right, I think that's it for now. Oh, and watch Sally – last week she fed Craig's spellings to the hamster.'

I felt slightly queasy and my bottom was stuck in the tiny chair; at least I could rest my chin on my knees.

'OK, thanks,' I said weakly.

'Now, what do I need to know about your class, Andy?'

Guy Calvert approached my desk with a hopeful smile and thrust his writing towards me with big dirty hands. English was not his best subject. Guy was a gentle giant of a lad, whose dad kept a prize herd of Holsteins in the fields around the school. He was stout of arm and face, and had the most amazing sprout of thick, frizzy, black hair, sticking up like wire wool. His nickname was Bogbrush and his younger brother, Ivan, revelled in the delightful title of Baby Bogbrush. Seeing Guy reminded me to ask him about his sibling's unpleasant reputation for vomiting, as recently described by Emma.

'Your brother's in Reception, isn't he, Guy?'

'What? Ivan? Aye, he's in Miss Torrinton's.'

'I've heard he's sick quite a lot – is that true?'

'Byyy, he's a'ways pukin'; does it at 'ome, 'n all.'

'What causes it?'

'N'body knows. Me mam's tekkin' him to the doctors but they say thes nothin' wrong wi' 'im. He keeps doin' it, though.'

I groaned inwardly.

The English lesson with my own class had taken my mind off the approaching dread for a short time, but the respite had been all too brief. I looked down at Guy's writing. The words had been pummelled into the page, as usual (pens only lasted a few days with Guy), and the thick, black lettering was hard to read. Guy shifted uncomfortably from foot to foot. I felt really sorry for him; he was a lovely lad, but all his ability was in practical things, as befits someone who had helped on a Dales farm since he could talk. He always knew what he wanted to say, but he had terrible difficulty with expressing ideas in writing. Spelling was a particular trial for him: his bs and ds were always reversed, however hard he tried. The diary extract before me was typical:

I helped Uncul doddy to fix the brainpipe wiyl my sister went to drownies.

I had run out of ideas to help Guy overcome this problem – I really needed advice from someone with more experience of teaching basic spelling. At this moment a rare flash of inspiration came my way: I would ask Emma to have a look at Guy's work while she was in my classroom during our swap over – she knew plenty about teaching writing. I sat back and smiled at my scheme. Guy looked at me and broke into another hopeful grin; I didn't have the heart to disappoint him, so I slashed a huge tick across his page and wrote, 'Excellent'.

The intervening days passed swiftly and the afternoon I'd feared finally arrived. I stood awkwardly among the miniature furniture in Emma's room and watched the tiny children file in from playtime, each one turning to stare at me and many breaking into nervous giggles or creeping with raised shoulders to whisper to their friends. Sue had organised all the materials for the activities and set everything out on tabletops with brilliant efficiency, and she now ushered the children on to the carpet for afternoon registration. Emma obviously had them well drilled and they each answered politely as I went through the list of names. Perhaps this wasn't going to be so bad after all; well, they did know me a little from assemblies and playtimes.

I launched into my intro: 'Now, hands up who knows my name?'

Twenty-three voices chorused in slow unison, 'Miissstterr Seeeeeed.' Not a single hand went up.

'Please remember to put your hand up when you want to speak.'

A hand went up immediately. 'You're tall.'

Another one followed it. 'How tall are you?'

Before I could answer two more hands went up.

'You're not as tall as my dad.'

'I'm going on holiday next week.'

I raised outspread palms before I was drowned in the tide. 'Whoah, hands down now. I need to tell you what we're going to do this afternoon.' A hand shot up again. It belonged to a cheeky face with blonde pigtails, the one who'd started the tall business, I noted.

'We know what we're goin' to do – Miss Torrytun's told us earlier. My name's Sally.' I tried to recall what Emma's rule was for blonde kids called Sally, but decided that I needed to talk instead of think, in case they took over again.

'Well, it's good that you know what you're going to do, but I'd better tell you again just to be sure.' I trundled through Emma's list trying to make each activity sound really exciting. While I was speaking, I glanced up at the children and noticed a most peculiar phenomenon. They were coming nearer. The front row, with Sally at the helm, was imperceptibly bottom-shuffling across the carpet towards my chair. The rows behind followed suit, surreptitiously closing any gaps that appeared. The strange thing was that they didn't seem to know that they were doing it – they continued to look at me, and even kept their arms folded, as they closed in. I decided to ignore this migration and get them going on the activities as soon as possible.

'Now, is there anyone who doesn't know what to do?'

A hand shot up. 'I need a wee.'

Sue stepped in and whisked a sandy-haired girl away. The space she left disappeared in a flash. I moved my feet back and pressed on.

'Right, who is a Daffodil?'

Sally pulled a face, 'Yer what?'

I glanced down at the list. 'I mean, who is a Daisy?'

Five hands went up. One belonged to a tidy-looking boy at the back, who, figuring that his hand was up, proceeded to speak. 'I've got a parrot.'

I was just about to respond when Sue reappeared.

'Shall I take the groups over to the tables to start their activities, Mr Seed?' Her authority and efficiency rapidly took command and within two minutes every child was busily engaged around a table. What a relief. I could see why Emma and Joyce were always spouting admiration for Sue. She was a short, bob-haired, always-smiling marvel, never still and as organised, thoughtful and resourceful a person as I'd ever met. She came over to me and apologised for butting in. 'I hope you didn't mind, Andy – it's just that some of them were getting restless. By the way, did Emma mention that break is at two fifteen, not two thirty?'

I enjoyed the next fifteen minutes, touring the large semi-open-plan room and asking the children how they were getting on. I tried to be wildly enthusiastic about the messy paintings on the art table, and listened carefully to descriptions of all the hi-tech features of an alien spacecraft that looked like a random arrangement of bottle tops stuck on an egg box. I observed machine guns being manufactured and tested on the Lego table and heard a customer demanding her money back with menacing threats in the miniature grocer's shop in the corner.

Most of the noise was coming from the water tray, so I went over to investigate. A diminutive boy in an oversized yellow jumper, who looked no more than three-years-old, was crunching a toy boat into an island of bottles.

'NNNYYYRRROOOWWWGGGHHH!'

'Hello, what's your name?'

'VVVRRRUUURRRMMM!'

'Have you got a speedboat there, then?'

'DDDVVVSSSHHHJJJ!'

Well, he seemed happy. I went back to the other side of the room where Sally was conducting a survey among her group as to whether boys smell. The room seemed noisy and chaotic but at least no one was crying or fighting. At this point, a little girl approached me with a freckled but serious face.

'Mister, Ivan's been sick and Kerry's trod in it.' Reluctantly, I went to look. Ivan had indeed been sick and, yes, Kerry had trod in it. Kerry must have been an athletic girl: she had managed to visit nearly every part of the classroom since Ivan's ejection, as evidenced by the neat set of beige footprints all over the red carpet. I called for Sue, who was obviously well used to dealing with these situations.

'It's OK, leave it to me, Andy,' she said, dashing over to a small green boy sitting in the book corner and whisking him to the toilets.

I was just wondering whether I should go for a mop and bucket when the little girl – the original messenger of doom – reappeared, this time with an accomplice. 'We found some more sick, Mister, in the sand tray.'

Oh well, I thought, at least Kerry won't have trod in it this time. I began to move towards the sand tray when a gaggle of four or five excitable children ran into me, inevitably led by the freckly girl. This time the chief informant delivered her report more breathlessly, 'Mister, there's some in the Wendy house. And can we play with the hamster?'

The smell was beginning to choke and I tried to get the children to sit down rather than dash round on a vomit expedition. But no one was listening to me; there was too much squealing and excitement by this time. The throng of roving reporters was continuing its game and growing in numbers and animation as it followed the trail. They no longer came to me but simply rushed around in a mob shouting the latest news across the room.

'There's some here!'

'It's on the nature table!'

The rest of the class echoed each announcement with a series of lurid 'ERRs' and 'UGGHHs' of increasing intensity. A mixture of despair and terror surged up in my chest as mayhem ensued. *Oh Lord, help me – where is Sue?* I looked round. She was coming through the door cuddling Ivan, who had obviously lost a lot of weight. At least he seemed to have stopped.

Somehow, I managed to calm the class down and get them back into their chairs. I hurried over to Sue.

'How is he?'

'Oh, Ivan's fine now, aren't you, love?' The little moon-coloured face nodded below his crinkly hair. I stood well back.

'Has he, er, finished?'

'Yes, I think so – but I just missed a big one as I went to get the mop.'

'Where?'

'It's not good. I wouldn't look if I were you.' Naturally I turned round to look. There were very few surfaces unaffected by the assault, it seemed. Kerry had also done her best to further distribute things across the floor and the wandering announcers had spotted the main areas of damage. All, that is, except one. There was one place where it seemed that Ivan had truly saved his best till last, where his stomach had made one final bid to become incontestably empty. It was the place where teachers put things safely out of children's reach. Where I put my jacket and piles of books to mark, and the register and pots of pens, paperclips and staples.

It was the teacher's desk.

I turned back to Sue who was biting her lip. I reached for the bell, hoping it wasn't slimy, and gave it a ring; I didn't care what the damned time was – they were going out to play.

The rest of the afternoon passed quietly enough. I followed a very long playtime with a very long story time in a haze of disinfectant, and then sent them out on the dot of home time. I almost couldn't bear to look at the room. Sue had done a superhuman job to clear up Ivan's output but the destruction covered a much wider sphere: there was sand in the water tray and bits of carrot in the sand tray; some of the African carvings had been carved some more; and the tadpoles had been set free; the stuffed animals had been interestingly regrouped; and the fossils decorated with felt tip. I didn't want to go near the desk.

After half an hour of frenzied tidying, scrubbing and rearranging, I glanced up to see Emma, looking serene. To my amazement, she didn't mention the awful smell or crumpled displays. Being Ivan's teacher, she was no doubt immune to the pong. She didn't even ask me how I'd got on. Instead, she enthusiastically showed me a great pile of wonderful collages, drawings and prints that my class had done with her.

'Even Sheena was quite well behaved – that Ritalin must be taking effect.'

I mustered a few feeble words of admiration out of my depression and asked if I could look at them properly later.

'I'll tell you how it went after a cup of tea,' I said. I needed to escape that classroom as quickly as possible. It was a great relief to sit down in the peace and relative fragrance of my own room. I glanced through the pictures – they really were good. I spotted Guy's work right away, with his distinctive chiselled style. On the back it said '*Guy Calvert. Me and mum taking the bog for a walk.*' Oh well, at least Emma wasn't perfect then. But I didn't care about the b and d reversal thing now, I was just ludicrously grateful that Guy was in my class and not Ivan, that I taught big children and not those uncontrollable, free-range, miniature ones. I would be extra nice to Guy and all of them the next day, I decided.

This crumb of comfort didn't last long, however. The door opened and Joyce walked in, beaming brightly. 'Heard you had an eventful afternoon, Andy. Well, it'll do you good to get a bit of experience with infants under your belt, you know. Speaking of which, Emma has a wedding that she's desperate to go to next term . . .'

At home that night, I recounted my dreadful day to Barbara, who had thankfully recovered some of her colour and energy, despite carrying the considerable extra weight of our forthcoming child.

'You poor thing. I hope you washed your hands really well afterwards.'

Tom was tugging at my sleeve to play on the floor with his farm toys but I was completely shattered and couldn't move from my recumbent position on the sofa.

'Are you all right?' said Barbara. 'You do look awful.'

'I think it's those Reception kids, they've just done me in.' I tried to move but felt a pain from my gut.

'Ouch.'

'What?' said Barbara, looking gravely suspicious. 'You haven't got tummy ache, have you?'

I tried to sound calm, knowing her dread of sickness. 'It's OK, I don't feel sick, I've just got a pain sort of in my side.'

'That's really odd,' she said, lifting Tom away from me. 'Does it hurt when you touch it?'

I tried. 'Not really, it's just a kind of dull ache.' The pain was now there all the time.

'Perhaps you should go to bed and lie down properly.'

I moved to get up but felt a sudden pulse of real agony from my gut. I couldn't help groaning, which brought a look of fear to poor Tom's eyes.

'I don't like the sound of this,' said Barbara. 'I think we should call Doctor Paxton.'

'It isn't that bad,' I said, clutching my abdomen as another spasm made me groan.

'But this is ridiculous – you're in real pain – it could be something serious.'

'Well, call him then but he'll never come out and I don't know if I'll get to the surgery.' But Barbara was already on her way to the phone. While she rang I slumped off the sofa and started to crawl towards the stairs, heading for the bedroom. The pain lessened for a moment and I thought about our antiquated GP.

Reginald Paxton had worked in this part of Swinnerdale for nearly forty years, delivering many of the valley's babies and handing out prognoses with a grizzle. He was infamous for his reluctance to make home visits, unless a patient was near death, but as I edged up the staircase I could hear Barbara fiercely taking on the challenge.

'No, I can't take him to hospital, he can barely move and it's over twenty miles away – he could be seriously ill! . . . Well, I don't know, it could be appendicitis, a twisted bowel . . . But you're the doctor, you need to come and look at him . . . No, Doctor Paxton, we will not wait until the morning, my husband needs medical attention now . . . No, not an ambulance, it'll take too long from Ingleburn, you're just three minutes away and it's . . . Right . . . Yes . . . Thank you.'

As I pulled myself up on to the bed, I heard her swear and add, 'That man!' Next she called Iris and asked her if she could come over and put Tom to bed, then she waddled up the stairs to see how I was.

'He's coming but I nearly had to threaten to make a complaint. Anyway, how is it?'

'Not too bad.' But I wasn't being honest: it was getting worse; a dreadful, deep, griping pain from inside.

She reached to hold my hand, biting her lip. 'He'll be here in a minute.'

We heard the doctor's car pull up and Barbara called down as he came through the front door without knocking. He clomped into the bedroom with the archetypal old leather bag and a profound scowl. 'Right, shirt off.'

I struggled to move so Barbara helped with the buttons while Dr Paxton prodded me under the ribs. 'That hurt?'

'No, I've just got a pain all the time.' Barbara eased the shirt away as the crusty physician ordered me to lie down. I did so slowly.

'I need you to relax,' he said, once more poking my midriff uncomfortably.

'I can't, I'm afraid – my muscles are all tense.'

'Just lie back and let them go.' It was more a growl than a request.

'I'll try,' I said, squeezing my eyes shut tight.

He pushed against my stomach hard. 'No good, I can't feel a thing, come on.'

Barbara had told me that Dr Paxton had all the bedside charm of an executioner. She wasn't exaggerating.

He huffed, 'This is impossible, I can't even make a proper examination.'

'What do you think it is?' asked Barbara, looking increasingly worried.

'That's the problem; I can't make a diagnosis if I can't tell what's going on.'

'Well, what might it be?'

'There's a possibility it could be a burst appendix. You'd better take your husband to hospital just in case.' He stood up and reached for his bag. That was clearly it.

Barbara rushed downstairs to meet Iris who had just arrived and I heard the two of them frantically discussing what to do while the doctor exited with barely a goodbye. Iris insisted that Don drive me to the hospital. Tom started to cry and I clutched my stomach as another piercing paroxysm shot through my insides.

The medical staff at Bilthorpe Hospital lifted me on to a trolley bed and rushed it through to an examination room where I was put in a gown and told that a doctor would be along very soon. The journey had been difficult, with Don quite tired and irritable himself, while the bumps and twists of the dale's snaking road added to my discomfort. Barbara had said that she'd come along later when Tom was settled, Iris having kindly offered to stay the night if necessary.

'Mr Andrew Seed?' It was a weary-looking bespectacled woman in her fifties. 'I'm Doctor Harrison.' She then proceeded to interrogate me efficiently while gently analysing my whole body, realising that I was in too much pain to relax fully. She called in a colleague and they spent five minutes pressing my abdomen with strong fingers and whispering to each other. They reassured me throughout and I felt confident that I was in good hands.

Dr Harrison surveyed my face. 'Hmmm, bit of a mystery this. I'm fairly confident that it's not your appendix. You don't have a temperature and it's not your stomach.' She touched her chin. 'When did you last evacuate your bowels?'

I would normally have made some kind of quip about consulting my diary but the ache wasn't conducive even to bad wit. 'I, er, can't remember, erm . . .'

'Well, have you been today?'

'I don't think I have, no.' I wondered whether they were going to do something horrible to my bottom.

She had one more poke at my innards then asked an orderly to push me through to a ward. Doctor Harrison spoke to the duty nurse and I feared the worse.

I was transferred to a permanent bed by a pretty blonde nurse who smiled reassuringly but refused to divulge further information.

'We're just going to try something,' she said.

'Will it hurt?' I mumbled feebly.

'No, not at all.' They always said that. She went over to a cupboard, no doubt to fill up a blunt, foot-long syringe or sharpen some kind of hooked implement. Maybe it would be anaesthetic before the major surgery they didn't dare tell me about.

She came over, pulling pale rubber gloves over her hands. My heart rate accelerated. She also had something in a metal dish. They were bound to wheel in a devilish device any moment and push a tube or spiky probe into a hole that was much too small. I prayed that God would help me to be brave.

'Right, Andrew,' she said, beaming. 'Can you lift your gown up to your waist?' Here we go . . . 'That's it. And lie on your side, please.' They clearly didn't want me to see. The nurse reached into the dish. 'Now can you raise both knees together.' I did, shaking. 'That's it,' she said. I just caught a glimpse of what looked like a fat, yellow bullet in her gloved hand. 'OK, I'm just going to put something in your back passage – it won't hurt.' *Liar*, I thought, breathing in tiny gasps. But she wasn't lying: I hardly felt a thing, except a slight coldness. 'That's it, you can lie down and relax now.'

I quickly covered up and leant on to my back. 'What happens next?'

'Right, well, that suppository is going to make you go to the toilet.' She pointed at a door ten yards away. 'It's just over there, look, and it's a special one that doesn't flush. We need to look at your bowel movements to see what the matter is, all right?'

I nodded, much relieved that there would be no pointy metal things at this stage at least.

The nurse continued, 'It shouldn't take too long to act. Will you manage to get there yourself?'

The pain had eased just a little. 'I think so,' I croaked.

She looked doubtful. 'Anyway, I'll be around, or just press the red button, OK?'

After fifteen minutes, I felt another raw spasm, then heard a lot of gurgling noises from deep in my nether regions. An abrupt, overwhelming urge to visit the loo outshouted all other sensations in my body and I slipped off the bed and stumbled to the door, hoping that the nurse wouldn't notice in case it was one of those foul explosive ones.

It was. I just kicked the door shut and yanked the gown upwards in time before my rear went volcanic. I hoped that no one in the ward could hear what was going on as I gripped the straining bar that some far-sighted hospital designer had thoughtfully incorporated into the special privy. There was one last excruciating spike of torture as I passed what felt like a rosette-winning marrow. It crashed into the collecting bowl with a thump that can't have been far off the Richter scale, and was followed by a series of unpleasant noises straight out of a *Carry On* film.

Then it stopped. I released the bar and felt strangely buoyant. The pain was gone.

After ablutions, I shuffled out of the little room and found the pretty nurse who was writing on a pad.

'I've, er, done,' I said.

'Oh good, and how do you feel now?'

'Much better, thanks. In fact, the pain's gone altogether.'

'Excellent, right, well you go back to your bed and I'll get the doctor to come through as soon as I can.'

I now noticed the other men in the ward and nodded to a couple as I made my way back feeling, to my amazement, completely well. The nurse walked over to the toilet: I didn't envy this part of her job at all. She was in there quite a long time and I heard a few noises, and then she came out, looking a little pale, and made her way to the internal phone. I could just make out parts of the conversation.

'Doctor Harrison? Yes . . . Mr Seed . . . Yes . . . He seems fine . . . OK . . . *Massive* stool . . . Yes . . . Never seen one like it . . . Taken a sample . . . Right.'

The doctor appeared ten minutes later and came over to me.

'I hear there's been some spectacular action. How are you feeling?'

'I'm fine now – the pain's gone.'

'Well, that's good news. Let's examine you again, then.' Once more she prodded and poked my midriff but this time the tension was gone and she nodded as she pressed. 'No pain there?' I shook my head. She moved her hands, 'Feel that?'

'Yes, but it doesn't hurt.'

She felt my forehead, stood up and looked satisfied that I wasn't about to croak. 'Let's see what you produced, then.' She disappeared into the toilet. '*Good grief!*'

Half an hour later Barbara arrived. She dashed in, looking anxious as she saw me propped up on the hospital bed.

'How are you?' she said.

'I'm a lot better now,' I said in an unnecessarily frail voice.

'Does it still hurt?' I shook my head. 'Have they done anything?'

'Just tests,' I shifted uneasily.

Her eyes darted about, looking for lesions or injection lumps.

'Do they know what it is?'

'Yes, I think so.'

She just waited and stared. 'Well?'

I wanted to hide under the covers. 'A big poo.'

'What do you mean, a big poo?' She shook her head.

'It blocked my lower intestine.'

There was a moment's silence. 'You mean to say you were constipated?'

'It was a really, really big poo, the nurse—'

'You mean I drove twenty-five miles out here, and so did Don, with me worrying that I'd be the mother of two fatherless children, and Iris had to cancel her Mothers' Union meeting and Tom went into a screaming flap, all because your bum was blocked?'

I nodded but Barbara wasn't watching. She was holding the end of the bed frame and I could feel the whole thing tremble as she launched into an explosive horse laugh, complete with snorting, squeaks and gasps for breath. Everyone on the ward craned over and the nurse rushed through thinking there had been an incident.

It was worse than a day in the infants.

Chapter Fourteen

Oliver

I shook Adam Metcalfe's big rough hand and zipped up my coat. I was back at Black Busk Farm and had just stepped out of the car into a biting wind.

'Ooof it's cold for April,' I said lifting a sleepy Tom out of his seat.

'This is positively tropical for Reddle,' laughed Adam. 'We had more snow last week.'

I took Tom inside the fortress-like farmhouse so that he could play with the Metcalfe children, then apologised to Ruth that Barbara wasn't with us.

'She's just too tired, sadly. It's a shame because she really wanted to see some lambs.'

'No worries, she can come and see them another time. You go out with Adam and I'll keep an eye on the bairns – they'll be fine.'

I thanked her and ruffled Tom's hair but he didn't seem to notice, he was already happily immersing himself in a pile of toy tractors and animals. Outside I put my woolly hat on and went to find Adam, who was unchaining a small bright-eyed collie from its kennel.

'How's that difficult lass gettin' on in your class, then?' he asked.

'Oh, Sheena? Well, there's been quite a big change since I last spoke to you. She's been put on this drug called Ritalin and it seems to have calmed her down. There's been a lot less trouble from her recently.'

'That's good, your prayers must have worked then.'

'Well, er, if I'm honest, I forgot about praying for her.'

He laughed gently, 'Don't worry, I didn't.'

We walked across the road and through a muddy gateway into a small field that was scattered with trailers and broken feeding troughs.

'Have you finished lambing, then, Adam? I noticed it all seems to be over round Applesett.'

'No, I've quite a few to go yet. We're always late up 'ere. Down the dale yer looking at March mainly and lowland places are lambin' in February or even January, but it's usually end of April afore we're done.'

'A busy time, then.'

'Busiest of the year. It's always cold, windy, usually wet and we often get snow up here. Come on, we'll go up on the hillside and check the yows.' He picked up a long metal crook and pushed open a gate. The dog flew through, eager to run and chase, but Adam brought her back with a growl.

'How's it been going?' I asked, already struggling to keep up as he strode up the rising hillside.

'It's been a bad year, sad to say. Lots of lambs have died . . . not enough twins.' There was no bitterness in his voice, just a stoic resignation. I wasn't sure what to say.

'So where are the lambs born, then?'

'Out here, mainly, on the pasture. A few o' the creaky ones are in the shed. We'll see some in a minute.' He pointed up to a scatter of fat, scruffy sheep standing higher up on the coarse, boggy fell. I stepped over a rabbit hole and there was a sudden clatter of wings and a dark grouse burst up from under our feet, making me jump. Adam smiled and then slowed down, once more reigning in the dog, who was crouching, ready to spring forward. A moment later he stopped and shielded his eyes.

'Gulls,' he said, pointing towards the ridge, where two white birds had landed. 'I don't like seagulls and crows – they usually mean dead lambs.'

Before I could answer, the wiry farmer put two fingers in his mouth and generated a piercing whistle. Immediately, the sheep looked round and scuttled, while the gulls fled. The dog slid forward, unable to resist its herding instinct. Adam shouted some indecipherable commands and it held back, twisting round gymnastically, bridling with energy before dropping down.

The mucky-fleeced Swaledales moved away further up the hill and we could see one wobbly lamb struggling to keep up with its mother. The dog edged forward as we walked up to where the gulls had been. In among the tufts and mud were three dead lambs, one red and torn open. They were a forlorn sight, their thin wool wet over slender bodies. Once more, I didn't know what to say. Adam held back the dog with his stick and turned away.

Further on we saw a single black-faced ewe, cowering. Once more Adam gave a shrill whistle and it jolted sideways. I asked what the whistle was for, realising that it wasn't a signal to the sheepdog.

'It tells me if the sheep has a lamb. You can't always see because they hide in the rushes to stay out of the wind, but if the yow jumps round when I whistle then it means they have one. They're nervy and protective.'

Sure enough, as we approached we saw the small shaky figure of a new-born lamb, its whiteness stained with traces of membrane and its cord still dangling. The dog ran behind to stop the sheep escaping so Adam could move in for a closer look. The mother scuttled warily, trying to watch both man and dog, while the lamb stood on trembling legs unsure what to do.

'That un's OK but it's just one again,' said Adam. 'Let's go down to the shed.'

The cold wind pushed us down the hillside and back towards the lonely farm, tight in the valley bottom between the fells. There were no primroses or violets here: the place was seemingly last on spring's list, yet I could tell that Adam was grateful for everything that he had. I thought again about Sheena and what an insignificant problem her behaviour was compared to the raw battle for survival going on here on these wild moors. Yet I needed to remember that she was a girl of only nine with a challenging medical condition, living in difficult circumstances. Adam at least had his close family around him.

Inside the small draughty barn there were rows of pens and the constant bleat of numerous sheep and lambs. It was good to be out of Reddle's stinging gusts and I wandered round, looking at the anxious faces of the ewes and their more inquisitive lambs, some of which hopped on to bales of straw for sport.

'So there's something the matter with all of these?' I asked.

'Aye, more or less,' said Adam, walking down a row and pointing.

'Lame, not enough milk, scourin', scourin', scourin', not enough milk, scourin' and that one's all right.'

'What's scouring?'

'Sheep scour: the runs to you.'

'And what's up with this one?' I said, indicating a scraggy-looking sheep with fat horns and grey matted wool.

'Her? She's a one-titted yow,' said Adam, enjoying my bewilderment. 'Mastitis.'

At least I'd heard of that. Just then I saw a large, plastic barrel move. Inside were two tiny, orphaned lambs, shuffling round and looking up expectantly.

Adam dished out some feed to three fretful ewes. 'You'll be tellin' me next you don't know how to count sheep.'

'What do you mean?'

He went down the line of pens with his finger. 'Like this: yan, tan, tethera, pethera, pimp, sethera, lethera, hovera, dovera, dick, yan-a-dick, tan-a-dick, tethera-dick, pethera-dick, bumfit, yan-a-bumfit, tan-a-bumfit, tethera-bumfit, pethera-bumfit, jiggit.'

This time I laughed, 'You've made that up. You are not telling me *that's* real.'

'Don't you know that? Very old is yan tan . . .'

I was about to say something but I knew from the way he said it that he was telling the truth. I just looked at this young, craggy shepherd and shook my head.

'Come on,' he said. 'Let's have a big cup o' tea.'

At school on Monday, I announced a special project that I had been planning for some time.

'Right, Class Three, I want your full attention. Put everything down, sit up straight and look this way.' Most of them did. Bernadette was on the floor searching for her pen top, Chris had already forgotten the first part of the instruction and Sheena was guiltily fiddling with something under the table.

'This week we are doing something special and we'll be working on it in every English lesson right through to Friday.'

Yvonne's hand shot up, 'What is it?'

'Well, I'm about to tell you that.'

'I think I know,' whispered Vanessa to Fay.

'Would you like to share your ideas, Vanessa?' I said, causing her to blush a little.

'Is it a play, something to do with Easter?'

'No, it's not a play; we're going to make something.'

This precipitated a few more hands in the air.

'You mean a big model?' said Victor, starting to look a little excited. 'Like that sewage works one you did before?'

'Er, no, it's not a model.'

Yvonne blurted out again, 'Is it a big murial on the wall, or summat like that?'

'You mean mural. No, it's not any kind of art. Remember, I said we are going to do it in English lessons.' There was a lot of head scratching and looks of confused expectation. I began to regret building it up so much. 'We are going to make a newspaper.'

There was a short baffled silence before Yvonne said, 'Eh?'

'We are going to write our own Class Three newspaper and I'll be sending you out to find news, do interviews, carry out research, take photos, write articles, put together sports reports, make crosswords and that kind of thing.'

It was foolish of me to expect as much enthusiasm as I was feeling but I couldn't help being disappointed by the vacant expression on most of the faces.

'But how will we make a newspaper, Mr Seed?' asked Glyn. 'Don't you need big machines and computers and things?'

'Don't worry about that part of it. We'll just make one newspaper by sticking lots of things together on to big sheets of paper, then we'll get Mrs Marsett to photocopy the whole thing.'

Most of the faces still looked blank. I obviously needed to do a lot more explanation. I produced a copy of the *Hauxton & Bilthorpe Gazette* and started to point out the various elements that made it up. After five minutes, I sensed that attention was drifting, so I put the paper away.

'Right, any questions?' About twelve hands went up. 'Yes, Lee?' I said, pointing to the sensible, pale-eyed boy.

'Can I take the photos?' All those with their hands up vented into noise.

'Awww, I was gonna ask that!'

'So was I . . .'

'Can't we have two photo people?'

'It's not fair.'

The following day I divided the children into groups and gave them each a card explaining their task on the newspaper. I also brought a big pile of different papers, both local and national, so they could look through them for examples of what they were supposed to be producing. I told everyone that they could write a news story, provided they had some news, and that if they finished their own task as well they could choose to produce something for the puzzle page or joke section or create a cartoon strip.

Eventually, after a thousand questions, clarifications and the dismantling of yet more misconceptions, everyone in the class at least started to give the appearance of working. Oliver Crotone then came up to me. He was a quiet boy with jet black hair, the son of the Italian chef from Ristorante Bari in Hauxton.

'Mr Seed, I'm writing a book review but I do have some news as well. I'm not sure which one I should do first.'

'Well, is it a big, exciting news story that could perhaps go on the front page?'

He hesitated, 'No, it's not exciting. I don't think it should be on the front page.'

I was just about to ask him what the story was when there was a kerfuffle from the other side of the room. I went over to discover that Sheena had accosted Lee as he passed with the camera and offered herself as a saucy model. After I had assured poor Lee that under no circumstances would he be required to point a camera at her in any state of undress, I returned to my desk where Oliver was still waiting, along with a queue of other confused junior journalists.

'Just do your book review first,' I said to him. 'Then write the news story after.' He nodded, then disappeared, and I quickly answered the other queries before setting up a card label on my desk saying *Editor*.

After a short while, the first drafts of news stories and articles began to arrive. I had suggested that everyone write their initial efforts in rough before writing them out neatly or typing them up on Eileen's battered old spare typewriter which we'd borrowed. It was clear right away that there was going to be considerable redrafting.

With some apprehension I had sent out Sheena and Eddie to interview the school secretary, suggesting that Eddie take the notes. They returned after fifteen minutes looking excited. Sheena was shaking a jotter.

'We've done it, Mr Seed. Eddie's wrote it all down what Miss Marsett said.'

'I don't know if it's long enough,' said Eddie, snatching the jotter.

'We did loads!' said Sheena, scrunching her face.

I put out a hand. 'Well, let the editor have a look, then.'

They were right about it being brief; there were just three questions and answers:

Q. What's it like being school secretary?
A. Very nice. I enjoy the job because there are lots of different tasks.
Q. If you got sacked, how would you feel?
A. I would be very upset.
Q. Is your job easy?
A. It's not difficult but there are lots of things to remember.

It was a start. Reluctant to send Sheena back out of the classroom as an investigative reporter, despite her improvement, I suggested that they think of a good title then both copy it out carefully and we'd use the neatest one.

'Can I 'ave a go on the typewriter?' asked Sheena, spying that it was unmanned. I nodded, feeling I should once again give her more responsibility now that the Ritalin was having a positive effect. After this, more pieces arrived on my desk, all compensating in enthusiasm for what they lacked in quality. Chris produced a news story about his mum burning the chicken and asked if it would make the headline. Next, Lee arrived with a long and phenomenally boring football match report for the sports pages, detailing just about every pass and tackle in Cragthwaite's 11–1 obliteration of poor Ingleburn Catholic Primary. Libby, having interrogated a touchingly honoured Pat Rudds, presented me with the alluringly titled 'The Life of a Cleaner'. It was not only well written but lent me several new insights into bleach.

I was beginning to become concerned that the entire newspaper might just be about school when Guy arrived with a typically black, chiselled scrawl. It was about his farm and it was rather sad.

> Carf killd
> Yestaday at Gill Farm a trajidy hapend. Sum cows trampld on a carf in shed. and now the carf is ded.

It had taken him half an hour and I could see that he was still sweating from the effort, but it was a good story and at least the bs and ds were the right way round. I corrected the spelling and grammar, then told him with a pat on the back that it would make the front page.

'I'll try an' get a photo of the shed, tonight, shalla?' he said, smiling.

'That would be really good, Guy.' He went away with a spring in his step and Vanessa and Fay shuffled forward holding an ancient hardback tome.

'It's the school log book for 1875 to 1886,' said Vanessa. 'Mrs Berry gave it to us.'

'But look what we found,' said Fay, opening up the heavy volume and pointing to a section of magnificent leaning script. I had to lean in to decipher it:

> *21st October 1877. With feelings of the deepest regret I have to record the death of Thomas Kirby. He fell off a wall in the boys' urinal at about 1 of the noon and expired about 7pm.*

'Wow, that's amazing,' I said; 'and tragic. A great find, girls.'

'Mrs Berry said it must have happened at the old school,' said Vanessa. 'I thought we could do a list of all the most interesting entries from this log book.'

'Excellent idea – that would make a great article.' I was suddenly buoyed, thinking that the newspaper would be a success after all, perhaps even good enough to sell to parents. But something was itching at the back of my mind and then it registered – death. First the lambs at Reddle two days ago, then Guy's calf last night and now, dug out from a century ago, the shocking demise of a boy; an ordinary child just like those sitting in front of me now. I mused for a moment on how the children in this rural island took death in their stride much more readily than most, before the cries for attention became too loud and brought me back to the present.

On Wednesday, the remaining first drafts of contributions to the *Cragthwaite Chronicle*, as the children had voted to name our journal, were piled up on my desk. There was far too much to mark so I took them home. Bernadette had excelled herself with a paragraph for the pets' page all about her mischievous ducks and her rabbit named Stinky. Mervyn, meanwhile, had penned a controversial comment piece suggesting that the Queen should sell one of her castles and give the money to beggars. 'At least it should generate a few letters to the editor,' I thought, before laughing at an advert for the classified section:

BMX bike for sale. Good condition but no wheels or seat.

There were more treats in the pile including an out-of-date weather forecast, a recipe by Jess for 'baken and barely soup', a whole page of jokes too rude to print and a prize quiz in which question eight was, 'How do you spell Mississippi?'

On Thursday my spirits were raised once more when the resourceful Vanessa and Fay handed in a quite magnificent school history piece entitled 'Lessons from the Logbook'. They had found a whole series of fascinating entries detailing outbreaks of scarlet fever, mass absences on market day, visits from The Sanitary Authority and gruesome strappings. Then Victor brought in a crossword he'd made at home and several children contributed beautiful drawings for a local nature page. I was delighted with how it had turned out.

There was just one piece missing, Oliver's book review. I sought him out, mentioning deadlines, and he apologised for not handing it in earlier.

'I did do it yesterday but I've been trying to finish my news story,' he said.

'Oh yes, I'd forgotten all about that – is it finished?'

He hesitated and half-covered his writing book. 'Sort of, but I don't know if it's any good, Mr Seed.' It was clear that he was worried in some way. I smiled and held out a hand.

'Well, perhaps I should just have a quick look at it? I could probably help you to make it better, if we need to.'

Hesitantly he slid his arm off the book and passed it to me. I opened it up and read:

Goodbye Nana

My nana passed away on Saturday. She was 79. I loved my nana because she was always kind to me and my sister. We played at her house every summer and in the other holidays. She was a good cook. She made the best cakes. My nana was my mum's mum and she lived on her own. Her name was Edith. She was always happy and I liked it when she told us stories. Nana's house was old fashioned and her garden had lots of flowers. I will miss my nana.

I tried to hide the fact that I needed a tissue but one or two children had noticed. It was one loss too many. I handed the book back.

'It's perfect, Oliver. No need to change anything.'

* * *

A few days later the various typed and handwritten pieces, along with photos and puzzles, were cut out and assembled on to large sheets of paper and glued into place by Vanessa, Nina and Lee. With great ceremony I let the trio carry these page masters through to Eileen in the office, who had been briefed beforehand about copying them thirty times each. Joyce had agreed that we should charge people for the cost of paper and printing, and so excitement mounted further in the classroom when the copied pages were returned for stapling so the *Cragthwaite Chronicle* could go on sale.

'It looks ace!' declared Eddie, as he held up a completed copy. 'I can't wait to show my mum.'

'I'm gonna buy three,' said Yvonne. 'Ma dad wants one and me auntie and I want me own copy 'n' all.'

The print run was sold in no time at all and another twenty copies were, too, much to everyone's glee. Several parents approached me in the following days to say how much they'd enjoyed reading the publication and how well the children had done. After such a difficult school year, I greatly enjoyed the warm glow of satisfaction that came with a successful project, yet my abiding memory of the newspaper would always be Oliver's tender little report.

Chapter Fifteen

Kirsty

Easter saw daffodils open in low breezy clumps across the green in Applesett and the air finally warmed, bringing us cheer as we enjoyed the much-needed break from school. Barbara, now with only three weeks before the baby was due, was huge and struggled to walk more than short distances. I took Tom out every day for a toddle to see Big Alec's lambs, play on the swings or splash at the edge of the waterfall. Everywhere buds were opening, bringing that sense of freshness and optimism that always accompanies spring.

When the last day of the Easter holiday arrived I sat down in the cramped little study and frantically tried to organise my plans for the forthcoming summer term. There were parents' evenings and reports to think about, sports events to arrange and a whole series of mini-projects that involved being outdoors. My desk was piled with papers, timetables, charts, lists and record books. I just wanted to shove it in a box: admin wasn't my thing.

I heard some tired footsteps coming slowly up the stairs and Barbara appeared with a cup of tea.

'Hey, I should be making you tea,' I said.

'You should, but you never do.' It was only half true. 'How's it going?'

'Badly, I just can't seem to concentrate.'

'Do you *have* to go back to work? Can't you just stay here and look after me?' She put her arms on my shoulders and slid forward. I twisted round and put my hand on her tummy.

'It feels like you're about to pop. How do you manage to carry this great puddin'?'

'I wish it would hurry up and pop. I don't remember Tom being this heavy.'

'What's Tom doing?'

'Don't know, don't care – I'm going for a lie down.'

I hoped she was kidding. 'Are you all right?'

'Yeah, just tired. Tom's having a snooze, so he's fine.'

I doodled for a moment and wondered what it would be like having two young kids in the house. Would it be havoc or just more of the same? I cast the thoughts aside and tried to concentrate on the twenty-three children who I'd be facing the next day.

At school the following morning I was heartened by three or four children saying how our class newspaper had been passed around entire extended families during the holiday and had been enjoyed by all. It was a cheering start to the term but, as is often the case, there was one dissenting voice.

It came from Kirsty Suggett. She was the oldest girl in my class and renowned for her earthy sense of humour. She accosted me after the register.

'Mr Seed you took out all me jokes from the paper!'

'Kirsty, I had to, they were too rude.'

'They weren't rude, I told one to Mrs Berry and she laughed.'

'Well, the editor decided that the parents might not all agree.'

'They only mentioned bums and trumping and—'

'I know what they mentioned, Kirsty. I'm sorry. Don't you know any clean jokes?'

'Depends what you mean by clean . . .'

I shooed her outside and tried to get myself prepared for the day.

The next six hours were a whirl of talking, instructing, explaining, correcting, remonstrating, waiting, inspiring, rebuking, sympathising, despairing, writing, reading, marking, exasperating and gulping tea. When three o'clock arrived I wearily called the children over to the minute, carpeted book corner and sat them down for a story. This was my favourite part of the day and I felt soothed to be able to sit down and read a book, knowing that the children themselves would be tired, calm and ready to enjoy a good tale.

I was starting a new novel, *Room 13* by Robert Swindells, which had been recommended to me by a librarian in Ingleburn. It was about a class of ten-year-olds going on a residential school trip to Whitby and having some very strange and creepy experiences in the old hotel where they were staying. I thought it would be a pleasant change from the usual tame adventure or animal stories that the class were used to.

I began the story and the children were immediately engrossed in its account of the various young characters, just like themselves, setting out on an adventure. Right away they warmed to the main protagonist, a girl of twelve, and irked at her adversary, a loud-mouthed, hostile boy. They delighted in the description of the eerie Victorian guest house with its old turrets and rickety stairs. When the bell went and I closed the book there was a big groan of disappointment.

'Can we have some more tomorrow?' asked Kirsty. 'It's mint.'

'We most certainly can,' I said, smiling, glad that I had done something right.

The following day, I mentioned the book and announced that we could have a slightly longer story time if everyone worked hard and quietly. The plan was a success and everyone responded well, including Sheena. At ten to three I asked everyone to tidy away then sit down.

'Right, well, you have all been excellent today, more or less, so let's go and sit in the book corner for story.' There was a small cheer and the class rapidly arranged themselves on the pink carpet. 'Who can remember what happened in the book yesterday?' I said. Nearly all the hands went up. After a quick recap I began reading and, once more, the children were rapidly transported to the seaside and to the dark, malevolent hotel where Fliss, the heroine, wakes up in the night hearing weird noises. She walks up the old, spiral staircase and finds a door that wasn't there before. The following morning her friend appears looking pale and acting most peculiarly. What's more, she has two small red marks on her neck . . .

Class 3 were completely silent and still, staring at me, some with mouths slightly open, as I drew out every last breath of suspense from the story. The book was beautifully written, only slightly scary, with a masterful tongue-in-cheek reworking of a familiar vampire tale and splendid realistic detail. Once again, when I had to stop there were long groans and calls for me to carry on for just a little bit longer.

The following day the story moved away from the hotel as the children and their sanguine teachers explored the quaint fishing port of Whitby. They toured the harbour with its salty trawlers and windy piers, visited the whalebone arch and Captain Cook's statue, then traced through the narrow, cobbled streets past tiny shops selling jet and up the 199 stone steps to the wonderful churchyard with its sailors' graves. Finally they climbed the last part of the precipitous Esk Valley to wander through the desolate and evocative clifftop ruin of Whitby Abbey.

After this the story returned to the mysterious events in the hotel where Fliss realised that she would have to battle Dracula if she were to save her friend. It was gloriously daft but Class 3 loved it. I read to them every day that week and on Thursday, after I described how the children in the story spotted an ancient shipwreck as they searched for fossils at Saltwick Bay, just along the cliffs, an interesting notion came into my head.

The children had enjoyed the book so much and were fascinated by Whitby itself so why shouldn't we do a day trip there and follow a trail of locations described in the book? It was a somewhat tortuous journey to Whitby from Swinnerdale, despite the town being in Yorkshire, but it would be a wonderful way to celebrate their interest in the book. At lunchtime I aired the idea in the staffroom, where Hilda, Val, Emma and Sue were munching through sandwiches.

'Well, it's no pottier than your other schemes,' said Val. 'I'm sure the kids'll enjoy it.'

'Too many hairy bikers in Whitby for my liking,' said Hilda.

'Although, you do get the best fish and chips in the free world.'

'Ooh I love it there,' said Emma. 'It's not grotty like some places on the coast – it still feels like a proper fishing port. And I love the Frank Meadow Sutcliffe gallery with those sepia Victorian photos of fishwives and lifeboatmen with scraggy beards.'

'Aye, they even had hairy bikers then, you see,' said Hilda.

I was pleased that they didn't pooh-pooh it. 'Well, I think it'll make a great trip.'

'Have you asked Joyce?' said Val. 'And when do you intend to go?'

'I've not asked her yet. When to go is a problem: I really want to go before Barbara has the baby.'

'It would be best to do it soon while the book's fresh in their thoughts, as well,' suggested Sue. It was a good point; my mind was made up.

Joyce loved the idea and said the only problems might be hiring a coach at short notice and getting parents' permission. How heartening it was to have the full support of the headteacher, unlike in Raven's day.

A week later I stepped down from the choky old bus and smelt the sea air, accompanied by Mrs Lund and Mrs Towler, Chris and Bernadette's mums. Herring gulls squawked overhead as I called my class to come and line up on the pavement on Whitby's West Cliff. Their eyes were bright with excitement, especially Kirsty's.

'Where are we going first, Mr Seed? Ooh, look, a ship. What's that thing? Are those the whale bones? I can smell chips. Come on, you lot, hurry up!'

I lined them up and explained what we were going to do, telling them that I had a special surprise for the last part of the book trail.

'Is it "The Dracula Experience"?' asked Yvonne. 'I've been there already.'

'You'll have to wait and see,' I said, thinking *well that's blown that, then . . .*

For the next five minutes Yvonne explained to Kirsty all about the town's new vampire museum and what she could expect to see there. I walked behind, listening.

'There's all these wax models and creepy sounds and that.'

'I aren't scared of vampires anyway,' said Kirsty. 'I'm aching for a pee, though.'

After a toilet stop, we explored West Cliff, admiring the bronze statue of Captain Cook high upon his pedestal, skipping through the whalebone arch and gawping at the magnificent view of the coast. Every child was desperately trying to spot the Gothic guest house described in the book; it was the one place whose location we didn't know.

'It is that one?' said Bernadette pointing to a stately Georgian terrace.

'No, too posh,' said Vanessa.

Lee pointed at a small hotel, 'What about that?'

'Too modern,' someone called.

'There?' suggested Sheena.

'That's a bus shelter,' replied Mrs Towler.

'No, *there*.'

'That's a shop.'

'Oh, I give up, then.'

We followed a steep path to the harbour where the children ogled candy floss and inhaled the aroma of battered fish and vinegar. We walked up the West Pier, admiring the lifeboat and lighthouse. Great waves rolled in from the fearsome North Sea and slapped against the boulders piled below the pier's stone walls. The children shouted into the wind and abandoned their walking partners before I called them all back for packed lunches in the bandstand.

Twenty minutes later we crossed the famous metal swing bridge over the Esk and explored the old town on the east side of the river, passing the little jet shops, like the class in the story, before reaching the renowned 199 stone steps up to the church. Every child counted, determined to check that the number was correct, and regularly blocked the way for elderly tourists descending in search of fish and chips. As we ascended, the view opened up again over the jumbled red rooftops of the port, with its hidden alleys and quaint inns, and screeching gulls vying for the best chimney pot vantage.

'It is one hundred and ninety-nine!' cried Kirsty, reaching the top first.

'I counted two hundred,' said Mervyn. 'I think.'

Yvonne, some way behind, stomped her foot. 'Oh, I've lost count – I'll 'ave to start again.'

'Oh no, you won't!' I called as she turned to go back down. Two grey-haired ladies chuckled from a bench at the side. Yvonne gave up and eventually the class assembled again for a head count. I said that they could have five minutes to explore the churchyard and look at the gravestones like Fliss and her friends had done in the book.

Sheena, who was still purple from her exertions climbing the steps, looked horrified. 'Am not treadin' on graves. Thes dead people in there!'

'They won't mind, honestly, Sheena.'

'I'm scared, I don't want ter.' It seemed genuine and she declined even when Mrs Towler offered to walk round with her, so I let her sit on a bench by the church.

Fifteen minutes later, the children were roaming through the gaunt remains of Whitby Abbey, perched hundreds of feet above the town on a windswept headland. They were given strict instructions not to climb on the ruins and most of them obeyed. I found a wooden seat and spent a couple of minutes just watching them revel in the freedom of being out of school in an evocative location. Part of me wanted to draw them together and tell them about the history of the place and the legends associated with it and explain what the different parts of the building were used for, but something held me back.

'When are we off ter find fossils, Mr Seed?' It was Kirsty again.

'But we've only just arrived at the abbey.'

'I know but I want to get an annomite.'

'Ammonite.'

'That's what I said: annomite.'

'We'll be going in five minutes.' Time was short, not least as we still had to fit in the surprise visit which, thanks to Yvonne, wouldn't be a surprise to anyone.

After a gusty clifftop walk to nearby Saltwick Bay, the children rushed down the steep path and on to the rocks, desperate to find fossils, once again as Fliss's class had done in the story. The crumbling cliffs had left a beach strewn with thousands of boulders and smaller fragments of soft, shale-like rock, which could be broken open hopefully to reveal hidden treasures.

'There's the shipwreck, look!' cried Jess, pointing to the skeletal remains of a large boat half-buried in sand and water. Beyond it was the beast-like hump of Black Nab, an infamous hazard to passing ships. A moment later, Chris gave a whoop and held up a small fragment of an ammonite.

'Awww,' called Kirsty. 'Where did you find it?' Chris pointed to the base of the cliff where fresh rocks had fallen after a recent storm, and soon the whole class was clustered there, bashing stones in a mad frenzy to find a petrified stegosaurus. I appealed for calm and suggested everyone spread out. Within a short while, others began to find small fossil pieces and Guy uncovered a handsome complete specimen.

'I've found a *massive* one!' called Eddie.

I went over and looked. There was a beautiful imprint of a large ammonite with the familiar grated spiral, about five inches across. There was just one problem: it was on a boulder several feet wide.

'How can I get it?' he asked.

'You can't, I'm afraid, Eddie. This rock probably weighs two hundred kilograms.'

'If a load of us carried it we could.'

Mrs Lund laughed, 'You'd need a JCB for that, lad.'

'My dad's got a digger,' said Guy.

'Sorry, but we're going to have to leave it here, magnificent though it is,' I said.

As expected, this prompted the usual refrain.

'It's not fair!'

Oh well, I thought, I hadn't heard it for a good four minutes.

Some of the children could barely climb the stepped path back up the cliff they were loaded with so much rock. I persuaded a few to leave some of their less spectacular finds behind as we needed to be at the 'museum', as I described it, for three o'clock.

When we arrived at 'The Dracula Experience', most of the class were tired. They soon perked up, however, when they saw the outside of the building with its great posters of bats and green-eyed vampires.

'Are you sure this isn't going to be too scary for them?' asked Mrs Towler, sounding doubtful. 'We don't want them all going home with nightmares.'

'I'm sure it'll be fine,' I said, trying to convince myself. 'Yvonne's been before and she said it was quite tame.'

'Yeah, I went last year,' said Yvonne, who had clearly been listening in. 'But it's changed since then – I think they've done it up a bit.'

'I 'ope it's scarier,' said Kirsty.

I raised my eyebrows and went in to pay with the school cheque-book. The waiting children bounced with excitement outside, many leering with hooked fingers and fangy faces.

The man at the ticket booth assured me that it wasn't too frightening and ushered us all in, asking the children to keep quiet so that they could hear the sound effects, and warning us that it was quite dark inside. I asked Mrs Towler to lead the way, with Mrs Lund in the middle and myself at the back of the line, keeping near to Sheena, who was beginning to become rather excitable. I also asked Yvonne and her partner for the day, Kirsty, to stay at the back since others were accusing her of spoiling it all by giving a commentary on what was coming next.

After a few fake cobwebs near the entrance we entered a space with well-lit displays all about Bram Stoker and his novel *Dracula*, partly set in Whitby, which inspired the attraction. There was a lot to read and most of the children only gave the boards a cursory glance, eager to find out what lay in store along the gloomy corridor ahead. I signalled for Mrs Towler to move on, as Sheena declared the place boring, but the atmosphere soon changed as everyone was shrouded in darkness and we heard the sound of footsteps and distant screams. I heard one or two children blurting out in mock fright but it was all light-hearted and jovial.

'Watch out for the secret door mentioned in the book,' I said as we turned the corner into a wider space which was even darker.

'They didn't have those before,' whispered Yvonne to Kirsty, as they watched model bats flitter above.

'Where's Draclia?' said Kirsty, sounding distinctly unimpressed. 'I want to shout "boo" at 'im.'

Up ahead I heard a few children jumping with fright as a door creaked loudly and an animatronic figure in a black cloak scooted past. We then passed some rather comical dummies, dressed up as vampire victims before the shadows revealed a realistic tall wax figure in a top hat with a glistening grin.

'Is that one real?' I heard Victor ask up ahead.

'No, but it's very good, isn't it?' said Mrs Lund.

The other children just in front stared at the figure then hurried past uneasily. Sheena walked up to it and was just about to poke its face when I reminded her about the 'no touching' rule.

'That's real that vampire man,' she said. 'I saw 'im move.'

'Don't try and scare people more, Sheena, they're just wax figures.'

'Was that ugly one there before?' said Kirsty to Yvonne, stopping for a closer look.

'Dunno, can't remember,' said her friend through the gloom.

I was just about to tell Kirsty to hurry up when the fanged figure stepped forward, lifted its arms and made a rasping sound at the nine-year-old. My own heart leapt with fright and next to me Yvonne jolted, half-collapsing with shock, but Kirsty herself stood rooted to the spot, opened her mouth and let out a shriek of almost military power. The poor costumed actor who had so skilfully maintained his stillness, reeled backwards, his eyes betraying considerable pain, while the rest of us slapped our hands to our ears involuntarily before the piercing screech ended. I moved towards the frozen girl, stumbling in my deafened, half-blind state, while the children who had been ahead piled back in noisy desperation to find out what had happened.

A few moments later, calm was restored and the house vampire apologised profusely, while I reassured poor Kirsty, although none of us could hear properly as our ears were ringing like a Whitby storm warning bell. She was still shaking as I hurried the children through to the exit, wondering what on earth had possessed me to read a scary book to the class.

On the long bus journey back, I sat next to Kirsty, despite Yvonne's protestations. She was pale and quiet and just stared ahead blankly, as any victim of a vampire would.

* * *

'How was the trip, then?' asked Barbara, as I arrived home late and picked up a crusty-eyed Tom.

'It was good: one child has become a zombie, we made a tourism employee deaf, we added to the coastal erosion and we learnt no history.'

'Right, just the usual, then.' Her face was drawn. 'Well, you can tell me all the details later but I need to lie down. I was going to do something to eat but, well, I didn't. Tom and I just had some jars of stuff. Just get whatever you can find.' She waddled off towards the stairs, holding up her giant belly. I made encouraging noises and went to look for some food, wondering how long this baby would take to appear and whether it was really twins or more.

There wasn't a long wait. Four days later Barbara started making funny noises early in the evening, then calmly told me to call Iris then fetch the hospital bag. Just ten minutes later, with our babysitter installed, we headed outside and I prayed there was enough fuel in the car and then prayed it would start. I turned the key and heard the petulant engine cough a few times. Barbara's squeezed eyes told me that a contraction was on the way. I tried again and the Alfa rumbled to life, its exhaust rattling ominously. We turned on to the road, both thinking about the hospital twenty-five miles away.

The birth was drawn out over several long hours with poor Barbara once more losing a considerable amount of blood at the end and suffering severe pain as the baby refused to make an easy entrance into the world. I was shuffled away to one side as various doctors and midwives came and went before everything happened quickly and a bulbous white child was pulled into the world. Barbara, barely conscious, was just able to register that it was a boy, healthy and fine, as she was whisked away for stitches. I sat helpless, as before, and felt rather guilty that it was I who was handed the swaddled child first.

'Ten pounds,' said someone. 'No wonder it was a struggle.'

I just stared at his wonderful puckered face and mouthed a thank you to God. After just a few minutes he was put in a cot and I moved into a waiting room, unaware of time. I called both sets of exultant grandparents and then Iris, who whooped before showing great concern for Barbara. I next called Joyce who told me not to come to school for a few days. After a long wait, a nurse led me through to see Barbara who was sleeping, her face colourless. There was a drip attached to her arm but I was assured she'd be OK.

I arrived home in the early hours and hardly slept at all: little did I know that for several months this would be the norm.

Chapter Sixteen

Alvin

We called him Reuben. He arrived home with Barbara, who needed a few days recuperation in hospital after losing so much blood, and wasted no time in grabbing everyone's attention. First of all, Tom was in total wonder, staring at his new brother and sticking out a finger for the balloon-cheeked infant to grab, which Reuben did with a startlingly powerful grip. Then Iris came rushing over the green when she saw our car, demanding a cuddle and cooing feverishly as she picked him up, only for our new son to turn crimson-faced and start bawling as if his feet were on fire.

Perhaps it was wind, perhaps it was colic, or perhaps it was a protest at being turned out into a bright, noisy world before he was ready, but Reuben Seed cried from the moment he found out what his lungs could do. The first time I picked him up at home I felt the tension and distress in his little body as he opened his mouth to wail. I did the things that had worked for Tom – walking around and jiggling him gently, murmuring soothing words as I held him on my shoulder – but his response was to dig sharp little fingernails into the skin of my neck and yowl all the louder.

Barbara bravely struggled with breastfeeding for a few days but he refused to cooperate and she was too weak from the birth for a drawn-out battle, so the house was filled with bottles, powdered milk, teats, sterilisers, bottle warmers and more, and I was given strict instructions not to let him gulp a squeak of air as Barbara passed him over for my first go at feeding. I was quietly excited.

'Hold him up a little; not that much. Cradle his head; hurry up or he'll start crying. Don't let the bottle drip on him.'

Reuben sensed milk and began to agitate his head with an open mouth in search of sustenance. I pushed the teat on to his lip and he fastened on to it, sucking like an industrial vacuum cleaner.

'Good grief, the bottle'll be empty in ten seconds at this rate,' I said, looking up.

'Just concentrate and watch that he doesn't choke.' A trail of milk was leaking out of the corner of his mouth and on to my arm. He stopped sucking for a moment and I pulled the bottle away, thinking that he needed a break. Within a second his eyes contracted tightly and his mouth creased ready to howl.

Barbara pushed the bottle back, 'Quick!'

'All right, all right,' I said, pretending to be in control.

A few moments later the bottle was empty. Reuben gave it a few more cursory sucks then stopped. He looked bloated and queasy.

'Sit him up, he needs a burp,' said Barbara. I put down the bottle and tilted him forward forgetting quite how floppy new babies are.

'Support his head!' screeched my wife, and I guessed that this wasn't the best time to bring out my gag where I clap rhythmically and chant, 'Reuben's head, Reuben's head!' football-style. Instead

I patted his back, like I'd done with Tom, and waited for a little milky belch. None came, so I lifted him on to my shoulder before Barbara could issue an order and jiggled him once more, applying further gentle pats.

'Don't overdo it,' she said.

'He's fine,' I replied, just as a gurgle sounded behind my ear and I smelt the familiar queasy odour of baby sick. Barbara lifted him away and I removed my shirt which was newly patterned with white lumps and streaks.

Barbara passed him back to me once I'd changed and he'd been mopped, and I delighted in feeling his soft wispy hair on my cheek and taking in that wonderful fragrance that babies possess when they are clean at both ends. After a few more minutes his eyelids drooped and he was incontestably ready for a nap. We crept up the stairs together to our bedroom where his traditional wooden crib had been placed. It was an old German one and had been beautifully prepared by Barbara's mother. I carefully laid him down and we tucked him up, noticing how his pudgy body already nearly filled the little cot.

'Ahh, he's so sweet like that,' said Barbara. We stayed and looked at him lovingly for a moment, so serene, then we both thought about coffee. I had only just turned away when the noise started: like a little siren rolling into action he delivered the first wail.

'You pick him up, I'll put the kettle on,' said Barbara.

The next few days saw this pattern repeated amid a stream of visitors. Our parents came and chuckled at Reuben's wobbly jowls and suspicious eyes, then hugged him until he could take no more.

John and Mary Burton from Buttergill called by in their blue Land Rover and dropped off a big box of pies, casseroles and cakes. They didn't hang around to make a fuss, knowing that the house was hectic.

Billy Iveson, our retired, mushroom-collecting neighbour, dropped in with some rhubarb and advice that a drop of tea in his milk would sort the colic.

'How did you know he had colic?' asked Barbara.

'A certain lady at the shop, who else?' he said winking.

With May almost round the corner and the sun peeping out between scudding clouds, I put Reuben into his pram and headed out with Tom to the shop for some fresh air, thinking Barbara could do with a short break. It was fresh, indeed, with a gusty breeze, but Applesett looked wonderful with the green showing verdant colour and the trees on the side of Spout Fell unfurling into full leaf. Several people scuttled out of their doors for a first look at the village's latest inhabitant.

'Byyy, he's a whopper!'

'Looks like his daddy.'

'Rugby player you've got there, lad.'

In the shop I picked up some milk and disposable nappies, having battled through on towelling ones with Tom and recently given up. Mrs Dent wanted the full, gory details of the birth and she pummelled me with questions.

'How long was the labour?'

'Did she 'ave pain relief?'

'Was it that red-haired midwife with the lisp?'

'Is it true she lost half of her blood?'

'Is Barbara on iron tonic?'

''As she got the runs?'

'Were there any other complications?'

'What's he sleeping like?'

At least the last one was easy to answer.

On the way back up the village, I let Tom have a go on the swings. The poor little lad had been rather neglected over the past few days. As I pushed him, John Weatherall's dented Transit drew up to the smithy nearby and he climbed out, stretching before walking over towards us.

'Now then, who's this little fella?'

'This is Reuben.'

'Reuben, eh? Can't say we've 'ad too many o' them in the dale. Mebbe a hundred years ago,' he said, smiling. The fat baby eyed him with distrust, his diminutive fist seemingly coiled for a quick pop if need be.

'Bonny kid,' he lied.

'You busy, then, John?'

'Always busy, lad, always got five people waiting.'

'The same five?'

'Eh?'

'Never mind.'

'Oh, while we're on the topic o' bairns, you don't need a babysitter, do you? It's just that our Holly is looking to try and earn a couple of quid, you know. She loves kiddies, 'n' all.'

'Well, we usually ask Iris Falconer but she's out some nights so, yeah, I'll talk it over with Barbara. How old is Holly now?'

'Sixteen,' said John walking back to his van and waving.

At home, Barbara was enjoying sitting down with her feet up and the TV on.

'Good walk?' she said.

'Yay, hwings!' said Tom.

'Hmmm, really good,' I added. 'It's lovely now the weather's warming up – loads of people came out to admire our bouncing babby.'

'And was he well behaved?'

'Not a peep from him: he really likes being wheeled around, I reckon.'

'Good, well there's a way for you to get some of that exercise you're always after.' Before I could say anything evasive she asked about Mrs Dent.

'Did she give you a grilling?'

'It was like the Spanish Inquisition,' I said, going into Monty Python mode. 'I exaggerated everything that happened so you'll get loads of sympathy from everyone.'

'You daft noodle.'

'Noogle!' said Tom, pointing at me, just as Reuben began to grizzle. Barbara picked him up and put a finger near his mouth to see if he was hungry. He would have snapped it off if he'd had teeth.

'Oh, and John mentioned that his daughter Holly is keen to babysit.'

'Hey, that would be great. Iris has done so much for us and I know she's missed some of her meetings – I really don't want to ask her too much and it would be nice for us to try and go out once a fortnight maybe. She's a lovely girl, Holly, too.'

'How do you know her, then?'

'Well she's been here three or four times, when Tom was a baby.'

'Has she?'

'Don't you remember, when all the village girls came round?'

'I remember some girls coming round but I can't remember who was who.'

Barbara shook her head as she went to make up some milk, 'And they put you in charge of kids . . .'

I spent the afternoon and most of the evening on school planning, then finally sat down with Barbara, who was looking decidedly weary. We gave Reuben his final feed at eleven and both yawned after our hefty baby had finally burped and so we could head up to bed. I laid him down in the crib and tiptoed away to the bathroom. When I returned he was half asleep, twisting his face ominously. Barbara was already in bed, exhausted. Almost silently I undressed and crept under the covers but I could hear little grouching sounds from across the room. I didn't even try to get to sleep and, sure enough, two minutes later, the start of a whimper signalled that it was time to pick him up.

I paced the room for ten minutes with Reuben on my shoulder and that at least kept him from breaking out into a full blub. He gave another little belch and I hoped that this was it: I carefully placed him down and crept back to bed.

Barbara poked me hard in the back and I awoke from a heavy sleep to hear Reuben beginning to break into another cry. Barely conscious, I dragged myself out of bed and picked him up, sniffing to test if there was anything noxious in his nappy. There wasn't but he squirmed and grizzled, once again spiking my neck with his tiny fingernails. A few minutes patting and carrying wasn't going to be enough this time so I took him downstairs so as not to wake Barbara, and began to pace the living room. The wall clock, which my crusty eyes could now just register, said 3.20 a.m.

By 3.44 he had finally stilled and I gently ascended the staircase, hearing a distant cough from Mrs Boo next door on the way. I wondered if Reuben's crying had also kept her awake. The old floorboards creaked under the bedroom carpet and I hoped that Barbara, at least, would be undisturbed. Slowly I lowered my week-old son into his padded cradle and asked for divine assistance in his staying there until at least six o'clock.

It was at the precise moment that I let my head fall on to the pillow that it started.

'Waaaaaaaaa . . .'

I left it for two seconds and pretended it wasn't happening. But it was. Barbara showed no sign of shifting so I gave up any more hope of sleep and went over to the cot.

I arrived at school the following day in a half-trance, realising as soon as I'd walked through the door that I'd be bombarded with questions about the baby. Eileen was first.

'Lovely to have you back, Andrew, how are things?'

Joyce appeared and quickly joined in. 'Have you brought a photo? How's Mum?'

Then Val passed by. 'Bloody Nora, you look terrible. Baby OK?'

I somehow managed to get through the day and was eternally grateful that Barbara took over night duties that evening. The rest of the week passed in a blur but somehow my body and mind adjusted and, after that, school life returned to normal; well, as normal as it ever could be with Alvin Rutter in Class 3.

Alvin loved Science, but he was permanently terrified. He was terrified that experiments would go wrong; he was terrified that expensive equipment would break in his hands; he was terrified that he might have to touch a minibeast; he was even terrified that the tables and graphs in his book weren't straight. But, all the same, he loved Science.

The next class topic I had planned for Science before Reuben came along was *Flight* – it had always been a favourite subject of mine – and I decided to get the work off with a bang by setting up a special competition involving bottle rockets. A bottle rocket is basically a large plastic drinks bottle containing a measure of water, into which air is pumped. The bottle is set upside down outside, air is fed in and when the pressure reaches a certain point the rocket blasts upwards with a spectacular spurt of water and noise. It was a sure-fire way to impress the children, and distract them from their interrogations about the baby, and I was greatly looking forward to it.

When I announced to the class what we were going to do, there were whoops of excitement and cries of 'Yesss!' from everybody. Everybody, that is, except Alvin. From the moment I began to tell the class about the bottle rockets, I could see that Alvin was becoming agitated. When he was worried, his face began to grow twitchy and he would start to slide from side to side in his chair, as if desperate for the loo.

I tried to put Alvin's mind at rest by detailing how safe my initial demonstration would be, and relating how everyone would be at a secure distance outside, and that the noise was not really loud at all. The rest of the class looked more than a little disappointed as I went through all these precautions – they *wanted* danger, but poor old Alvin was the opposite. Talking to him made me feel like I was trying to reassure an anxious mother that the matter of her six-year-old daughter abseiling down Blackpool Tower was a mere trifle.

When the day of the demonstration arrived, there was great ebullience from the class, especially when I produced a foot pump, lemonade bottle, watering can and a length of plastic tubing with a rubber bung fixed to one end. I warned everyone about good behaviour and lined them up to go outside. I was tingling with excitement as much as they were. Alvin shuffled over to me looking very perturbed and asked if he could go to the toilet.

'Poor kid,' I thought, 'it's nerves, but I bet he still enjoys the show – any child would.'

The bottle was soon set up in the middle of the football pitch. It was one-eighth full of water for 'fuel', and resting against a set of cricket stumps, ready for launch. The rubber bung was pushed firmly into the bottle and the pump was standing by. I looked up to check that the class were all behind the touchline and up wind; there was a cheeky wave from Jess and several thumbs up. I began to pump. A gush of air bubbles spurted from the tube into the water at the bottom of the upturned bottle with each press of the foot pump, and the pressure soon began to build. Some of the children let out little squeals of nervous delight and others had their fingers in their ears. An ordinary plastic lemonade bottle can take a surprising amount of pressure, and soon an impromptu countdown began as the rocket took longer to go off than expected.

'Ten, nine, eight . . .' I carried on pushing at the rusty pump, 'seven, six, five . . .' and before 'four' had been uttered there was a splattering roar of water and air, and the bottle was a hundred feet or so in the air in a fraction of a second. Most of the class missed its ascent because of the incredible speed, but fingers quickly darted up, and all of them saw it tumble from the sky to land with a clatter against the wooden fence. A brief cheer went up, with cries of 'Do it again!' and 'Can I have the next go?' 'Awww . . . *go on* Mr Seed!' It was a tremendous success.

My plan was to let everyone have a go later in the week. I lined up the children ready to walk back to the classroom, where I would tell them about designing their own rockets, with additions like nose cones and fins, for a competition to see whose bottle would fly the furthest. As the class crocodiled across the faded tarmac netball court, a lone figure appeared in the doorway and began heading towards us. It was Alvin: he had missed everything. When he reached the group there was fear on his face – a combination of dread at the thought of what cataclysm had just taken place on the field, and fear at being told off for hiding in the toilet. He made a half-hearted attempt to produce the word diarrhoea, then trotted to the back of the line still trembling.

I gave the class one week to produce a two-litre pop bottle, and design and make a rocket. There were some extravagant ideas: nose cones with parachutes, wings, go-faster stripes and grand, home-made launch pads. As usual, some were more successful than others:

Mervyn filled his nose cone with Plasticine for strength and then added metal fins – in the end, it resembled a V2 doodlebug and probably weighed about the same. Bernadette's rocket had chronic pressure problems when pumped up – in all likelihood something to do with the slits she had made in the bottle to attach the fins.

Despite these eccentric examples, the finished rockets made a superb display of colour and inventiveness – it was almost a shame to fire them towards a fate of sure destruction. Even Alvin's terror had been overcome by a creative urge to produce a splendid Saturn V-inspired effort, complete with USA stickers and cotton reel boosters.

On the day of the competition I carefully outlined the rules to the children: the launch pad would be set at an angle of forty-five degrees, everyone would pump the air into his or her own bottle and a long measuring tape would be used to discover the champion rocket. I had made contingency plans for Alvin to avoid another marathon loo visit; he would be the Official Measurer. This would give him special responsibility and allow him to stand even further away from the launches than the rest of the class. He seemed quite honoured when I broke the news to him, and several members of the class were very thoughtful, saying things like, 'Awww – I wish I was doing that!'

It is often said that children can be cruel to each other, tormenting non-conformists and mocking idiosyncrasies, and I had seen this happen during the year with the overweight Glyn suffering at the hands of Sheena, but experience had shown that kindness was just as prevalent. On many occasions children would rally round a classmate – even one who was not a friend – with great sensitivity;

they somehow sensed fear and anxiety, and acted with tremendous care and loyalty. And so, with Alvin suitably boosted by his special role, the class marched through the door, each one holding a handsome model rocket as if it were a first-born child.

A magnificent spring day awaited us outside: the air was cool and crystalline, with a soft sun illuminating the sombre fells and dappling the heavy stone roofs of the village. What a privilege, I thought, to be here, now, with these children so full of excitement and enthusiasm in such a beautiful place. I sucked in a refreshing chestful of Dales air and addressed the skipping astronauts, reminding them where to sit during the firing.

The first few shots went well: Libby's rocket attained twenty-seven metres and Oliver's twenty-four. The class were kept busy by writing all the scores in a chart while they waited their turn. Alvin stood about sixty metres beyond the end of the tape, a tiny shivering figure who came running in after each landing to determine the distance. After seven or eight goes, Alvin's fears began to ease and he gradually drew closer with each launch, realising the absurdity of staying so far away; he was also getting tired.

The next name on the list was Guy's and there was a robust cheer from his mates and cries of, 'Go, Bogbrush!' as he lolloped forward carrying a colossal rocket. Guy was the only one who had not managed to find a two-litre bottle – his, rather, was a monster three-litre one. I'd figured that its extra width would slow it down and so I had allowed him to use it. As befitting his practical farm-boy nature, he had not held back with structural additions to the design: huge blobs of glue-gun adhesive held six enormous triangular fins in place, and there were dozens of thick plastic tubes gaffer-taped around the fuselage. He had also painted it purple.

A few titters rose from the class as Guy wedged the rubber bung into the neck of the bottle with a mighty heave of his thick arm. I usually gave the bung an extra twist for each child to make things fair, but I couldn't move the bung in Guy's rocket – it looked like it had been hammered in. Guy had also opted to fill his bottle one-third full of water, instead of the usual one eighth or so. 'Oh, well – his choice,' I thought. 'It'll never leave the ground.'

'Shallus start wi' pump now, Mr Seed?' said the hefty, scrag-haired youth. I nodded.

Guy slammed the bottle on to the launch pad and began kicking down furiously on the foot pump. I decided to stand back a couple more paces. The corpulent bottle took much longer than the others to build up pressure, despite Guy's manic pumping, and several of the class jeered then started a slow handclap. Alvin's bravery was growing by the minute, meanwhile, and he stepped a few paces nearer for an improved view of the great bubbling missile on the launch pad.

Guy was enjoying all the attention and announced to his mates that he was now targeting Alvin's head. I was just about to have a quiet word to discourage him from such talk when the ground shook violently and a hurtling volley of muddy water stung my eyes. After the initial shock of the explosion, I blinked several times and saw Guy, completely soaked, but with fist punching the air and eyes tracking the rocket, which was now a stratospheric maroon blur, trailing shreds of torn card and plastic in its wake.

The next few moments I will never forget, happening as they

did like some vivid slow-motion dream. The class held its breath as the bottle shot towards Alvin, who was over fifty metres away. My mind was trying to calculate whether this distance was scientifically possible, but I couldn't stop looking at the hapless boy target. At least at that range – even if it did reach him – he would have plenty of time to move. But Alvin moved not at all. He was frozen to the spot. The panic on his face betrayed a desperation so great that his body's only reaction was complete physical shutdown.

'Move Alvin . . .' I silently called to myself as the rocket tore directly towards him. Guy, meanwhile, was like a striker who has dribbled round the goalkeeper and now faces an open goal, his euphoria total at the moment of impact. Then suddenly, miraculously, Alvin's figure came to life, just as the missile seemed certain to hit him square in the chest. He instinctively ducked at the last moment and the rapidly dipping bottle whacked him with a resounding 'pop!' on the top of the head. The class shrieked with delight, Guy leapt high in triumph, and Alvin's involuntary spasm became a tottering dance before he steadied himself and began breathing again.

To my shame, I bore tears of laughter which I couldn't disguise as I ran over to Alvin. He tried to smile but was still shaking when I arrived.

'Can someone else measure the other ones, Mr Seed?' he said in a crumbling voice. A chair was produced for him, followed by Guy, demanding to know if the extra distance gained from the bounce off Alvin's head would count or not.

I let him count the distance, but I also let Alvin go to the toilet an awful lot during Science that term.

* * *

When I arrived home I tried to recount the story to Barbara but struggled because I kept bursting into laughter. She shook her head and reminded me that we'd arranged for Holly Weatherall to come round to talk about babysitting and meet the children.

I answered a knock at the door and welcomed in a pretty, petite girl. She had a diffident manner and her mother's wavy fair hair and striking green eyes. After a brief chat, she went over to play farms with Tom, and Reuben was brought in, having just had his nappy changed.

'Ahhh, can I have a cuddle?' asked Holly, going up close.

'Course you can,' said Barbara, handing him over, 'but don't be surprised if he starts crying – it's his speciality.'

She carefully took hold of Reuben and he gave her a check over with his dark eyes. I expected his bottom lip to flip out and loud noises to exude, but nothing happened. Or rather, it did: the newborn tyke watched her and approximated something close to a look of approval. He was too young to smile but in terms of his usual expression of disgust, this was as low on the register as we'd ever seen.

Holly made a series of faces and funny noises which kept him happy, then took him over to Tom and knelt down and started to talk about what games the boys might play together when Reuben was older. We knew we were in the hands of a master.

Chapter Seventeen

Bill

With a blissful wash of warm breezes and misty sunshine, April handed the dale over to May. At home Reuben continued to suffer from colic and we continued to suffer from sleeplessness, but life went on and we struggled through, being young and foolish as we were.

The new month brought along two significant events, one at Cragthwaite and one at Applesett. In school, this was the traditional time for assessment tests to be taken, and at home the village was busy preparing for the Whitsun Fair.

Joyce had decided to continue with the short English and Maths tests that Howard Raven had carried out for decades. These were simple and painless exercises and Val favoured them, too, as they only took an hour each. There was to be one change this year, however. The government of the day was trying to improve Science education in primary schools and, to this end, they had devised a set of standardised tests for juniors which were being piloted around the country. Our school had been randomly selected to try out the experimental papers.

'We may as well do them with the other tests,' said Joyce, handing over a couple of large plastic-wrapped packages to Val and me in the staffroom one afternoon. 'I haven't read the guidance booklet, but I'm sure they're straightforward.'

I opened the bag and picked out the teachers' guide. It was forty-eight pages long. Val swore quietly and threw her bundles on to the floor. It soon became clear that whoever had written these tests was used to preparing secondary school exams, probably A-levels: they were frightful. There was a thick booklet for each child to complete, filled with long, complicated questions, graphs, tables and diagrams.

'I think my class are going to struggle with this,' I said.

'I can't do half of these myself!' wailed Val, who had now decided to have a look at the papers. After a few depressing minutes of turning pages, it was decided that we'd just hand them to the children and get it over with, with the minimum of fuss – whoever had written the papers was clearly round the bend.

The following week I was busy rearranging the desks in the classroom, separating each one as far as possible, in preparation for the tests. When the children arrived, they seemed quite excited by the new arrangements; only one or two looked a little apprehensive, Alvin included, knowing that it was the morning of the tests. At least he'd be calmed by the lack of a practical element.

'After break, there's going to be an extra test, in Science,' I announced. 'This is nothing to worry about, even though it's quite long.' I didn't really want to say anything about it at all. 'Are there any questions?'

A hand went up at the back. It was the stocky figure of Bill Redshaw. 'Will we 'ave to do experiments and stuff like that?'

'Er, no, I'm afraid not, Bill – it's just a written test like the Maths and English.'

His shoulders dropped in disappointment. Bill was another farmer's lad and a person who was wonderfully practical. He loved subjects like Technology and Science where he could make things and test them out. Bill also enjoyed helping other people and when he saw me picking up the bundles of test papers, he immediately offered to help give them out.

'Well, I don't like writing much, Mr Seed, but I'll do me best,' he said, picking up a stack of booklets. Both he and I knew that writing was definitely not his strength.

When the Science test was finally under way, I found myself scuttling around the room, as hand after hand went up asking for help. The children simply weren't used to this type of lengthy exam-based approach. The test guide obligingly explained that teachers were allowed to help with reading questions but not give help with answers or any aspect of the science involved. I dashed between Guy, Bernadette and Chris most of the time, although I suspected that several others who needed help were simply not asking for it.

A quick tour of the room, glancing over shoulders, substantiated my fears: Eddie was writing gibberish; Sheena was doodling on the inside cover of the booklet; and Hazel seemed simply to be ticking random boxes wherever she could find them. I consoled myself with the knowledge that at least two-thirds of the class were busy writing what appeared to be sensible answers, then went back to reading questions for the trio who were now propping up their tired arms at the elbow.

Back in the staffroom at lunchtime, I could see that Val had clearly undergone a similar experience to mine. With a growl, she hurled a pile of completed papers on to a chair, and ripped open her handbag for a cigarette. I decided not to say anything.

Looking at the children's answers, it soon became apparent that the content of the tests was at a much higher level than appropriate. It didn't take long for my mood of despair to lift, however, when I began to read some of the interesting responses to the questions my class had produced:

Q: What is the function of the human heart?
A: It poops all the blood around the body.
Q: Explain how being close to people who smoke can damage your health.
A. 2 cm.
Q: Why was there a sound when Kate plucked the elastic band?
A: boyoyoyoyo!
Q: How was the sound different when Sam plucked the longer elastic band?
A: wowowowowo!
Q: Explain why the magnet did not attract the plastic paperclips.
A: Magnets won't attract plastic paperclips because they are made out of wood and the steel paperclips are made out of aluminium.
Q: Seeds are dispersed away from the parent plant. Why is this?
A: So they get used to being on their own.

But of all the answers, my personal favourite came from Bill:

Q: Explain why the temperature of the solution in beaker D was exactly 18°C the following day.
A: No.

Even Val cheered up a little when I read them out.

I passed Bill in the cloakroom at lunchtime. 'How did you find the Science test then?' I asked.

''Orrible – especially that question about beakers. Why did you give us them tests, Mr Seed?'

'It wasn't my idea, Bill, I'm sorry. We can't always have things our own way, can we?'

'Aye, suppose not.' He turned away and then called back. 'Oh, Mr Seed – will I see you at the fair on Monday? My Uncle Alec does the tractor rides: I always go and help out.'

'Yes, OK, Bill, I'll probably see you there.'

Applesett Whitsun Fair was another event where the whole village seemed to turn out in force. Mary Burton, as one of the organisers, had asked if Barbara and I would do a shift running the Roll a Penny stall if Holly Weatherall helped us look after the children. She explained the workings of the day and how the money raised was divided between the chapel, village hall and sports club. We were delighted to help and when Bank Holiday Monday turned out to be a glorious day of May sunshine, there seemed no finer place to be. The morning was frantic, with activity all over the village green. Marquees were erected, stalls were set out and signs placed everywhere telling people where to park. With the becalming Holly holding Tom's hand and Reuben quiet in his pram, we set up the large square Roll a Penny board on some bales of straw and returned to Craven Bottoms for a bite of lunch.

In the early afternoon we walked out on to the green again with our two boys, Reuben in his pram, to stroll around and see the events. Cars were already arriving and visitors were streaming into the village, completely changing its normally tranquil atmosphere. Outside the pub, a tall red-and-white maypole had appeared, and a circle of white-cotton-clad girls were prancing around it in fits of nervous giggles, each one trailing a long ribbon. I could hear someone sounding a little agitated about last-minute practice. Tom stared at the group, considering whether he wanted a go.

'We must come back and see that later,' said Barbara. 'I used to do maypole dancing before I turned into a flabby mother.'

'I want to see everything,' I said, feeling a boyish excitement. At that moment our voices were drowned out by the roar of a tractor coming up the green. It was driven by Big Alec Lund and pulled a huge green trailer covered with posters advertising 'Tractor rides up Buttergill only 50p'. Bill Redshaw was standing in the trailer looking very important. I gave him a wave and could just about make out a cry of 'Now then, Mr Seed!' as he trundled past.

Outside the chapel there was a hubbub of activity. Mary Burton was orchestrating a small army of mainly elderly ladies carrying boxes of cakes, jams and pickles on to a line of trestle tables in front of the railings. There were sweets, jelly and ice cream, home-made buns by the thousand, local cheese, hot dogs and piles of dusty second-hand books. Behind them a large painted board proclaimed 'Chapel Sing-Along 4.30pm All Welcome'.

Further along, there was already a queue of people developing at the Tombola, and next to that were the other games, among them Bash the Rat, Lucky Dip and Guess the Weight of the Jar. Opposite these stalls, the road had been taken over by a group of frightful-looking Morris dancers, dressed in long, black wigs and cracking huge sticks together with glee. I picked up Tom, who looked somewhat distressed.

'Still want to see everything?' grinned Barbara, knowing my lack of enthusiasm for such troupes.

At the top of the green, a cluster of the village's older men were giving a quoits demonstration, something I'd never seen before. Large metal rings were aimed at a small spike in a square of clay and hurled with great accuracy. Beyond this were signs pointing towards exhibitions of dog running and sheep shearing up the Buttergill road. I smiled as I looked down at the village hall where cream teas were being served, thinking back to when Barbara and I had unsuccessfully overseen the same operation two years before. The village was now thronging with people warmed by a dazzling sun and cooled by a clean breeze rolling off the fells. It really was a wonderful sight.

A few minutes later I took over the running of the Roll a Penny stall from Billy Iveson, while Barbara pushed Reuben home for a feed. It was surprisingly popular, although all the coins ended up in the same corner because of the slope where it had been set up. After ten minutes, Holly appeared and offered to walk round with Tom.

'That's kind, thanks,' I said, turning to Tom. 'Would you like to see the fair with Holly?'

'Yay, in buggoo,' he said, looking pleased.

'Oh right, he wants to go in his pushchair,' I said to Holly. 'Little mite has walked round quite a lot today.'

'That's all right,' she said, smiling. 'I'll go and fetch it.'

'But wouldn't you rather be going about with your friends?'

'Nah, I'd rather go round with Tommy.'

She headed towards Craven Bottoms to get the pushchair, promising to return for Tom, and I tried to tempt a passing family into parting with some of their cash.

After an hour or so, John Weatherall came along to take over the game.

'Alreet, lad? Have yer a partner for the egg throwin', then?' he asked.

'What's the egg-throwing?'

'Oh, it's the best part o' the whole day. You'll see what it is, but you need a partner to join in. It'll start in about half an hour, opposite the pub.'

I was intrigued. 'OK, then, but what about you?'

'Oh, don't worry, I'll be there – never miss the egg throwin' – I'll get the missus to take this over for a bit.'

I wandered off, looking forward to finding out what it was, and also pondering where I was going to get a partner. My eye was caught by another strange activity: a group of hefty young men were launching bales of straw backwards over their heads, attempting to pass them above what looked like a pole-vault bar. I was relieved that John hadn't suggested I have a go at that. It must have required enormous strength.

On the way back home to see if Barbara was all right, I once again heard the roar of Big Alec's tractor. It came round the corner from Buttergill and coughed to a halt right outside our house. Behind, the giant green trailer was full of children, strawberry-cheeked with excitement. Bill was there, too: he jumped down from the trailer and helped Alec open the back and lift everyone down. He was in his element. Alec put a piece of card in the tractor cab window saying 'Back at 4.15'. He then hurried off down the green, probably for some refreshment. I called across to Bill.

'How's it going?'

He skipped over, first picking up a cloth bag from the trailer. 'Grand, Mr Seed – you having a good day? I reckon we've made over a hundred quid on these rides. Some kids've been four times.'

'That's fantastic. Is it your break time now, then?'

'Aye, I'm going to get an ice cream and a can. See you later.' He ran off towards the chapel and, seeing that Barbara was busy showing off Reuben to an admiring gaggle of grannies, I wandered towards the pub to make sure I was in time for the egg throwing.

A small crowd was gathering outside The Crown. Several members of the darts team were there, as well as most of the young men and farmers from the village. I was just about to ask Dave Duggleby what was going on when the pub landlord, Dennis Helliwell, stood up on the stone mounting-block outside the building and shouted for attention.

'Right, quiet, everybody! It's time for the big event of the day. We'll be starting egg throwing in ten minutes!' There was a small cheer from some of the beer drinkers on the tables beside him. 'If you want to take part, you need to buy an egg from me now. They're 30p each. And no cheating with hard-boiled eggs from home this year!' There was another cheer, much laughter and a gradual movement towards Dennis, who produced a large tray of eggs. I was more intrigued than ever, desperate to discover what it was all about. I was also very happy to be just a bystander, having made no effort at all to find a partner.

Once everyone who wanted to take part had bought an egg, Dennis vanished behind the pub and then reappeared carrying two large coils of rope. He marched over to the open part of the village green across the road where most of the contestants were assembling. Once more, he went into shouting mode:

'OK, stand opposite your partners if you're playing. Everyone else stand well back!' Two straggly lines of men formed and Dennis picked up one of the ropes. John Weatherall stepped forward and took the end of the rope while Dennis uncoiled it between the lines. The rope was then lifted by the two men and everyone in one of the lines told to step back, staying level with the rope. The same odd procedure was then carried out with the other rope and the opposite line of people. Everyone was told to spread out along the ropes, but to stay opposite their partner. Finally, everything seemed to be ready: the two lines, each of about twelve people, stood five yards apart.

'Right, have a quick practice then!' called Dennis. John Weatherall immediately lobbed his egg towards Big Alec, who was obviously his partner. Alec took an easy catch, expertly cushioning the egg with his great hands. With a quick flick of the wrist, he then propelled the egg back to John, who stepped neatly to one side and captured it with a swift pull back of the arms. Several other people began to throw eggs to their partners, some more gingerly than others.

Once more Dennis barked for everyone to listen. 'Now then, the rules are very simple and most of you know them anyway. The eggs must start on my right. Throw in order from this end when I give the signal. If you drop the egg but it doesn't break, you're OK, still in. If your egg breaks, you're out. After each round, we move the ropes back a few yards and then go again. Last pair with an unbroken egg wins a six-pack of beer.'

This sounded like fun, but I was still glad to be just a spectator. A large number of people had now wandered down to see what was going on and a wide circle had formed. Dennis looked at the crowd and gave one last shout:

'Any last-minute entries? I've plenty of eggs left!'

Two men sheepishly moved forward, pushed by large, cackling females. I smiled along with everyone else. Then I stopped smiling. Out of the circle came a small, running figure. It was Bill.

'Mr Seed, Mr Seed. Can I go with you on the egg throwing? Oh, go on, please. I'll buy the egg!' There were about 150 people listening and watching. I still nearly said no.

Two minutes later I was standing behind a rope while a nine-year-old boy threw an egg at me. I tried to copy John's catching technique, and miraculously the egg stayed intact. The competition proper then started. The eggs were swiftly and nonchalantly exchanged by the experienced locals; others took more time, but no one dropped one. Bill and I were the last to go. This time I had the egg. I tried to throw it as gently as possible and watched with horror as it seemed to be dropping short. Bill smartly dived forward and took the egg in one piece, just above the ground. There was a long 'Ooooohhh' from the watching crowd. I apologised, recalling with some relief that Bill was very good at cricket.

Dennis, with help from a couple of the spectators, then picked up the ropes and moved everyone back. There was a great deal of banter from the players, and Round Two was under way. This time I had to catch the egg. John and Alec made the extra distance seem like nothing, John even taking the egg in one hand to admiring cheers from the pub. One or two others following him were not so successful. One throw was too low and hard, but the egg bounced on the long grass and somehow survived. An over-exuberant throw then saw an egg sailing right over the catcher's head to land in a splash of yellow on the green. There was another cheer and the watching crowd shuffled back a little more. The next two throws were successful and then we saw the first real victim of the game: a tall lad of about eighteen tried to catch the egg in front of his chest, but with insufficient cushioning. There was a luscious splat followed by a slimy dribble down his jeans, amid roars of delight from the crowd. We were next.

Fortunately for me, Bill's throw was a beauty, but I took no chances and stepped to the side, eager to avoid the fate I had just seen. The catch was clean and, with great relief, I felt the smoothness of the unbroken shell nestle in my palms. There was a smattering of applause. I was enjoying this now. Bill called, 'Nice one, Mr Seed.'

Next round. The ropes were moved back. I was now about eighteen yards away from Bill, which suddenly seemed a very great distance. This time, there were several dropped eggs and over half of the pairs tramped away from the lines amid laughter and recriminations. John and Alec were still there, of course. I was glad to have the throw this time. I looked at Bill and gave him a nod; he stood on the rope like an Olympic athlete at the blocks, with his hands held out in front. I lobbed the egg towards him, hoping that I wasn't going to hit the crowd, at least. Once again, my young partner was magnificent in his athleticism. He raced to the side and took the egg with a dramatic catch low on one knee. I punched the air.

In the next round, even some of the expert locals bit the dust. Big Alec went for an overarm throw but, once more, John made light work of the catch, displaying the egg neatly between finger and thumb above his head. There were some great diving catches and two spectacular egg-splattered misses. I was dreading my turn to receive. When it came, Bill gave me the thumbs up to see if I was ready. He looked miles away. He called to expect an overarm throw and it came. He launched the egg into the air in a huge arc. Why had he done it so high? It became a tiny brown speck and then hurtled down towards me. Everyone was shading their eyes and following its descent. What was I to do? I momentarily considered missing it on purpose, but that was cowardice. I heard calls of 'Howay, Andy!' and 'Steady on this 'un' and 'No chance!' The egg homed in. I reached up with quaking hands, determined to cushion the blow.

The splat was bigger than I thought. So was the cheer. I was clarted in shell, yolk and white. There was nowhere to hide. Bill was kneeling on the grass crying with laughter. I walked over, trying to shake the gunge from my palms.

'Sorry, Mr See . . . Mr See . . . Sorreee.'

I couldn't help joining in. When, after a very long time, he'd recovered sufficient sensibility, I asked him the question. 'Bill, we were doing really well – why did you throw it so high? I'm sure I could've caught a lower one.'

He wiped his eyes and looked up at me. 'Well, we can't always have things our own way, can we, Mr Seed?'

Big Alec and John went on to win the egg throwing in spectacular style and, soon after, people began to drift away from the Fair, back to their cars. There was then a mammoth clearing-up operation, with the whole village once more mucking in to collect litter and put away the games and tables and marquees. The biggest job, however, was collecting all of the straw bales which were strewn around the green. I stayed until late, helping load them on to Alec's trailer before I went home to see if Barbara was OK. When I went out again, dusk had descended and there were just three or four figures raking up the last of the loose straw off the grass. One of them, of course, was Bill.

Chapter Eighteen

Nina

For the past two years, June had been my favourite month in the Dales but this time round I was in no fit state to appreciate it. Reuben's colic had given both Barbara and me the gripes also, as weeks of sleeplessness finally caught up with us and we became irritable and too weary to care about things that had previously been important.

Barbara was exhausted and we wondered if we would have managed at all, if not for the help of the wondrous Holly, who spent hours keeping poor Tom amused while we carried, pushed and patted his bawling younger brother. At school I found myself sitting at my desk when previously I'd spent all day on my feet touring the room and checking up on every child's work.

'I didn't even have the energy to read a story at the end of the afternoon yesterday,' I said to Barbara one evening in between yawns.

'What did you do with them, then?'

'I just said, "Do what you want for the last fifteen minutes, as long as there's no dismembering."'

Usually she would have laughed or reprimanded me for being

irresponsible but instead she just made a little sound and rubbed at the shadows under her eyes.

To make matters worse, after a relatively serene couple of months, the old Sheena had resurfaced. There were stories circulating in Cragthwaite about bullying in the village and pilfering from the shop, and at school she became argumentative and moody once more. This culminated in her entering the classroom at lunchtime when I was in the staffroom and flinging all the books off the shelves in a fury induced by Mrs Hyde sending her to the head's office for swearing.

Joyce herself was in a meeting with one of the governors so, in despair, I went to see Val.

'She was fine a couple of weeks ago; well, manageable anyway – I don't know what's happened,' I said.

'I suspect she's stopped taking the Ritalin, the daft beggar.'

'Her mother's got virtually no control over her so I can easily imagine that happening. This is all I need . . .'

Val's expression betrayed some rare sympathy. 'Well, I'll talk to Joyce about it and see if there's any way we can give her the tablets here.'

'Thanks, Val, that would be a real help.'

'She doesn't have a friend in the class, does she?'

I half-laughed, 'Would *you* be friends with Sheena?'

Val ignored the remark. 'It's just a thought – you haven't got a nice lass that you could talk into befriending her, have you? It's worked for me in the past, that's all – kids without friends often end up getting into more and more trouble.'

'Right, thanks, I'll have a think.'

I left the room concluding that there was nothing to lose by trying Val's plan. Not only that, but there was one girl in Class 3 that fitted the bill; the only girl who could do it – Nina Marsh.

Nina was by far the most mature girl in the class and someone it had been a delight to teach throughout the school year. She was bright, sensitive and artistic, with a wonderful temperament to match her abilities. As I thought about her, I couldn't recall telling her off or even having to correct her once: along with Fay, she really was a teacher's dream.

I didn't waste any time in approaching Nina the following lunchtime and asking her to give this Herculean task a try. She sat down in the classroom looking rather apprehensive, an earnest girl with long, red hair.

'Right, Nina, I have a very special job for you but it's not an easy one. The reason that I'm asking you is because you're a very kind and sensible person, and I know I can rely on you.' This speech appeared to arouse a little suspicion but she kept quiet. I wasted no more time. 'It's about Sheena. She's, well, having a lot of difficulty with her behaviour at the moment, as I'm sure you've noticed, and she needs help to, er, stay out of trouble.'

Nina nodded, looking at me with big eyes, but said nothing.

'I think one of her problems is that she doesn't really have any close friends. I think that Hazel tries hard to be nice to her, but Sheena hasn't responded all that well. By the way, I know you won't mention this to anyone else in the class, will you, Nina? It'll only make things worse if the others find out.'

'No, I won't tell anyone,' she said in a solemn voice.

'Right, well, I've talked about this with Miss Croker and I'm asking a really big favour here but I wonder if you would be willing to try and be friends with Sheena. I know she can be difficult sometimes but if you could make a real effort then she would have at least one friend and then she might not be so, er, miserable all the time. What do you think?'

She looked at me and nodded, 'I think it's a good idea, Mr Seed. I wouldn't like to have no friends. I'll talk to her when I go out and try really hard to be nice to her.'

'That's very kind of you, Nina,' I said. 'I think it'll help everyone.'

The last time I had seen Adam Metcalfe I mentioned to him that if he ever needed help on the farm on a weekend or during the school holidays then I'd be glad to go over to Reddle to help him out if I could. I remember him asking if I'd done any farm work before and I admitted that I'd only done a bit of fruit-picking and that I wasn't any good at all with animals. He smiled at the time and thanked me for the offer but now, to my amazement, he was on the phone, asking if I fancied lending a hand with leading hay bales on Saturday.

'I might if I knew what it was,' I said.

'It's lifting 'em on a trailer basically – and stacking 'em in a barn after.'

'Well, it sounds like something I could manage.'

'Aye, it's not hard; there's just a lot o' bales, that's all.'

'But I thought you didn't have any grass for hay at Reddle.'

'It's not at Reddle, it's at Warton-in-Gawdale – I rent some meadows down there. We cut it all yesterday and the forecast's good for tomorrow so we're crackin' on.'

'Right, well, I'll come down if I can, but I'll need to check if Barbara is OK to be left with the kids.'

'No worries, just come on if you can. There'll be seven or eight hopefully. The field is the first one on the right just past the church in Warton.'

I had no idea where the village was but went through to talk to Barbara, who was watching TV with a dozing Reuben slouched over her shoulder. He was only a few weeks old but already looked to have doubled in size. Tom was rolling on the floor with his favourite teddy, sucking his thumb.

'That was Adam, he wants to know if I can help with stacking bales of hay on Saturday. I said I'd check with you first – I don't want to leave you with the boys all day.'

'It's all right because Holly's coming over. I asked her yesterday so I could try and do a few decorations.'

'Oh, right, OK, I could do it, then . . . The trouble is, I'm so tired I don't think I'll be much use.'

'Well, even if you only last an hour it'll be a help. I think it'll do you good to get out and get some fresh air and exercise, too; you look so pale.'

I agreed it was a good idea and so, late the next morning, I found myself steering our rusting Alfasud through the high twisting roads of the upper dale towards Reddle and beyond. The lumpy fields were draped with buttercups and the grass was a vivid green where the sun illuminated it from between the scudding billows of white cumulus above. In the valley bottom, a number of fields either side of the river were shorn bare, their straw-coloured squares standing out among the pasture like missing jigsaw pieces.

The road climbed out of Swinnerdale and into the bleak vale of Reddle with its dark, wild fells and blocks of dense forest. It was a dramatic spectacle with wind-pushed clouds tracing shadows across the bare moorland. I passed the little huddle of stone barns that made up Black Busk Farm, then stared up as the fearsome bulk of one of Yorkshire's highest fells, Arkle Pike, came into view like some great upturned pudding. Beyond this there wasn't a person, car or building in sight.

I stopped and checked the map before reaching a remote junction. Turning right, I headed into a long, narrow valley whose name I didn't know. Here the dry-stone walls changed from muddied grey to white and the hills were scarred with a brighter, sharper rock. The whole scene was dazzlingly beautiful in the piercing June sunshine. Adam had certainly picked a good day to get his hay in.

Ten minutes later, I found myself motoring into a proud stone village, Warton-in-Gawdale. I couldn't miss the spired church and nor could I miss Adam Metcalfe, standing beside his old red tractor in the meadow next door. I looked for a place to park but he called me to drive in through the open gate. Next to him was a squat, muscular man in his fifties and beyond them a Land Rover and flat trailer.

'Now then,' said Adam as I climbed out the car. 'You found us.'

'Yes,' I said, nodding at the other man. 'I've never been down here before. It's a lovely place.'

'This is Frank,' said Adam, as the burly man reached forward and crushed my hand with his huge, leathery one.

''Ow do,' said Frank as I grimaced through the pain.

Adam looked around. 'Aye, wish all my land were like this. I've happy memories of the village, too – this is where I courted Ruth.'

'Didn't waste no time there,' laughed Frank. 'What age did yer marry?'

'Nineteen,' said Adam. 'Barely outa shorts . . .'

We heard chugging and a blue tractor rumbled through the village. Both Adam and Frank waved to the young driver who stuck out a saluting arm.

'So which fields are we doing?' I asked, noticing that the meadow we were in was grazing pasture.

'The next two, up the rise,' said Adam. 'I'm just waiting for my cousin Ray to bring the other trailer. Then we can row up and get baling.'

We walked over to the big trailer higher up the field and sat down for some sandwiches. Clearly there was no hurry and Adam explained that we couldn't start too early as the hay would still be damp. Flies buzzed about our faces as we admired the view.

'Grand day,' said Frank, looking up and watching the fluffy clouds scudding across the sky above a glorious broad vista of hills, trees and farms. A group of lazy cows stood in the field across the road and the sound of bleating sheep drifted in from all around.

After lunch Adam climbed into his red Zetor and Frank and I followed the little tractor on foot as it struggled up the steep field and squeezed through a narrow gateway at the top. Reaching the gate I saw the two large hayfields with their piled rows of cut grass lined over the yellow ground. Adam reversed the tractor towards a machine with two great red metal spiders attached to it, and he and Frank connected it, explaining that this was a hay bob for rowing up the lines ready for baling. I stood and watched their quiet, brawny expertise as they heaved the contraption into position and pressed the power drive into place.

Adam hopped back into the cab and steered up between the rows of hay, dropping the two spinning spiders down to flick the dried grass into tidier lines.

'Shoulda brought me rake,' said Frank, as he walked around the edge of the field kicking loose strands on to the piles.

I copied him going the other way. 'What about nettles?' I asked, seeing a clump that had been mown next to the hay.

'Nettles are bad – kick 'em in t'edge. Nettles and dockin's bad, clover good.' I looked up and noticed that there was a hedge along two sides of the field, making me realise that we were actually on the far western side of the Dales here, even though dry-stone walls were still predominant.

Frank walked back to the gate, after going just a few yards, so I did the same.

'We used to do most o' this by 'and,' he said. 'It was cut by machine but we raked it into cocks, then rows, then piled it up in big pikes. A lot more men worked on farms then, aye.' I was about to ask him about the other changes he'd seen when we heard a noise behind and saw a large jeep turning into the field by the road pulling another long, low trailer. A minute later another red tractor appeared towing a dirty yellow machine which I recognised as a small baler. Frank explained that this was his neighbour, Arnold. The Fergie, as Adam later referred to the second tractor, huffed up the field and edged through the gate into the hay meadow, with about an inch to spare either side of the fat wheels.

Adam had already finished rowing the first field and came over to help set up the baler with its strange steel sledge, and to greet Ray, his tall, quiet cousin who had just joined the group. I felt slightly awkward and out of place among these hairy men of the soil who had known each other all their lives. There was a lot of tinkering, checking, pulling and pushing of levers, straps and locking pins, then the dented, yellow contraption was pronounced ready and Arnold climbed into the Fergie and started the engine. The baler came to life as the tractor edged forward along the first row of hay, with wheels, cranks and shafts turning and throbbing noisily.

'Aye up, a freebie!' called Frank with delight as the machine spat out an old bale which had been left inside since the last operation. It tumbled into the metal sledge at the back and I tried to deduce how the whole thing worked. The assembled watchers discussed the relative merits of the newer big bales and these old small ones, with Frank declaring that many farmers now wanted to switch back since small bales were much easier to move around.

The baler deposited the grey-green blocks of dried grass around the field with surprising speed and, within a few minutes, Ray went to fetch his jeep and trailer. Adam soon returned from the other field and the hay bob was detached so that he could hitch up the second trailer to the back of the Zetor. By this time two more cars had arrived in the field and there were eight people in total, including a willowy girl and a friendly faced man, who was unquestionably Adam's brother.

'Is it Andy?' he said, holding out a hand, which evidently wasn't that of a farmer. 'I'm Peter. Good of you to come down and lend a hand. Where do you live, is it Kettleby way?'

'It's Applesett – about ten miles further down Swinnerdale.'

'Oh, yes, I know it – big green. I've been to the chapel there.'

'Are you not a farmer like Adam, then?' I asked.

'No, not me; I just help out now and again. I sell insurance. Do you want to borrow some gloves, Andy? I think you'll need them.'

He gave me a pair of thin cloth gloves as the two vehicles manoeuvred into place, lining up their trailers with the first piles of bales in each row. I stayed with Frank and Peter, following the Zetor, and the work began in earnest. It was easy at first – although the bales were much heavier than I expected – since we only had to heave them a short distance on to the low trailer. Frank stayed on the trailer stacking the bales while Peter and I threw them on board. The thin twine bit into my fingers each time I lifted one and I soon realised the need for gloves, although I noted that Frank with his great leathery palms had no problem.

After the tractor had moved on through the first row and the trailer was two layers deep, the task became much more challenging as we had to lift the bales higher. The wind blew dust into our eyes and flies were everywhere. Rabbits in the next field scattered at the sound of the Zetor's hard diesel chug and a sparrowhawk sat on a wire scrutinising the hay for fleeing mice.

'Over there next!' called Peter to Adam, who was taking great care to position the trailer as close to the piles as possible.

'No, that one's nearer!' shouted Frank, nearly falling from the growing stack.

Adam climbed down from the cab to give Frank a rest and let him drive and the Zetor headed for a huge sycamore in the corner of the field. The blocks of hay were now six deep on the trailer and I copied Peter, using a shove from my knee to launch them up eight feet to the top.

'Get that one under the tree would yer, Andy,' called Adam from his travelling perch. I walked over to the lone bale which was much greener than the rest and leant over to pick it up. I could barely move it – the thing must have weighed twice as much as the others. Gritting my teeth I hauled it in swings towards the trailer, watching it bow under its own weight and the twine nearly come away. I then struggled to pull it up on to my knee, knowing that there was no way I could lift it on to the stack. I heard laughter from above and realised I'd been tricked.

'Doesn't dry out under trees,' said Adam, smiling. Peter then came over and together we heaved the brute bale upwards. I stood up and rubbed my aching back, looking across and observing that the other team had already filled their trailer.

Half an hour later, we headed back down to the road after a short break for drinks. I asked Peter where the bales were being taken and he pointed out a great stone barn at a farm just across the road. I wandered there, following the others, every muscle protesting and my forearms patterned with welts and irritating little scratches.

'You'll wear long sleeves next time, like me,' said Peter, watching me rub them.

Inside the cavernous barn the jeep pulled through a big arched doorway and parked the first trailer next to a raised floor covered in a wire mesh. Adam threw four bales down and arranged them as a landing pad, while most of the helpers climbed on to the mesh to do the stacking. I much preferred the idea of throwing bales down to picking them up again so I climbed up the lofty trailer pile and joined Adam as he dropped each bale on to the angled arrangement below so that they rolled into the dusty shed. There were hundreds to do and I quickly realised how tough farming was, bearing in mind that we were doing this in good weather, too. Everyone worked harmoniously and there was a spirit of good humour right through the day. No one minded my awkward endeavours and, despite the back-breaking effort involved, I enjoyed it tremendously.

At seven o'clock, after a mighty feast brought by Adam's sister Elaine, my body had reached its limit. There was still half a trailer to unload after another tour round the second hay field, but I needed to get home and have a long bath. Adam gave me a big pat on the shoulder and said he was really grateful for my help.

At home, Barbara looked less tired and had clearly enjoyed working on her wooden Christmas decorations. However, she laughed when she saw me, 'Just look in the mirror.'

I nearly didn't recognise myself: I really was a walking scarecrow, with grass-filled hair, a blackened face lined with smears of sweat and a bright red nose and ears. But I didn't care.

'How was the haymaking, then?'

'Really good,' I croaked. 'Erm, how's Reuben been?'

'A little better. Holly was a marvel and stayed nearly all day, playing with Tom and she did a feed, too. I told you she's a lovely girl.'

But I wasn't listening. My head had flopped against the mirror and my eyes were shut.

* * *

Two weeks later I was speaking to Joyce about Sheena.

'She's definitely been better since Nina befriended her,' I said. 'That girl is a wonder – she talks to her every playtime and partners her in PE, all sorts of things. She's so sensible about it, too.'

'We must give her a little gift of some kind at the end of term.'

'That's a good idea. Er, what kind of thing?'

'Oh, don't worry, I'll take care of it,' said Joyce, writing it down in a notebook. 'Oh, and I want to ask Sheena about the Ritalin this afternoon. Can you send her through.'

'Right, I'll do it when she's got her book from the mobile library.'

The mobile library was a service provided by the County Council for rural schools and every four weeks a large van arrived in the car park and the classes took turns to go on-board in small groups to choose three books each. Usually I just sent the children from the classroom in threes, knowing that the librarian on the van would keep an eye on them.

At two o'clock, I sent Nina, Eddie and Sheena to go and change their library books, giving them five minutes. Normally, I would have asked Eileen to supervise Sheena but I felt so confident that Nina would direct her away from trouble that I decided to risk sending them alone. However, three minutes after they'd gone, I suddenly realised that I'd forgotten to tell Sheena to see Joyce after going to the van. The rest of the class were working diligently on illustrating some poetry so I took a chance on leaving them for a moment.

I slipped through the door and sprinted round to the front of the school where the mobile library was parked. Glancing through the door at the back I saw Eddie and Nina but there was no sign of Sheena. I rushed through the front entrance to see if she was with the head, just as Eileen spotted me.

'It's all right, Andy, Sheena's in with Joyce.'

I thanked her with relief and nipped back outside to tell the two children in the library van to be quick. As I approached the door of the vehicle, I heard some distinctly dirty giggling from inside so I crept up the steps and into the van to see what was going on. Nina and Eddie stood with their backs to me sharing a book, pointing and sniggering. The van driver was round the front wiping the windscreen. I stole a little closer.

'Euurrgghh,' said Nina, 'have you got one of those?'

'Yes, but mine doesn't look like that,' replied Eddie.

The floor creaked and they turned round, jolting in surprise. Nina's face blushed an extraordinary colour and she hurled the book on to a pile near the front. Neither said a word as I reached forward to see the cover. It was entitled *All About Growing Up*.

Eddie bit his lip and stared at me. Nina looked down, with her hand over her mouth, trembling slightly. I was just about to ask them if they'd chosen something else a little more suitable when her control collapsed and she spluttered into the filthiest laugh I had ever heard, tilting her head back rudely and causing Eddie to snort with embarrassment. Only when Nina lost the ability to breathe did she calm down. By this time the driver had rushed round the back to see what the commotion was about.

'It's all right,' I said to the confused librarian. 'They just found a, er, really good book.'

I walked back to the classroom shaking my head but quietly pleased that Nina Marsh was normal after all.

Chapter Nineteen

Derek

I turned the key for the twenty-fifth time and despaired. The Alfasud was not going to start. It was a quarter past eight on a cold, damp morning in late June and I should have been on my way to school. The old Alfa was a cheap buy from my aunt in Manchester just before we came out to the Dales and our very first car. It was nominally white in colour, but large patches of rust were gradually becoming dominant, giving it the appearance of a Guernsey heifer.

Under the bonnet things were even worse and I remember one day finding a sycamore seedling which had sprouted in a pile of accumulated gunge beside the engine. When my father asked me how the car was doing, I replied, 'Not bad apart from the tree growing inside it.' We laughed about whether it might qualify as having a real wood interior. It had also lost its aerial, chopped off by Barbara in a freak accident when it was caught up in the boot door at a petrol station, to the extensive amusement of the family queuing behind us.

The Alfasud was also very temperamental and particularly hostile to dampness of any kind. It was, after all, a car born of southern

Italy, a child of blazing summers and mild Mediterranean winters – it was not used to the frequent driving squalls of the Yorkshire Dales and, inevitably, today it was under protest. In the end, I gave up and ran indoors. Barbara was carrying Reuben who, at long last, was sleeping a little better and crying a little less.

'The stupid car won't start,' I wailed.

'Are you going to ask Iris if you can borrow the jeep again?'

'I'll have to – there's no other way for me to get to work.'

We often wondered what we'd do without our neighbours, Iris and Don Falconer across the green. They were wealthy by Dales' standards but remarkably generous and had become good friends since we'd moved into the village. Like us they were incomers, so we shared a special bond and often talked about how, although the true locals were warm and welcoming, there would always be a distance between ourselves and them. 'Your grandfather has to be buried in Skirbridge church to be fully accepted here,' Don was fond of saying.

After a quick phone call, I arrived at the Falconers' house to find Iris standing outside the large double garage looking somewhat flustered. She appeared to be pointing a TV remote control at the doors.

'I'm really sorry, Andy,' she said, 'Don's just had these new automatic doors fitted and I can't seem to get them to open.'

She tried again, jabbing her arm forward. 'You're welcome to borrow the car if we can get it out.' I was just about to offer to have a go when there was a clank followed by a deep whirring noise. One of the double doors began to rise. There was nothing behind it. I looked inside the cavernous garage and could see the giant Toyota on the other side. Iris was still jabbing away with the remote. After another five minutes in which we both pressed various buttons and heaved at the door unproductively, I looked at my watch. It was twenty-five to nine.

Iris noticed my anxiety. 'Can you manoeuvre the car across?'

I went inside for a look. There was a gap of about two feet in front and three feet behind the bumpers.

'I'll have a go,' I said.

I climbed up into the seat of the blue jeep, which felt as high as a lorry cab. The engine started first time with a booming rumble; I thought about the wheezing Alfa, then turned round and looked back at the gleaming new garage door behind me – it seemed like the back of the car was already touching it. I lowered the electric windows and called to Iris to give me a signal to stop. She smiled and waved. I let out the clutch and inched backwards – at least the car had power steering. The great fat tyres twisted on the concrete floor with an ugly crunch. Suddenly, Iris put her hand up and yelled. I stopped then threw the steering wheel round and edged forward until I heard the bull bars on the front jab against some boxes of magazines. I had moved across the garage about nine inches. Iris seemed to think it was going well. I waggled the gearstick back into reverse and repeated the move. The deep chug of the car's huge diesel motor reverberated around the garage. What if I got it stuck diagonally?

At quarter to nine, after an epic series of miniature shunts, the back end of the hulking four by four finally emerged into the daylight. I was sweating as Iris clapped and waved me away down the drive. About halfway to Cragthwaite I realised that I'd left my bag at home: it was much too late to turn back, although I might as well have done, because as I turned the corner out of Skirbridge the road was full of cows. This was a common feature of the dale: milking herds frequently crossing roads or walking down lanes from field to milking shed and back, and traffic just had to wait. Normally I would have missed this event by a good half-hour, but my lateness had incurred a further wait. I stopped and regarded the fat Friesians lolloping towards the car – at least they were coming this way so I wouldn't have to follow them for half a mile at a snail's pace.

There were, I'd discovered, two approaches taken by motorists to cows on the road in Swinnerdale. Visitors and incomers like me invariably stopped and pulled over to give the beasts maximum leeway. They usually waited in their vehicles with charmed amusement at this rural scene, even if it did lengthen their journey. Locals, however, thought differently: they were simply not prepared to let a few cows slow them to a halt and so they usually just barged their way through the herd, expecting the animals to move aside for their vehicles. It helped, of course, that most of them drove Land Rovers or meaty trucks. At this point it occurred to me that I was in a hefty four-wheel drive myself. And I was late. I slipped into first gear and gingerly motored forward, determined to be a proper local.

Pleasingly, the first few cows paid the jeep ample respect, swaying their course to accommodate mine, and soon enough I was moving steadily if slowly through the great tide of black and white bulk. Then came the first problem. Cows are never alone: they are always accompanied by at least two million flies, and several hundred of these parasitical fiends decided to investigate the interior of the Toyota through its open windows. I quickly shut the windows which had the effect of trapping the mini swarm inside, so I opened them again. Another five thousand came inside and started examining my face. I stopped the car and flapped manically.

I was still only in the centre of the herd and, to make things worse, the cows didn't seem to regard the stationary car as a threat and one or two began to buffet the sides with their voluminous abdomens. A large individual stopped in front of me and, turning sideways, raised its tail nonchalantly. A torrent of liquid manure, remarkable in its volume, gushed forth, landing rather too close for comfort. I decided to rev the engine to deter them, but in my state of insect-tortured paroxysm, I hit the accelerator rather more forcefully than I'd intended. The jeep's three-litre diesel engine gave a monster bellicose roar, causing one particular cow to jerk away in terror. I watched in misery as its black, fridge-sized rear end obliterated the jeep's off-side wing mirror. The day was getting worse.

As the last of the herd trailed past, I opened the back windows and powered the car forward, hoping to blast the irritating flies outside, while still clinging to the irrational hope of reaching the school by nine. At least half of the flies were duly sucked out, but I forgot about what the cows had left on the road.

I arrived at school at ten past nine. I didn't want to look at the car as I stepped out of it but my eyes wouldn't obey: it was no longer blue – it was poo. All over. The beautiful metallic paintwork looked like it had been attacked by Jackson Pollock in his Brown Period. But I had no time to do anything about it now; I raced inside, darting into the gents for a quick check in the mirror. My white shirt was speckled with pungent, yellow-brown streaks on the right-hand side. I reached for my bag to change into my track-suit and then remembered it was at home. What had I done to deserve this?

Joyce was standing in my classroom by the door and she didn't look happy. I muttered an explanation but she dashed straight out saying that she was expecting an important phone call. The children looked agitated, too, and were, of course, full of questions about my late appearance.

Yvonne got in first, as usual. 'Where 'ave yer been, Mr Seed? We been waitin' AGES.'

'Mrs Berry was in a right bad mood,' said Eddie.

'Has she done the register?' I asked.

'Yeah,' said Yvonne, 'but why are yer standin' sideways?'

'And what's that yellow stuff on yer shirt?' said Rachel, leaning across for a better view.

'Quiet reading everybody,' I barked. 'No more questions.' The children already had their reading books out but at least half of them were peeping over the tops of the pages at me and giving furtive sideways glances. I loaded a serious glower and fired it broadside. All of the eyes quickly fell into books, although few stayed there.

I scribbled down what I could remember of my plans for the day and tried to compose myself while the class were quietly occupied. But something in the classroom was making concentration impossible. It was a smell – a dreadful sickly stench. At first I thought it must be the smears of cow muck on my shirt but a surreptitious sniff revealed those to have a quite different and infinitely less offensive pong. I looked up and noticed that some of the children were sniggering and waving their hands in front of their noses. Others were pulling contorted faces. Then there was the scrape of a chair and Derek Milner came out towards my desk.

'MrSeedI'vetroddenindogmuckagain.'

Derek didn't speak, he gabbled. He was a lovely, gentle boy, but he was incapable of leaving gaps between his words. This did make conversation difficult, especially as the person listening to Derek usually required three or four seconds to mentally unravel his staccato utterances. The problem was that Derek was never prepared to wait this long for a reply and always burst in with another jabber before the listener had a chance to speak. This, of course, created a vicious circle in which the poor recipient of Derek's attentions was driven crazy trying to decipher each sentence and remember the previous ones, while Derek kept up a manic verbal attack on the basis that he wasn't getting a response. This occasion was no exception.

'HaveItotakemyshoesoffandputthemoutside?'

Being already under severe stress, I decided to take radical action: I put up both hands and bellowed, 'STOP!'

Poor Derek nearly fell backwards with shock, but at least he shut up. Although I had only caught half of his original declaration, it was immediately apparent what the problem was. I looked down at Derek's shoes and saw what I feared. Poo was clearly the theme of the day. I opened all the windows and sent Derek outside to take off his shoes, although I was unable to think what we would actually do with them. He came back in and walked over to his table in his socks.

'Derek, go and put your plimsolls on – we can't have you walking around without something on your feet.'

'MrSeedI'veforgottenmyPEkitagainI'msorry.'

I picked out PE just in time and raised my hand again, diving in with, 'OK, you can look for some plimsolls in lost property at break.'

I watched Derek sit down, quite unfazed by this whole episode. Most children would have been mortified to bring such an evil stink into the classroom, but Derek was somehow unperturbed. He certainly was a character: accident-prone, bright, imaginative, and a great authority on astronomy. Stars and planets were the love of Derek's life. He was always offering to bring in his telescope and give talks to the class about the Milky Way, but no one could understand him. On the whole, though, the class were very tolerant of his machine-gun speech and a few could even keep up with it.

After assembly and Maths it was break. I sent the children out to play and had a go at scrubbing the dappled muck from my shirt. The yellow stains spread into wide blotches and the wet fabric was uncomfortable. Then I remembered that I needed to see Joyce to give her a proper explanation for being late. I was just about to head out of the classroom when the door opened and two red-faced boys clumped towards me. It was Derek and Mervyn.

'MrSeedMervyn'sbeencallingmeaduratplaytime.'

'I never called him a dur, honest!'

'Youdidyouliaryouwerelaughingaboutthedogmuck.'

They probably carried on after I ran past.

I somehow survived the rest of the morning without any further calamities. Joyce's usual joviality had returned, much to my relief, and she chuckled at my far-fetched explanation for being late. Eileen then lifted my spirits further by offering to tackle Derek's shoes. Like Sue, she often noticed that something needed doing and quietly got on with it without being asked. She was a godsend. Derek and Mervyn had eventually calmed down and apologised, too: perhaps the day's tide was turning. Even the weather had brightened up.

The first lesson of the afternoon was games, and it was now dry enough for the children to go on to the playing field. There was a cheer as I asked them to get changed to go outside. I was pleased, too, as I'd be able to try out some more of the activities that I'd learnt on the PE course at Shreeve Hall. Derek approached me again. I looked down at his feet and saw two plimsolls: one white and one black, and both left-footed.

'MrSeedIhaven'tgotmyPEkitrememberItoldyou.'

I picked out PE again and stopped him just in time. 'This really isn't very good, you know, Derek – it must be the third time you've forgotten your kit this term.' I was surprised to find myself repeating the familiar PE teacher's mantra so easily. This pause to think was brief but costly – it allowed Derek to nip in with a second gabble.

'CanIhelpyougettheequipmentoutinstead?'

I raised a hand – it felt like I was communicating with an ancient Native American. 'No, you'd better help me get the equipment out, Derek.'

I consoled myself with the thought that if I let him join in with the plimsolls he'd found in the lost property box he'd only be able to run in circles anyway.

I lined everyone up ready to go on to the field. Yvonne looked me up and down and said, 'Why aren't you changed for games then, Mr Seed – forgotten your kit as well?'

I should have known that the games lesson was not going to run smoothly.

I asked Derek to bring out the hoops from the PE store and told the rest of the class to warm up by jogging around the playing field. Inevitably this turned into a race, and some of the boys began pushing and tripping each other up in an attempt to finish first. The less athletic decided to walk around the circuit, which forced everyone to wait for them to finish. Then Derek appeared – at least I thought it was Derek. It was hard to tell because he was carrying so many plastic hoops that positive identification was impossible. One arm was extended out to the side like a hook, carrying about ten hoops, but he was clasping at least another twenty-five, and for some reason these were around his body. The hoops had slipped down on to his legs, causing him to waddle with tiny comical footsteps. As soon as the class saw him they began to roar with laughter. I expected him to trip up and spill the lot, but somehow he stayed on his feet.

By this point, the lesson had lost all its discipline and the children were painfully rowdy. I decided that a bout of vigorous exercises would be the best way to dissipate their energy and cast my mind back to some of the stretches and movements that Jeff Osbourn, the County PE Adviser, had shown us. After a series of star jumps and press-ups, I asked Guy, who enjoyed this kind of activity, to show the class how to do squat thrusts by resting on his hands and feet and kicking his legs back and forward. They had only done a few when there was a volley of wind-breaking by someone at the back, followed by muffled sniggers. I couldn't bear another commotion so I sent them all off running to the bottom goalpost and back.

When the children returned, several asked if they could try the squat thrusts again, since they had barely started them last time. I assented but once more the abdominal strain involved produced the same result, my suspicion being that Sheena was heavily involved. I pointed to the goalposts and ordered them to run down again. All in all, they jogged down the field four times that afternoon before a very curious thing happened. Oliver and Victor returned back to me first and, after a moment to regain their breath, they dropped down to a crouch and tried once more to perfect the squat thrusts. The rest of the class followed on and did the same. I was just beginning to think about moving on to some team games when a resounding trump rent the air. Without my saying anything, every child stood up and started running to the goalposts.

After school I recounted the tale to Hilda and Val in the staffroom. It quickly became apparent that Val didn't find flatulence amusing.

'It's the bloody smell that gets me: it always seems to linger round the blackboard. It's like working in the trenches sometimes.'

Hilda shook her head and muttered, 'Well, as my grandfather used to say, it's a sorry arse that can't rejoice from time to time.'

I laughed and flopped down into a chair with a cup of tea, greatly relieved that a school day containing so many minor traumas was over. I thought about how it had all started with the obstinate Alfasud and this reminded me that I still needed to clean Iris's dung-spattered jeep and do something about the wing mirror.

Half an hour later I was back in the classroom gathering the day's marking and bemoaning the absence of car washes in Swinnerdale when the door opened and once more Derek Milner shuffled over to see me. What now? He was holding his shoes and I was holding my breath, desperately trying to concentrate in order to decipher the inevitable babble.

'MrSeedIjustwantedtosayI'vereallyenjoyedbeinginyourclassthis year.'

It was very fast, but I understood. Good old Derek, I thought, even if his shoes did still smell.

Chapter Twenty

Hazel

The classroom door creaked open and in walked Hazel Bowe, looking sheepish. It was the lunch break and I was catching up on the piles of marking that had somehow accumulated in the last two days. I wasn't surprised to see Hazel; she was a regular visitor to my room at break times and was always anxious to be given a job, even though she knew that she should really be outdoors.

'Would you like me to tidy up the reading books, Mr Seed?' she asked hopefully.

'Go on, then, but do it quietly because I'm very busy.'

She nodded and slid forward, evidently pleased to be away from the rowdy playground. We both knew that she also preferred adult company and often came in to the room for a quiet chat.

Hazel was a small, soft-eyed girl with long fair hair. Her clothes always looked slightly grubby and I sensed that she suffered from neglect; I knew that her father was permanently off work and at home with a back injury, while her mother worked all hours as a cleaner trying to make ends meet. They lived in one of Cragthwaite's small cluster of council houses and their lives had been thrown into turmoil for the past nine months, ever since Sheena and her mother had moved in next door.

It was Hazel who furnished Joyce and me with details of what Sheena was up to in the village and at home. This gave us a fair indication of what we could expect at school. Recently there had been a spate of door slamming and mighty rows to add to the usual shouting and swearing that travelled through the walls into Hazel's house.

We had managed to persuade Sheena's fraught mother, herself surviving on a cocktail of anti-depressants, to bring the Ritalin tablets to school so that we could administer them in the office, but Eileen had suspected for some time that Sheena wasn't swallowing them, rather hiding them behind her teeth to spit out later. I once more had to sit her alone in the classroom, as her attention span had returned to virtually zero, but it was at playtimes that Sheena sowed a kind of poison through what had once been a happy village school, mainly by spreading rumours, breaking up friendships and making foul accusations against other children. The novelty of having Nina as a support had only lasted a few weeks; both girls knew that they were just too different and Nina unsurprisingly found herself unable to stick up for someone who so often wronged others.

'My mum says that Sheena scratched some cars in the village last night with a 50p,' said Hazel. She had managed about two minutes of quiet.

'How did she know it was Sheena?' Stupid question, really.

'Someone saw her and they went round to complain. I heard them.'

'Oh dear.' I decided not to say any more in the hope that I might finish the marking.

'My mum says Sheena's getting worse,' said Hazel, evidently deciding to continue even if I wasn't joining in the exchange. 'The police have been round again and she stays out really late at night.'

I said nothing. Hazel continued, 'I have tried to be her friend at school and at home, but she just keeps doing awful things. She was friends with Nina, I think, but not really proper friends.' She glanced over to see if I was listening. Part of me wanted to reply and engage her in conversation, especially as I knew how much she suffered with her unruly neighbour but, despite a sense of guilt, I needed to finish the marking, so I kept schtum and ploughed on through the Maths books. Eventually Hazel got the message and stopped her news ticker service. A moment later the bell rang.

At home, the colour was returning to Barbara's cheeks as Reuben had finally recovered from the worst of his colic and had shown indications of wanting to sleep for more than an hour at a time.

'How was your day?' she said with a smile as I trudged through the door after work one Thursday and scooped up the merry little Tom.

'Not too bad: we had the usual three parents in complaining about Sheena, and Mrs Hyde, the dinner lady, insisting that something had to be done. But what do we do?'

'Oh, let's not talk about school now; I'll make us a cup of tea and you can play a bit with Tom or lie down.'

'Sounds good . . . How about you? How's chubby Reubs?'

'Well, he had a good sleep again today,' she said with a hint of glee in her shoulders. 'I think we might get our lives back soon. I reckon he's a real character, too.'

'Rarlway Daddee!' said Tom, pointing at his wooden track, satisfied that we'd talked long enough.

'Oh, and Iris rang to say the jeep's wing mirror is sorted out with the insurance company,' said Barbara, going through a mental list.

'But don't we need to give them something for the excess?'

'I offered but Iris insisted not – you know what they're like.'

'Too kind . . . lovely people,' I said, flopping down on to the carpet and clicking some Brio together without looking.

'Your mum called, too,' continued Barbara. 'Your parents, your grandpa and both sisters are coming over for Tom's birthday. I suggested a picnic, up Buttergill maybe.'

'Good plan,' I said, trying to look enthusiastic about the wooden railway.

'I can't believe he's going to be two . . .' Barbara smiled as Tom sat on top of me, pulling out miles of track from the basket. 'Oh, there's one more thing. I heard from Mrs Dent that the BBC are filming some of that vet series here next week. They're doing up the village around the shop apparently. It's half-term, too, so we'll all be able to go and watch.'

I was interested but neither my brain nor body made any response.

Barbara gave up. 'I'll go and put the kettle on.'

When half-term arrived I treated myself to a couple of reviving walks around Swinnerdale. The first was to the top of rugged Spout

Fell, nearly two thousand feet up and presenting a memorable panorama both towards the flatter Vale of York and up to the majestic hills of the neighbouring valleys. The wind on the flat summit was ferocious, causing me to stumble at one point and hang on to the tumbling cairn which marked the highest point.

The second walk was a complete contrast, taking in the dense woods that enclosed the cataracts around Skirbridge where the River Swinner tumbled over a series of limestone ledges into the lower dale. Here it was peaceful away from the breeze and the green canopy painted soft dapples on to the moss and ferns, while pink campion and flitting birds caught the eye.

At one point the woodland path became a tangle of grasping tree roots where it edged the riverbank and, noticing that the water level was particularly low, I stepped out on to a raised section of the river bed itself, a rocky platform between branching gushes of water. There was no one around and the only movement was from a deft yellow wagtail, hopping over the flow for insects. Not for the first time I shook my head in disbelief at living somewhere so beautiful.

Back in Applesett the following morning, four large grey trucks and numerous vans arrived, some of them bearing the logo of the BBC. Tom watched and pointed with curiosity through the big bay window of Craven Bottoms as one parked just across the road on the edge of the green.

'Do you think our house will be on telly, Tom?' I said.

He turned round to check the size of the TV set, evidently confused. Barbara came through with Reuben who was half-asleep.

'Shall we go out and see what's going on?' she suggested. 'Mrs

Dent says they're dressing her part of the village up to look like its celebrating King George's silver jubilee.'

'Oh, right, which King George is that?'

'Well, it must be, er, George the fifth.'

'But I thought he was around in the First World War.'

'Well he was, wasn't he?'

'But isn't the vet series set in the fifties?'

'I thought it was the thirties.'

'Well, which George was king in the thirties?'

'Hang on a minute, you're supposed to be the teacher.'

'Yes, but I've only ever done Romans, Vikings, Egyptians and Tudors. I'm always confused about the Georges anyway: there's too many of them.'

'Oh, be quiet and let's go out or they'll have finished filming at this rate.'

We wedged our plump baby into his pram and set off, with Tom insisting that he could walk even though he usually moved at roughly the same speed as a clock's minute hand.

Just down from the pub there were people walking about everywhere, carrying cables, moving trolleys of props and heaving lights. Several young women walked around with clipboards and a whole gang of harassed-looking individuals knocked on doors asking people to move their cars. The locals stood outside their front doors in pairs, bemused at the goings-on, while technicians shouted.

Mrs Dent was in her element, standing next to the shop and pointing and nattering to several villagers, while two hefty men on ladders lifted an old-fashioned store sign into place to cover the existing one. Bunting was being arrayed everywhere, along with pale

Union Jacks and silvery flags bearing pictures of the king. An old green Alvis was being wheeled into place and a black delivery bike was carefully propped up against one of the cottages near the pub.

Barbara spotted Iris, who had also come down for a pry at some of the actors, and the two of them immediately began talking babies so I continued on down through the village with Tom. There was some commotion as traffic was blocked from travelling through the village, much to the consternation of visitors who wanted to see what was going on. I spotted old Billy Iveson, pulling his wheezy dog along the lane.

'Now then, Andy, what d' yer make o' this ter do?'

'Well it's chaotic but interesting.'

'Takes me back, in some ways – I recall the Silver Jubilee, alreet. We 'ad a street party outside pub. Nineteen thirty-five it were, aye.'

'How old were you then, Billy?'

While he was working it out, Tom pulled at my hand wanting to let go and I allowed him to wander since the road was now free from traffic.

'Well, I wa' still a young man. I would 'ave been, let me see, twenty-six.'

'Have you lived here all your life, then?'

'Apart from a few years when I worked on a farm up at Kettelby, aye. It's changed a bit, but not much. More cars, o' course. Never seen anything like today, though.' He scratched his wiry grey hair and looked around before pointing further down the lane and smiling. I turned to look and there was Tom, standing and staring at three old gents, dressed in rural garb of the 1930s, parked on a bench and clearly fed up with waiting for their moment. They looked hot in their tweed jackets and flat caps and, oddly, none of them seemed to have noticed the transfixed toddler in an oversized jumper just a few feet away. I scrambled for my camera and just caught the moment before my son turned away at the sound of a tractor in a nearby field.

'Are they hiring you as an extra, Billy?' I asked, thinking how he hardly looked any different from the trio of yokel actors.

'Nooo, the limelight's not fer such as me,' he laughed, before carrying on towards Buttergill to tread the route he took every day.

I went back to find Barbara, who was passing Reuben round to various women for cuddles. We waited about for another half-hour but there was no sign of any actual filming taking place and Tom was becoming bored. We agreed that we'd watch the results on TV and headed back to our house unsurprised that the BBC had stayed well away from it. Just as we reached the chapel there was a call of 'Cooee!' and we turned round to see Holly scurrying across the grass towards us. Tom waved excitedly.

'Hi, Holly,' said Barbara. 'Enjoying half-term?'

'Well, it's good to have a rest from school but I soon get bored.'

'You're not into all this filming, then?' I added.

'Well, it's OK but I've seen them do it before . . . I was just wondering if I could come round and play with the boys for a bit?'

'What do you think, Tommy?' asked Barbara.

He clapped his hands, 'Yay!'

We weren't going to disagree.

The last few days of a blissful half-term passed in a blink and I was back at Cragthwaite Primary sitting in the staffroom where there was only one topic of conversation: the fact that Joyce Berry had walked into Monday assembly with her skirt tucked in her knickers.

'Did you notice, Val?' said Emma.

'Course I didn't notice or I would have said something. I was too busy glowering at flamin' Sheena Baxter.'

'Well, I noticed but I was laughing so much I couldn't move,' continued Emma.

Sue went over and pushed the door shut. 'Careful, she could come in any moment, poor Joyce.'

Hilda, her face bright with merriment, was certainly making the most of it. 'Come on, the big question has been overlooked here.'

'Eh? You mean what she was doing previously?' said Val.

'No,' laughed Hilda. 'What colour were they?'

'I'm fairly sure they were pink,' I said, immediately regretting it.

'Mr Seed!' screeched Hilda. 'If you'd been any kind of a gentleman you'd have covered your eyes.'

'To be honest, I couldn't help looking,' I confessed. 'It's not every day you see a headteacher's bloomers.'

'The whole school saw them,' said Emma, 'but it's scandalous that not one of the teachers told her.'

'Who did tell her, anyway?' said Sue.

'It was that blonde lass from your class, Andy,' said Val. 'Whatsername – Hazel Bowe.'

'Yes, very brave of her,' said Hilda, 'but I know one thing: she would never have done it with Howard Raven.' At this point Val spurted her tea and that set everyone off whooping and howling so loudly that Eileen came running from the secretary's office to see what had happened. I left the room soon afterwards seeking fresh air: the thought of the previous headmaster in frilly undies was making me queasy.

At five past twelve Joyce came into my room with a message. As usual, Hazel was there, having once more volunteered for chores.

'Oh, Hazel,' said Joyce, 'I must say thank you again for being the only person in the school with enough gumption to tell me about my, er, skirt, this morning.'

'That's all right, Mrs Berry, I've done that meself so I know what it's like.'

Joyce smiled, 'You're a very kind, sensible girl – well done.' Hazel was about to say something else when Joyce turned to me, 'Andy, I've got Mrs Hyde at me again saying that the older children are getting up to too much rough and tumble outside. Apparently there are no more playtime balls to use.'

'That's odd,' I said, thinking that I'd seen four or five in the cloakroom box last time I'd looked. 'Where have they all gone?'

'On the roof, unfortunately – it's that flat part over the hall. Guy Calvert has put most of them up there by accident, she said. He doesn't know his own strength, that boy.'

'Oh dear.' I waited for the killer request.

She put a hand on my arm and leant in, 'Would you be a dear and go up there for me? You can borrow Pat's ladders – but I can hardly ask her to do it or we'll have no hall left.' I turned round to look at Hazel, whose wide eyes confirmed that Joyce hadn't lowered her voice enough.

'OK, then. I may as well do it this lunchtime.'

'Thanks Andy, I knew I could rely on you. Oh, and if you're looking for Sheena, she's standing outside my office. Apparently she told everyone's favourite dinner lady to, er, *something* off; I'm dealing with it next.'

I rarely ventured out on to the playground during the dinner break and right away I was struck by the huge amount of noise compared to the morning playtimes when a teacher was always on duty. There was a crowd of complaining children around the bulky figure of Mrs Hyde who, as usual, was shouting for everyone to be quiet, an act that raised the volume even further. Children were running and screeching, while on the field there appeared to be a game of rugby going on among the older boys using a tied-up jumper for a ball. The quieter children, including Rachel and Fay from my class, had wandered over to the fence, while small groups of girls sat on the grass making daisy chains.

It didn't take long for one of the infants from Hilda's class to spot that I was sneaking across the playground with a large pair of stepladders and very rapidly a small mob gaggled round.

'What yer doin', Mr Seed?' asked a carrot-headed girl.

'I'm going up on to the roof.'

'What for?'

'To get all the footballs down off there.'

'Can I come up, too?'

'No, it's not safe.'

'Awww.'

More children joined in.

'Can we hold the ladder?' said a Class 2 boy.

'Well, all right, if you're sensible.'

'Am always sensible, but Gemma here in't. Don't think you should let 'er do it.'

Gemma wasn't going to let this pass. 'Oi, at least I'm not a show-off.'

'You are a show-off, I'm not.'

'Get lost.'

I halted. 'All of you stop it, you're being silly. I've changed my mind: no one can hold the ladder because it's going to cause arguments. All of you run along and play somewhere else now.'

This caused a storm: 'But! Awww! That's not fair! I asked first! Pleeeease!'

I looked up and saw Mrs Hyde coming over, so dashed the last few paces to the wall, opened the stepladders and scurried up just as she accosted the rabble.

The flat section of hall roof was about twelve feet from the ground and I soon realised that it wasn't going to be easy to clamber over the parapet wall around its edge. I could reach the top of it easily enough but there was still about five feet of vertical brickwork to heave myself over. I considered the best approach while children from all over the playground and field pointed and came over to watch. With no one holding the stepladders they wobbled considerably as I stretched up to feel for a good finger hold and this stirred even more interest.

I now had one hundred spectators and the pressure was on. A few smart comments from Class 4 pupils brought reprimand from Mrs Hyde, who herself seemed to be quite enjoying the spectacle and was as eager as everyone else to discover the answer to the question of whether I would make it or not.

Grasping the top of the wall firmly, I put a foot against the brickwork and tested if there was enough grip to raise myself up. The sole of my cheap black shoe slid several inches, offering little reassurance that this was the best strategy. A few laughs and one or two gasps came from the audience, and Mrs Hyde ordered everyone back, clearly intent on limiting the casualty count to one.

Determined not to be beaten, I dug the edge of my right shoe into one of the lines of mortar and felt a little more support. It would need a push-off, though, so I kicked back with my left foot and heaved upwards, causing the tall stepladders to sway considerably and Mrs Hyde to yank two unsuspecting infants further from peril. My right foot gave way but I just managed to scrabble my left against the bricks hard enough to reach the top of the wall with my other foot and hook it over the parapet. After an undignified lurch I rolled on to the roof and flopped my feet down, to a rousing cheer and applause from the children. I thought about bowing but then noticed that there was a small rip in the knee of my trousers and both shoes were scuffed as though I'd been in a brawl.

Turning to look at the hall roof I was amazed by how complicated a structure it was. There was PE equipment everywhere but, before picking it up, I moved along the flat section of the roof to see how it joined to the rest of the building. The watching children dissipated as I moved out of view towards the back of the hall and along the edge of one of the classrooms. The view from here was stupendous and I surveyed some dark clouds rolling in from Hubberdale while shafts of sun spotlighted farms and fields across the other side of the valley. As always, the call of sheep drifted in on the breeze from the surrounding hills. I thought I could just make out Applesett in the haze, too, and thought about what Barbara might be doing there with Tom and Reuben.

A glance at my watch indicated that there was only ten minutes of break left so I quickly scooted around the roof picking up the numerous balls and other items which had migrated upwards over the years. There were plastic footballs of every colour, many flat, plus grey, weather-beaten tennis balls, sponge balls, netballs, rubber cricket balls and several small bouncy balls. I threw them down on to the grass, much to the glee of the children who had waited below hoping for such a harvest.

Among stones, dirt and bird droppings there were other things: a skipping rope, bean bags, an old leather shoe, several small bruised toy animals – some of them no doubt lost members of a Sylvanian family – and, saddest of all, a sun-bleached doll whose clothes were just crusted rags. I carried them all towards the parapet and looked for a safe place to drop them. I was just about to call Vanessa over to guard the haul when Hazel ran around from the back entrance with panicky eyes.

She stopped and looked up, evidently distressed. 'Mr Seed!'

'What's the matter, Hazel?'

'Sheena's run away.'

By the time I had scrambled down off the roof, nearly knocking the steps over again, and run round to the front of the school, Val had already been out in her car and rounded up Sheena from the village.

'She hadn't got very far,' said Joyce, a hand on her chest, looking very relieved.

'What happened?' I asked, still confused about the events.

'I had a word with her before lunch about language and treating dinner ladies with respect but she wasn't listening so I told her to come back and stand outside my office again after dinner.'

'Did she just run out of the door then?'

'Well, according to Eileen, Mrs Hyde said something to her when she came out of the hall which set a few tears off, then she just shouted she was going and walked out.'

'Did you have to run after her?'

'Andy, can you imagine me running?' I couldn't. 'I sent for Val and she got into her car and found her down the road.'

'Well, I probably could have spied her out from the roof but I was at the back. Anyway, where is she now?'

'In Val's room, just to be safe. I'll go and fetch her in a moment.'

'Shouldn't the bell have gone by now?' I asked.

'It should but under the circumstances I thought it best to extend playtime a bit.'

There was a slight pause, while we both thought about the six weeks of the summer term remaining. 'What are we going to do now?' I asked.

'I don't know, I just don't know.'

I returned to my classroom to try and organise myself for the afternoon. Hazel was there, her eyes red.

'What's going to happen to Sheena?' she asked.

'Mrs Berry's going to take care of her this afternoon.'

She wiped away a tear. 'I don't want her to get in trouble, Mr Seed.'

I felt my own eyes welling up. 'Nor do I, Hazel.'

Chapter Twenty One

Donna

July meant Tom's second birthday and Craven Bottoms being crowded with family, young and old, fussing round him and producing exciting presents, including a quite magnificent red and yellow pedal-powered tractor from my mum and dad. My younger sister, in keeping with the theme, created a delightful tractor cake using Wagon Wheels, while Barbara crafted a Swiss roll into a muckspreader, much to Tom's delight. My older sister provided a monster picnic, and four generations trundled up Buttergill in three cars to find a suitable picnic spot.

We decamped at the road's highest point and set out blankets on the soft grass nearby, with a wonderful vista across this narrow, cul-de-sac vale with its handful of farms and unparalleled peace. Overhead the plaintive cry of a sailing curlew added to the wildness of the spot. But it was cold. At first we tried to ignore the deadening breeze but, even with coats and hats on, our fingers numbed and, one by one, we admitted that somewhere more sheltered would have been better. Or indoors.

'Isn't July supposed to be summer?' murmured my grandfather from his folding chair.

'At least it's not raining,' I said.

Two minutes later it was. We hurled the picnic into the cars and hurried back to Applesett thinking about hot cups of tea and a fire.

At school Joyce had arranged for a meeting with Sheena's mother, Sheena and me. We sat in the head's office at four o'clock, everyone uncomfortable and unsure what to say.

'I just wonder what we can do better here at school,' said Joyce. 'We want Sheena to be happy. We want her to do well with her work and enjoy her days in the classroom and outside. We don't want her to be miserable and upset. We want the best for her.' I noticed that she made a point of not mentioning trouble or running away.

Mrs Baxter had her face down, as usual, and was struggling for something to say. Sheena for once looked placid, almost touched by Joyce's words. Her mum glanced up and half-opened her mouth but nothing came out. Instead, a large round tear formed across the bottom of her eyelashes and rolled into the corner of her eye. We watched it trace a fluid line down her cheek before it dropped on to her lap. Joyce stood up and reached across her desk for a tissue before gently pressing a hand on Mrs Baxter's shoulders and comforting her. I glanced at Sheena, who was almost crying herself.

'Just take your time,' said Joyce.

Finally Mrs Baxter spoke. 'What's really upset me the most is that she was doin' so well wi' the Ritalin at first. I don't know why she stopped takin' it.'

'Why did you stop taking it, Sheena?' I asked. 'It was helping you, wasn't it?'

Up to this point she had denied spitting the tablets out but the atmosphere in the small room had dismantled the pretence. We all knew it couldn't go on.

'I dunno,' she said in a small voice. It had none of her usual agitation.

I continued, 'Mrs Berry wants you to be happy and to do well. I want that, too, and so does your mum. Do you want to be happy and to do well?'

Sheena looked down and nodded.

'Do you think the tablets will help you?' said Joyce. 'They seemed to help you before.'

Looking up at the headteacher this time, Sheena once more gave a small nod.

A notion came into my mind. 'Did you know that there's someone in the class who wants to be your friend?'

'You mean Nina?' she said.

'No, someone else. A girl who really cares about you. She was worried you were going to get in trouble over what happened last week.'

'Who is it?'

'Well, I'm not sure she wants me to tell you. The best thing would be if she told you herself, probably. But she's, well, a bit worried.'

Sheena didn't respond but Joyce spoke softly, 'She's probably worried that it won't work out, Sheena. It's not easy to make friends with someone who's unhappy.'

'I could be 'er friend,' said Sheena.

Mrs Baxter grasped Sheena's hand. 'Oh love, can't you see that if you take the Ritalin it 'elps you and, well, people are more likely to like you.'

There was a moment's silence then Sheena leant over and hugged her mother. There were more tears and most of them were from Joyce, whose eyeliner was now smudged beyond rescue.

'I will take them, Mum, I will, I promise.'

Over the next week Sheena made an immense effort to behave at school, even apologising to Mrs Hyde and trying to read on her own in the classroom, something she'd never even attempted before. She took her Ritalin tablet each day and volunteered to the unfortunate Eileen a full oral inspection to prove that she'd swallowed it. Joyce heaved a sigh of relief and I prayed that it would continue.

I also hoped that Hazel would give Sheena another chance and this she did, and I was delighted to see the two girls together at playtimes. The noble Nina saw what was happening and left the pair of them alone. Perhaps now I could finally give the other children some attention, late as it was in the school year, and I could start by trying to do something for poor Donna Hugill.

Donna Hugill hated PE.

It would have come as a surprise to anyone looking at Donna that she could hate anything. She was a gentle soul: tall, willowy, softly spoken and with a long, innocent face of ethereal paleness. Donna loved animals, especially horses, and she loved the wild countryside around her isolated little farmhouse at the edge of Crackby Moor. She loved her friends, and most of the time she loved school. But she hated PE. And today was the worst day in Donna's year. It was Sports Day.

Since Tom's birthday it had been raining on and off for three days and the temperature was more akin to March than July. The grim weather had ruled out any chance of practising for Sports Day and so it was that I found myself surrounded by moaning children as we walked out on to the school field for the event itself on Monday afternoon, during a break in the downpours.

'Mr Seed why 'aven't we 'ad a practice? I don't know what races I'm in.'

'You're in all of them, Yvonne, like everybody else – that way it's simple.'

'Mr Seed I've hurt ma leg like: I can't do Sports Day.'

'Well have you brought a note, Bill?'

'I 'aven't, no.'

'I could ask your mum – she's over there sitting with the other parents.'

'Actually, Mr Seed, it dun't feel too bad – mebbe I'll give her a go.'

In fact, it would have been safer to let him sit out since he was wearing boots the size of breadbins and not a scrap of PE kit.

Guy pointed across the field. 'Mr Seed, what's 'appened to the parents? They're sittin' all funny.' I looked over to the running track where around fifty mothers, fathers, grannies, aunts and toddlers were seated on the dining hall chairs, which had been carried out and arranged in rows. Guy was right – they were sitting all funny.

'I don't know, Guy.'

'They look all low.'

And then it became apparent. As we neared the track I felt my feet squidge into the wet grass and looked down to see a bubbly ring of mud around my shoes. The ground was very soft and the parents, parked on chairs with spindly metal legs, were sinking into it. Several of them were wedged at an unlikely angle, trying to counterbalance gravity with comical leans, while others slowly descended with dark mutters before being forced to heave their half-buried chairs out of the mire and look for a drier spot. Mrs Sowerby, a lady of some width, looked like she was sitting on the ground, with her knees dangerously close to blocking her line of vision. Only the toddlers were having fun, skidding off their inclined seats on to the marshy grass with whooping glee. Some of the dads had given up and were perched on the wooden fence behind – an ancient structure which looked less than willing to provide unqualified support for the purpose.

Class 3 were soon arranged on a spread of large gym mats, beside the white tramlines of the running track and opposite the semi-submerged parents, whom they watched with fascination. I went looking for Hilda, since Joyce had asked her to organise the event, but before I spotted her a final grumble from one of the children caught my ear. This time it was more plaintive.

'Mr Seed, do I *really* have to take part in all the races? There's no point – I always come last. I've come last in everything, every single year.' It was Donna. I didn't know what to say.

'I'm sorry, Donna – Mrs Percival has organised Sports Day and I've just been told that everyone has to run every race. Just . . . just do your best.'

They were hollow words and we both knew it; she slunk back

to her corner of the mat with the look of a mourner and sat down into a tight ball, clasping her arms round her shins and rocking back and forth edgily. I had watched Donna suffering throughout the year in PE lessons, trying to catch, hit or kick a ball, or unsuccessfully marshalling her limbs to run or jump. Somehow, it just all went wrong and, despite my continuous encouragement, the poor girl possessed not a speck of confidence that she would ever improve.

For a second, I considered just leaving her out of the races and taking the consequences but at that moment my thoughts were interrupted by a tinny squawking from down near the finish line. It was Joyce trying out the megaphone she had borrowed from Ingleburn Primary. It didn't work: the batteries were almost flat and any muffled parp that it did produce was promptly blown down to the next field by the wind buffeting off the fells behind us. The trouble was that Joyce seemed to be the only person among the whole gathering who didn't recognise the fact: she just carried on announcing all sorts of special things to the sheep in the field, while the children carried on chatting and the parents continued sinking.

The whole school was now gathered by the track and waiting to start, but there was still no sign of Hilda, who had appointed herself as the official starter. The sky seemed to be darkening, too: fat clouds brooded over Spout Fell debating whether to spoil the fun. Then Hilda appeared, striding across the grass towards Joyce wearing her usual clothes plus a pair of pre-war plimsolls.

'Sorry everyone, it was me whistle: the pea was stuck again.'

Without further delay, Emma unleashed a gaggle of minuscule five-year-olds to line up for the Reception flat race, and we were away. The boys went first – it seemed like they were only running five yards – and they burst down the track, swapping lanes and looking sideways. My class cheered for their favourites, usually the smallest.

The girls ran next and Joyce parped away, probably announcing a winner. Then Hilda's class were lined up, this time halfway down the track, and my class knew they would be next. I watched them: some were nervously chattering away, while others, like the ferociously competitive Victor, steeled themselves for a mighty surge to victory. Lee and Oliver were stuffing orange glucose tablets into their mouths and countering complaints that they ''ad sweets'. I tried not to look at Donna in case she caught my eye.

Then came the call.

'Class Three, line up for the sprint: boys then girls.'

They stood up and shuffled along the side of the track to the start. Hilda fussed them into lanes and warned about the dire consequences of toes straying over the line. The boys took a lane each and looked forward, fists clenched. There was a fierce rivalry here and a lot at stake: the title of the fastest runner in the class. Mervyn fancied it, as did Victor and Lee, but Oliver was the one to beat. He was crouching like an Olympic sprinter while the others stood. Alvin next to him looked anxious, while Bill was trying to speak to Hilda.

'Mrs Percival, Mrs Percival! What are you going to say to start the race?'

'Ready, steady, go,' said Hilda. Derek, Guy and Chris set off.

They were tearing down the track amid screams of 'Come back, you wallies' and uproarious laughter from the spectators. Guy and Chris soon twigged and sheepishly crept back, but poor Derek belted on, convinced that he had outstripped all comers and won a famous victory. Emma saved him the embarrassment of actually crossing the line by stepping on to the track. The poor lad was shattered by the time he made it back to the start.

Hilda hushed the cries of the waiting girls for the handsome Oliver to win and settled the boys once more. Everything went quiet.

'Ready . . .' several feet nudged over the line, 'go!'

There was a brief storm of flapping arms and legs and they were away. I could hear a screeching complaint from Bill about Hilda's starting procedure dying away as he exploded down the track, bursting into the lead out of sheer rage. Victor then surged ahead but, as always, Oliver outstripped everyone to take the precious red sticker.

The girls were next: this was no less competitive, but the desire to win was not so manifest. Still, I could see robust concentration in the eyes of Vanessa, Libby, Yvonne and Fay as they lined up. A few cries of 'Come on Jess' died away, then a brief honk from Joyce.

'Ready . . .' said Hilda, 'steady . . .' At least half the girls lurched forward two or three paces. As they were reversing came 'Go!'

Vanessa streaked away, unperturbed, almost as fast as Oliver. The girls quickly spread out and, inevitably, Donna took up the rear, gently ambling along her lane before stepping on to a flattened molehill and suddenly finding herself with one shoe twice the size of the other. She still had ten yards to go after everyone else had finished. The kinder children and most of the parents gave her a mighty cheer to keep going, but the attention only made it worse.

The skipping races followed and I looked forward to the Class 3 boys' event which, as Val had intimated in previous years, would surely provide rich entertainment. I wasn't disappointed. Most of them knew how to skip but in their desire to win the race they simply abandoned any pretence of technique. Eddie's action was the best. Its comic effect was accentuated by his shorts – they were the largest shorts I had ever seen. Just their weight and air resistance alone must have added at least twelve seconds to all of his race times. In skipping terms, Eddie was a 'dragger': he lifted his elbows to their maximum and hauled the rope up his back, before slamming it down to whip his feet and then jumping two seconds late and about three feet too high. To his great credit, Eddie somehow kept going down the track like this, despite frequently entangling the rope on his giant shorts.

Oliver won again, despite substantiated accusations that he had only turned the rope twice along the eighty-metre track. Joyce kept the sheep informed.

I looked up the lanes and saw the girls practising: there was grace and rhythm here in abundance. Within moments, their race started and, to my great joy, I saw that Donna wasn't coming last. Two girls had tripped and stumbled, and Donna, although slow, had trundled past them. She finished second to last, but was it worth anything?

The sack race followed. For the boys, Bill was a master, bouncing like a rubber toy all the way to the line. Victor threw his sack down in disgust at only finishing third. Glyn meanwhile, had the sack with a hole in it and spent the whole race trying to force his foot through the fabric to make another hole so that he could run instead of jump. He managed, in the end, and came in last but happy.

Back at the start, Hilda told the Class 3 girls to lie down on their sacks – this peculiar way of starting the race seemed to be a tradition here.

'Go!'

Ready and steady seemed to have been retired. The girls jumped up and scrambled into their sacks. Except Bernadette. She had taken her glasses off for the race and was trying to get into the wrong end of the sack. She had evidently been given the sack which Glyn had adapted, because she did manage to find two holes for her feet. Unfortunately, no matter how hard she pushed, the rest of her body simply wouldn't follow, and she ended up scuttling down the track with the sack round her ankles like a pair of giant hessian knickers that had lost their elastic. Donna saw Bernadette and at least smiled, although she still finished last.

I looked around for Sheena, who had joined in well up to this point and who I hoped would perhaps pick up a sticker. She wasn't with the other girls and for a moment my heart jolted before I spotted her next to Joyce helping with the stickers. She had evidently had enough and had asked for a job at the finish. I wasn't going to argue.

The next event was the ubiquitous egg and spoon race. There were rumours among the boys that Victor had brought along chewing gum for nefarious purposes, but in the end all of them cheated anyway, placing dropped eggs back on the spoon with their hands, rather than scooping them off the ground as stipulated by Hilda. Victor won the race, but was given black looks for the rest of the afternoon.

As the girls lined up for their turn, I had real hopes that Donna might just pull off a surprise here: for once her slow, steady style might be the right formula. Hilda wished everyone luck and set them off. Vanessa stormed ahead but dropped her golf ball 'egg' almost right away. Kirsty burst through and did the same. A succession of different leaders emerged from the pack, but every time the promise of glory tempted them to rush, and the egg was dropped. Only Donna resisted, her steady crouched walk marking her out as a tortoise among hares. She soon moved out of last place as several girls chased their dropped eggs across the track and halfway down the course, she was actually in third place. I couldn't believe it: third! She would get a sticker for that. I dug my fingernails into my palms and shouted out, 'Keep going, Donna!'

Some of the watching boys cheered her, too. Nina briefly held the lead at this point but then dropped her egg and accidentally kicked it across the lanes. Donna was lying second. And then it happened. An unrestrained toddler burst out from the rows of parents and on to the track to retrieve Nina's golf ball. He ran straight across Donna's path causing her to stop with a jolt. Her egg flipped into the air and fell. A frantic mother stood up with the anguish of having to make a decision about collecting her fugitive child. She made a dash and swept him back to the seats. Donna bent down, her left arm still rigidly held behind her back, and tried to scoop up the egg with the spoon. Fay went past her, but she was still third – she still had a chance. But the golf ball was clearly not of a cooperative disposition. Donna chased and harried it with her spoon but it simply refused to play its part in the drama that so many longed to see. Two more girls passed Donna. Others who dropped their eggs simply placed them back and carried on. But Donna wasn't like that; she'd been told to use only the spoon and so she continued to scoop through the grass fruitlessly while the rest of the class overtook. Once more she was last. I turned and quietly stamped the ground in frustration.

The obstacle race was a disaster for her, too, as was the relay. At least by this time there was only one event left for her to endure: the three-legged race. Donna was paired with Fay, who was at least compassionate, if about six times faster, and the girls lined up and waited for a ribbon band to slip around their ankles. It was now three o'clock and I could see that Hilda was anxious to finish off the last few races quickly. She gave out the bands hurriedly and jogged back to the side of the starting line, holding her whistle at lip height; she had now given up 'go' as well as 'ready' and 'steady'. I looked along the line to see if the girls were prepared and noticed something very odd. Jess and Bernadette, standing side by side with their arms round each other's shoulders, both had the band around their left ankle.

I shouted, 'Hang on, Mrs Percival!' But it was too late, the shrill whistle cut me off and the girls started. All the girls except Jess and Bernadette, that is. As the others moved forward, they simply dropped to the floor as if they'd been shot.

Vanessa and Libby cantered into the lead shouting 'One-two, one-two' with military efficiency. A few other pairs began to establish a rhythm also, but Donna and Fay looked like they were kicking each other. They waggled their way down the track like two drunks, while poor Jess and Bernadette tried to rise, still bound together and giggling furiously. They readjusted their band to a superior left-right arrangement and tried to advance. They managed two steps before being slain again by the giggles. At least Donna and Fay wouldn't be last.

The afternoon was finished off with the parents' races. There were numerous casualties. A number of huge dads, belting down the track as if their bottoms were on fire, omitted to make any allowance for the fact that there was an ash tree eight yards beyond the finish line. There was an audible thud as someone's deceleration ran out of space, followed by what sounded like Joyce megaphoning the sheep to fetch a first-aid kit.

The mothers' race was worse. A large number of mums were dragged on to the track by their belief-filled sons and daughters, causing a pile-up at the start. Hilda suggested two to a lane. I was doubtful, especially when I saw Mrs Sowerby lining up: she needed three lanes on her own. I was also dubious about some of the footwear in evidence; the more sensible mothers opted for bare feet, but one or two lined up with heels. I almost couldn't look. On Hilda's whistle, Mrs Milner stormed ahead and was winning easily until she trod on the same molten molehill that Donna had encountered earlier. Her foot sank into the soft earth and she stumbled for several yards before ploughing a neat furrow in the turf with her chin. The following horde panicked. Some opted for hurdling Mrs Milner, while others tried to stop, and at least three didn't see her at all. There were writhing bodies strewn everywhere.

The children cheered. Mrs Sowerby came puffing up at barely a ramble. I wondered whether she would simply round the melee and collect her winner's sticker but, to her credit, she stopped and scooped up a number of bruised mums off the track. The sheep, thanks to Joyce, missed none of it.

Despite the hilarity of many of the races, I spent the following day thinking about Donna. Not only had she not enjoyed the day, but her prophecy had been fulfilled: she had been humiliated. I spoke to Joyce about it.

'I tend to agree with you, Andy; it could be much better. Maybe next year you could think of another way of running Sports Day – but, I warn you, the parents are great traditionalists here and won't accept too many changes.'

'But the trouble is, the same people win year after year and the same kids come last each time, too. The majority actually have no chance, really.'

'So what do you suggest?'

'Well, what about having another Sports Day as well, but one where the children perform in teams, so that the different abilities can be mixed up.' I'd heard from other teachers on the PE course about events like these.

'Sounds great: you can organise one for next year, if you like.'

I went away from Joyce's office greatly excited and began making plans immediately.

That evening I relayed the story of Donna and the rest of the day's events to Barbara.

'It was the same for me,' she said. 'Seven years of primary school sports days and all I had to show was a tatty certificate for finishing third in the wheelbarrow race in 1971 and that's only because Ian Rice lifted me right off the ground.'

'Just think, you'll be able to run the mothers' race at Applesett in three years' time.'

'Oh, I can't wait to go mincing down the village green and stumble into some dog poo.'

'Anyway, I want to tell you about my plans to revolutionise Sports Day: I'm really excited about it.'

Barbara listened, only yawning once, and agreed that it was a great idea. I scuttled upstairs and immediately began to sketch out exactly how a team Sports Day might work. It was only when I noticed that the clock had passed midnight that I stopped.

The following day I showed the plans to Joyce. I called the event Swinnerteams.

'It all sounds fantastic, Andy; I can't believe you did all this last night.'

'Joyce.'

'Yes?'

'We've got the rest of this week and the whole of next week to go until the end of term, haven't we?'

'Yes . . .'

'Well, I'd like to try out Swinnerteams next week.'

'But, Andy, you need lots of parents to run it, and there's all the letters to go out – it would be very short notice.'

'Look, I've done a rough draft of a letter already. Let's aim for Wednesday next week, send out the letter and see how many parents respond. We only need fifteen or so.'

'Well, OK, if you're sure, but it's going to be a lot of work.'

'I know, don't worry – I'll organise everything.'

Eighteen parents responded: it was on. I had planned twenty events for the children to try working together in teams, including skittles, golf, darts, putting a shot made from a bag of sand wrapped in old tights, a welly relay involving water, a sports quiz and, the highlight of the day, pulling a tractor across the playground. The events were to be spread out around the school, with each one run by a parent or teacher. The children, in teams, were to be given a list of events and a map, and the whole thing would be run on points that would be added up at the end. That way, no one would know who was winning. I also planned to mix up the teams in both ages and abilities so that everyone had a chance. I collected copies of the class registers and asked the other staff to identify the sporty and the not-so-athletic.

My class thought it was a wonderful idea and began to buzz with excitement when I told them about the tractor.

'What if it runs us over, like?' asked Bernadette.

'You get extra points for not getting run over,' I said. She seemed happy.

I was greatly relieved that Val liked the sound of Swinnerteams, too. She suggested that we make the children in her class captains of the teams, being the oldest in the school.

'Just what I was thinking,' I said.

'Right, I'll get them to design badges for their teams; they'll enjoy that. What are the teams going to be called, then?'

'I haven't really thought of names.'

'Well, what about something to follow a theme? My class is doing Space at the moment.'

'Brilliant idea – the teams can be planets.'

'What about Uranus?'

'I'll let you sort that one out, Val.'

Within a few days, I had organised Jack Calvert, Guy's father, to bring a small tractor and a long rope. He even offered to drive it round for a test pull to see if the children could manage it. I frantically put together scoresheets, maps and details of each event, and sent them to the helpers. I expected lots of phone calls from confused parents. Amazingly, none came. And then it was Wednesday.

In morning assembly, I explained to the whole school what was happening and organised the hundred or so children into their teams, so that the younger ones could see who their captains were.

'Now, you're all going to be moving around in and out of the school a lot, and around the playing field, so you must stay with your team all the time. Do you understand?' The Reception children did big nods, but I could see that Emma looked rather doubtful. There were numerous questions. A few children were shocked that a teacher wouldn't be with them all the time, although most relished the fact, and a number wondered what to do about going to the toilet or if they got lost.

I spent the rest of the morning with my class setting out equipment around the school, along with chairs, scoresheets and pencils. At lunchtime, the parent helpers began to arrive, clutching their maps and looking a little bewildered. Then, the throbbing chug of an old diesel engine heralded Mr Calvert's tractor. The children jumped with excitement and I sent them to get changed and put on their badges.

At quarter to one, all of the children were seated outside in their teams, with the captains busy counting numbers. I checked with them and everyone was present. The weather looked like it would hold. I gave a silent prayer and shouted 'Go!' All one hundred and four children shot off in about ninety different directions. There was lots of yelling and herding of infants, and for a moment I thought it was going to descend into instant anarchy, but then the teams re-gathered and started to walk to their first event. A minute later, the sun appeared. We hadn't seen it for days – surely this was a good omen.

I'd decided not to supervise one of the twenty events myself, but rather move around, checking that everything was running smoothly. It was a wise decision. Pluto had gone to the wrong starting event and Venus seemed to have disappeared altogether. The parents, however, soon got to grips with my strange points systems and began to encourage the participants. Most wonderful of all was watching the children in their teams encouraging each other: girls cheered boys, top juniors cheered Reception, and the most able carefully coached those who needed help. It was fascinating to behold.

Victor, as always, was desperate to win and I caught up with his team, Saturn, at the Skittles event. Predictably, he was ignoring his captain – a tall, fair-haired girl from Val's class – yet he was down on his knees carefully explaining to one of Hilda's infants how to score maximum points. I gave him a pat on the back and looked at the team scores. I announced that Saturn were doing really well. I said the same to every team as I went round.

After this, I called in at the Tractor Pull and came across Jupiter taking their positions on the rope. This was Donna's team. Jack Calvert was calling out advice from his cab.

'Right, let's have the littlest ones at the front, and you big 'uns at the back, that's it. Oh, now then, Mr Seed – grand day. Job's going well 'n' all. Furst team did twelve metres.'

'Fantastic, but don't let me interrupt you, Mr Calvert, I'm just observing.'

'Righto. Now, are you the captain, lad?' He addressed a strapping ginger boy from the top class.

'Aye.'

'Oh, you're one of Thwaite's lads from Chapelgarth, aren't yer?

'S'right.'

'You'll be the man f'job 'ere, then – you're the anchor so wrap the rope around yer and lean reet back. Everyone else get a good grip and when I shout 'eave, pull for all yer worth.'

He released the handbrake and called to start. The children strained like fury, their faces contorted with endeavour and their feet straining against the tarmac. At first I feared that the tractor wasn't going to move at all.

'Pull!' the big, ginger boy bellowed. The John Deere stole gradually into motion, rolling an inch at a snail's pace, but then picking up momentum once the inertia was broken. The children's faces lit up with joy to see that they were actually pulling a tractor. I was thrilled to see it, too. But, most of all, I was elated to see Donna enjoying herself as the team began to step backwards and pick up pace: her face beamed along with the little ones.

'Keep going! This is good, very good – six seconds left,' called Mr Calvert.

The ginger boy's face was purple with the strain and he was almost horizontal.

I couldn't help joining in the encouragement, 'Go on, heave!'

'Stop!' Mr Calvert pressed the brake gently and brought the old, green tractor to a halt. He climbed down from the cab and looked at the number chalked on the playground next to the front wheels.

'Fifteen and a half metres: unbelievable!' he said. Jupiter lifted their arms in unison and roared.

After an hour, I had visited all the events and seen every team in action at least once. They waved to me as they rushed past to their next sport. Everyone was enjoying themselves hugely: it was working even better than I had dreamed. The parents were delighted to see the teamwork and organisation among the children, too. Val and Joyce were just as enthusiastic. I headed back to the staffroom to begin making some tea, when I realised that there was an event I had missed after all – the darts – and it was in my own classroom. I raced over to the mobile just in time to see a small girl from Emma's class throwing one of the special plastic Velcro darts that Lee had kindly brought in for the infants. Mrs Collier, Yvonne's mum, was keeping score.

'Forty-five, Kelly, that's very good,' she said. 'Are you putting the kettle on, Mr Seed?'

'I'm on my way but I just want to see the dartboard in action first. How's it going?'

'It's going all right, really, except some of the juniors are having trouble with the real darts.'

I looked across to where I'd hung my own dartboard in front of one of the classroom displays. I'd also brought in a large piece of hardboard to protect the wall. It wasn't big enough. The display was covered in drawings of birds, and all of them looked like they had been blasted with a shotgun. There were holes everywhere: in the hardboard, in the work on the walls, in the wooden frame of the display, in the plaster above and below, in the lino floor, and even some in one of the desks which was a good ten feet away.

'It was a lot nearer, then I moved it,' said Mrs Collier, following my eyes and expression. 'One or two did manage to hit the board.'

After carrying round trays of tea and coffee to the adults, and making sure that all the children had had a drink, I headed for the scoring table to await the teams who had finished. To my amazement, Earth were already there, sitting neatly in a line and sucking ice-lollies provided by the PTA.

'We've finished – 'ave we won?' said a freckly girl from Class 2.

'I don't know yet, you might have done. I have to add up all of the scores to find out first. Have you enjoyed it?' They had.

I sat down and went through the scores. Their total was 4,668. It sounded very impressive. Soon another team finished and passed me their scoresheet. It was Jupiter. Then Val arrived.

'Do you want me to check these, Andy?'

'Please,' I said, losing where I was. Val picked up a pencil and traced down the column in about five seconds.

'I make it 4,568.'

'Oh, I'll recheck it.' I'd lost where I was again. 'Tell you what, you do Jupiter and I'll do Earth again.' We swapped sheets. It was 4,568.

'This one's high: 5,305 I make it,' said Val. I checked the figures methodically and reached the same total.

'Wow,' I whispered, with the ginger boy watching and grinning feverishly.

Three more teams arrived and, thankfully, so did two parents to help with the adding. Fifteen minutes later, the last team to finish came hurtling over and passed me their sheet breathlessly. Joyce put up her hands to quieten everybody and made a little speech to the assembled parents and children, giving me profuse thanks. It had been a great success. Then the last score was checked and the sheet passed to me.

'Do you have a result, then, Mr Seed?' asked Joyce. I stood up.

'I do,' I croaked. I could hardly speak. I thanked everybody briefly and congratulated the children on their magnificent efforts. A hundred pairs of eyes were telling me to shut up and announce the winner: they knew that they all stood a chance. Joyce reached down and picked up a wooden shield and box of medals.

'Right, then, top three in reverse order. With 4,977 points, a superb total, in third place, Pluto!' They stood up to a raucous cheer.

'The second team worked together fantastically well and had a great captain. They scored 5,109 points and it was Neptune!' The proud team rose and received their applause. Then the remaining teams shuffled with excitement. But would my cracking voice hold out?

'The w . . . the winners were just am . . . just amazing. They scored a massive 5,305. It was . . . it was Jupiter!'

Eleven children leapt into the air with spontaneous joy. One of them, jumping higher than she'd ever thought possible, was Donna.

The following day, Eileen brought me a letter. It was from Mrs Hugill, Donna's mother:

Dear Mr Seed

As I am sure you realise, yesterday was a very special day for Donna. Thank you so much for organising the event and I'm only sorry that I wasn't there. But I've heard all about it. She's like a changed child, it's the only thing she's ever won. She won't forget it. Thanks again.

Yours sincerely,

Margaret Hugill

I wouldn't forget it either.

Chapter Twenty Two

Rachel

It was the Tuesday of the last week of the school year and the staff of Cragthwaite Primary shuffled round the building in a zombie-like state, their energy supplies drained by giving all that they had to help the children of the village and its hinterland to think, listen, read, write, spell, add, multiply, measure, paint, skip, act, appreciate, perform, understand and remember, along with a thousand other things for which the patience of a saint was utterly insufficient.

In Class 3, unlike earlier in the year, I was disappointed that Sheena was absent. Since the meeting in Joyce's office and since Hazel had become a real friend, she had turned a corner, making a conscious effort to join in with learning activities and stay away from the endless disputes which had established her sorry reputation. On Friday in assembly, Joyce had presented her with a Headteacher's Award sticker for her efforts and I was delighted to see that she was genuinely pleased to receive it, her broad grin bringing an extra-loud round of applause from the more sensitive in the audience.

At morning break I walked through to the office to ask Eileen if there was any news about Sheena, particularly as she'd been away on Monday, too.

'I tried ringing home when I saw the register but there was no answer,' she said. 'Might Hazel know?'

'I've asked Hazel, but she just said that they were out on Sunday and the house was quiet last night, too.'

I returned to my room, wondering if they might have gone away for a few days. But surely Sheena would have said something: she loved travelling, all the more because she'd never really had a proper holiday.

The playground bell was ringing as I entered the mobile and the first child into the room was Rachel Sunter. Rachel was of medium height and medium brain, the archetypal steady plodder who is so often overlooked in a busy classroom where others demand attention for being loud, naughty, stuck or clever. She was a girl who just quietly got on with things, never making a fuss and generally doing her best. I gave her a smile, not least as she looked uncharacteristically animated.

'I can't wait for *Charlotte's Web* again this afternoon, Mr Seed: it's the best book ever.'

'Oh, right,' I hesitated, feeling guilty that I wasn't planning to read any of the story that afternoon, despite being three-quarters of the way through. There was so much to do before the end of term just three days away.

Rachel didn't sense my uncertainty but continued to acclaim the book. 'Wilbur's my favourite character, but I like Templeton the rat, too, and I love Charlotte.'

The story had certainly captured the imagination of the class with its American farm setting and tale of Wilbur the runt piglet who is first saved from slaughter by a girl called Fern and then by the genius of a large, grey spider called Charlotte who weaves words into her web and protects the innocent animal from the cruel insinuations of the other animals in the barn where they live. I really wanted to finish the book, not least as the children were enjoying it so much, but I was overwhelmed by what needed to be done before Friday: individual work folders had to be assembled, the classroom had to be thoroughly tidied for parents' evening, reports had to be given out and there were numerous projects to finish. I couldn't see myself getting through so much reading aloud but then I looked again at Rachel, whose face still glowed with that expectation of entering another world for just a few minutes at the end of the day and I wavered.

Thinking back, I hadn't read as many books as I would have liked over the school year: part of the reason was Sheena, who previously had never been able to sit still and who constantly interrupted the story or distracted the other children. And yet, wasn't I always stressing how important books were? I honestly believed that developing a love of reading was paramount in a child's education; that it was, in fact, the secret to learning.

Furthermore, I believed that it needed to start from day one. I called to mind the hundreds of times that Barbara and I sat down with Tom and read him picture books and nursery rhymes, and how we would soon be giving fat little board books to Reuben to chew and stare at the illustrations. It was vital, and yet Sheena had probably never been read to at home. What chance did she have?

So that was that: it was my job to enthuse and uphold the written word where it was trodden down or neglected. I was a compensator – there for the Sheenas for whom reading had no cultural relevance, but also for the Rachels who loved a good story and who longed to be taken to wonderful new places and meet enthralling characters.

I would finish *Charlotte's Web*.

My trance was broken by the rest of the class noisily entering the room, several of them down to their T-shirts and sweating; the weather had finally relented. I looked outside to spy out any stragglers and was amazed to feel the heat of the sun as it burnt away the last few wisps of clouds in a sky that was at long last azure. As I turned to head back inside, I heard Joyce call from down the path.

'Andy! I need a word.' I let the door close as she scuttled up the path, the lines on her face betraying some concern.

'Is something up?'

'I've just spoken to Mrs Bowe on the phone.'

'Hazel's mum?'

'Yes. She said that Sheena's house is completely empty.'

'Might they have gone on holiday?'

'They've taken everything. Apparently Sheena's mum had let it slip to a couple of people that she was thinking of doing a moonlight flit.' Her eyes closed for a moment. 'They've gone.'

I felt strangely dizzy and empty, not knowing what to say. Joyce put her arm around me, 'I'm shocked, too. Do you need to sit down?'

I noticed one or two faces peeping through the window.

'No, I'll be all right – I'd better get into the room.'

'Well, OK, but I'll bring you a cup of tea.'

* * *

On Wednesday and Thursday the unexpected heatwave continued, sending everyone outdoors and bringing a surge of visitors into the dale. At school there was no sign of Sheena and we had no way of contacting her mother; the children were also aware that something was going on.

'Mr Seed, where's Sheena? She 'an't been 'ere all week,' said Jess.

'Ma mum says they've done a runner,' blurted out Yvonne before I could reply.

I put out a hand to end more speculation. 'I don't actually know where Sheena is and nor does anybody else, Yvonne, so please don't go round spreading rumours.'

Yvonne turned to Hazel, 'But 'azel says their 'ouse is empty, like.'

I was about to tell Yvonne not to say any more when Hazel spoke up, 'It's true, Mr Seed, I think they've gone – all the rooms are empty and her mum's car in't there and . . . it in't fair.'

Kirsty put a hand on Hazel's shoulder and there was a moment of quiet before lots of children started talking in animated tones. I hushed them with some difficulty, making a mental note to see Hazel at break. It was an awkward situation but with so little term time left, I had to address the practicalities of preparing the children who would be moving on after the summer.

I arrived home at six o'clock on Thursday to find an empty sweltering house. Barbara had left a note:

Gone to the waterfall, taken picnic.

I quickly changed into shorts and a T-shirt, grabbed a cool drink then walked down to the bottom of the green to Applesett Force. The village seemed curiously deserted as I passed by the rows of stone cottages: there were plenty of cars but no people.

When I arrived at the waterfall, the explanation became apparent. It looked like half of the village had decamped to the dappled shade of the waterfall's steep ravine and people were everywhere, enjoying the gurgling melody and cooling effect of the water as it flowed down through pools and limestone steps. The falls themselves were thin and hushed as Buttergill Beck had dried up to a dainty stream, rather than the surging river it was in winter.

'Aye up, Andy, welcome to Scarborough!' It was John Weatherall, stretched out on a towel, a can of beer by his side. 'Your lass is down there – she's the one rubbing four bottles of sun cream on yer little tykes.'

I spotted them down near one of the upper pools and waved. Everywhere there were children splashing in the beck and pasty bodies laid out on lilos and towels, trying to get comfortable on the hard rock ledges and pebbled banks. Iris and Stewart were there along with Mrs Dent, Billy Iveson and Vince and DD from the darts team. There was a wonderful holiday atmosphere and the unmistakable sound of people having fun.

'Daddee!' called Tom as I approached. He was wearing just a nappy and paddling in the middle of a broad, shallow pool which someone had created by damming the beck with piles of stones. There were paper boats on the water everywhere. Barbara was resting back on a huge pile of towels and bags, while next to her Holly Weatherall in a bikini top and shorts bounced a red-faced Reuben on her knees.

'This looks fun!' I said. 'How long have you been here?'

'Since five – isn't it glorious?'

'I've been here since I got off the school bus,' said Holly. 'It's hardly ever this hot.'

I noticed a bag in the shade and suddenly felt very hungry. 'I hope there's some picnic left.'

'Don't worry,' said Barbara, 'there's a tub of things just for you.'

'Oh, you lovely person.' I delved into the bags.

'Come in water, Daddee!' said Tom, splashing violently.

'I will soon but Daddee needs a sandwich first . . . and very probably a snooze.'

After munching what was left of the picnic and having a cuddle with Reuben, I lay down on a towel and closed my eyes. It was truly a wonderful sensation. The music of the gently burbling beck was interspersed with joyful birdsong and distant torrents of laughter from tots playing in the water. The warmth of the sun massaged my face and not even the discomfort of the hard, lumpy slab of rock under my back could blemish the moment.

I heard Tom calling repeatedly for me to come and play, so with superhuman effort I pulled myself out of a half-slumber, took off my sandals and stepped into the water.

'Arrghh!' It was still preposterously cold. 'How can kids swim in *this*?'

'Remember we're 'ard locals!' laughed Holly.

'Don't be such a wimp,' said Barbara. 'I've been in twice: it's nice and refreshing.'

'Refreshing? It's glacial! And there are sharp stones at the bottom.'

'Dearie me . . .'

As I approached Tom, who was still standing in the middle of the shallow pool hitting the water with a stick, another even more unpleasant sensation reared up: a foul, unmistakable pong. I looked at my son who had guilt written across his face.

'Not done a poo,' he said, staring at me. His drooping nappy told another story. I couldn't face this: I turned to Barbara with the most pathetic, long-suffering expression ever seen in Swinnerdale.

Propped up on her elbows, she glanced at the grimacing Holly then took in a big breath. 'Listen, it's *only* because it's the end of term and you're tired and it's been a difficult year that I am even considering getting up right now.'

'I'll do anything . . . else.'

She shook her head in despair. 'Reuben did a squelcher just an hour ago and I've already done Tom's nappy twice . . .'

'I love you lots.'

'Hmmpphh, I should tell you to prove it . . .'

She slung the changing bag over her shoulder, stepped into the water and whisked the humming Tom away behind some bushes. The smell lingered and I wondered how long it would be before he'd be potty trained, after I'd mouthed a silent prayer of thanks for my wife and avoided Holly's eyes.

Further downstream there came a huge splash and the sound of older children screaming with delight and mock terror. I wandered back to the little packhorse bridge to see what they were doing. On the other side of the bridge there was a deep, dark plunge pool about forty feet across, surrounded by sheer rocks and ferns. On the water were two small inflatable boats containing laughing children, while several others were swimming around them. One of the older boys had climbed down to what Tom and I had named the pirate cave and on to a narrow rock ledge eight feet above the water.

'Look out!' he cried, then hurled himself off the crag and into the pool, narrowly missing one of the dinghies. Peering further over and down, I noticed that the level of the water was so low that it was now possible to walk under the bridge and up the riverbed to the higher levels where we were camped. I scrambled down to the pirate cave, avoiding the divers, and edged round on to the rippled limestone of the riverbed, ducking under the bridge.

Ahead of me was a series of mini cataracts, like an elegant stone staircase fountain, edged with delicate silver birches and moss. It was a viewpoint I'd never seen before and was quite magical. It was perfectly possible to climb up these steps through the falling water. I stood there for a moment thinking how my head would be underwater here if it were February and how I'd be swept away in a flash, and yet now it was benign and beautiful. It might not be like this again for years, I thought, and rushed back to suggest that Barbara and I take Tom to climb up it while Holly stayed with Reuben.

The new nappy was in place when I returned and the noxious one had been stashed in the dustbin of a nearby holiday cottage by the resourceful Holly. Tom was back in the water and pleased to see me but Barbara sounded very doubtful when I first suggested my plan about ascending the rapids on foot.

'Just come and have a look,' I said. 'It's ace fun – and we might not get a chance to do it again.'

'I've climbed up there before and it is really good,' said Holly. 'You just have to watch out for potholes.'

'All right, then,' said Barbara. 'But it better had be *really* good.'

Over the bridge again Barbara passed Tom down the steep slope to the pirate cave then made a huge fuss about descending the six feet or so herself. We stopped and admired the jumping boys for a minute, then ducked under the arch of the bridge with Tom's eyes wide with wonder.

'Oh wow, I see!' said Barbara, now able to appreciate the fairy-tale quality of the scene. 'Shall we climb it together, Tommy?'

'Yay!' he cooed, taking a parent's hand on each side and lifting his feet in joy. We splashed forward through the soft gush of the beck up to the first step and the diminutive waterfall that cascaded down it. The drop was only a foot, but a slippery obstacle, so we lifted Tom up in unison, dropping him down with a satisfying splash on to the next level with the customary chorus of 'Wheeee!'

This was repeated step by step as we mounted the glorious descending beck, squelching our way up through the falling streams of crystal-clear mountain water. As Holly had warned, there were a few potholes in the riverbed formed by hard stones spinning round in rocky depressions and grinding out cavities but it quickly became apparent that we had no inkling of just how large some of them were.

Tom was enjoying Barbara and me swinging him up to each higher level, and he launched his feet outwards as we lifted him, bringing them down hard into the beck to make a satisfying splash. We approached a low step on the rocky bed and pulled him to waist height as he chuckled winningly, his little feet waggling in the air between us. Then a truly surprising thing happened: as we plonked him down in the water he just disappeared, slipping out of our wet hands and plummeting down into a four-foot pothole concealed on the dark riverbed. Barbara gasped as our son's head sank out of view but his natural buoyancy bobbed him back up immediately and we grabbed his flailing arms and yanked him upwards. He was spluttering loudly, his eyes wide with shock and icy water pouring off his little trembling body.

Barbara enveloped him for a cuddle as he regained his breath, and several villagers raced over to see what had happened.

'There, there, it's all right,' she soothed, as Tom abruptly realised that he needed to cry. 'We won't take you up any more waterfalls . . . silly Daddy's idea . . . we'll go home in a minute.'

I didn't really know what to say. The best I could manage was, 'I think he needs another nappy.'

Friday was the last day of term and the final day of the school year, my third at Cragthwaite Primary. It was lunchtime and the teachers were gathered in the staffroom, as usual.

'Well, there's another one gone,' said Val.

'I thought we were supposed to be going to the pub,' said Hilda.

Emma rubbed an eye, 'I want to but I'm too kernackered.'

'I think we're all kernackered this year,' I added.

'Speak for yourselves,' chirruped Sue. 'I'm full of beans.'

'Full of wind 'n' all,' quipped Hilda.

'Oi, Mrs Percival, do you mind!' laughed Sue. 'Anyway, aren't you retiring, Hilda?'

'She retired five years ago,' said Val. 'We just can't get rid of her.'

Hilda put down her cup. 'Oh, come on, you know this place would fall apart without me – I'm the only one who knows where the governors keep their sherry.'

'And who would order the infant boys to wee straight if you weren't here, Hilda?' I added.

She grimaced, 'Oh, you know, I went in there yesterday and *the smell—*'

'DON'T START!' boomed Val, bringing a hearty laugh from everyone.

'Ah, that was good,' said Emma, exhaling. 'I needed a laugh.'

Joyce and Eileen came into the room.

'We heard that from the office,' said Joyce. 'If there are good jokes going we don't want to miss out.'

'Unless they're rude,' added Eileen, which made us hoot even more. We then compared the gifts that the children had bought us, which brought more hilarity, not least when I revealed that, once again, I really had received a pair of tartan socks, and then came the inevitable glances at watches as one o'clock approached.

I stood up and stretched, then turned to Joyce. 'What shall I do with all of Sheena's things?'

'Good question. We still haven't heard a jiffy. I've asked County what we should do but we definitely need to hang on to her books and other English and Maths work for her next school to see.'

'Not that she really did any work until the last few weeks,' I mused.

'What else did she leave?'

'Erm, PE kit – quite unsavoury that – a pencil case, a coat, and there are a few bits of artwork that I'd normally have sent home today.'

'Sad isn't it?' Joyce shook her head slowly. 'A year in a school and she'll have nothing at all to show for it.'

'I wonder where she's gone.'

We stood for a moment in silence before the bell rang and started us towards the door like Pavlov's dogs.

At three o'clock I was sitting with my class on the cramped square of carpet in the corner of the room which acted as a book corner. *Charlotte's Web* was in my hands and twenty-two children were sitting like statues, their eyes fixed on me as I read the final two chapters. Rachel was at the front, completely engrossed in the story of how Wilbur the pig, who once literally faced the axe, reaches the country fair and wins a medal, thanks to the inspired marvels of his friend Charlotte the wise grey spider.

A happy ending seemed inevitable and none of the children were prepared for the moment when, after she has produced her egg sac, Charlotte announces that she is dying. There is nothing Wilbur nor any of the other animals can do to save her: she has reached the end of her natural life. At first my class just stared, almost unwilling to accept this turn of events, but then, as the story progressed and Wilbur returns to the farm and Charlotte's babies hatch and are blown away at the end of their strands of silk by a warm wind, the truth sank home and tears appeared.

Rachel was first, wiping her full eyes, then reaching for a tissue.

Even some of the boys were sniffling quietly, their minds trying to comprehend that the hero of the story was gone and wouldn't be coming back. But Wilbur was still there, and he looked after three of the babies when they returned to the farm. There was hope at the end after all.

I drew the brush across the final section of sill and stopped for a rest. The sun was shining and it was the first weekend of the summer holidays. I was at the top of one of John Weatherall's extending ladders, painting the double-decker bay window at the front of Craven Bottoms. A warm wind was blowing, like in the story, and, rather than tiny spiders, this one brought the scent of the meadows, of hay and flowers, along with the songs of the Dales – the call of lambs and the rising piccolo of the skylark.

This elevated perch gave me an unrivalled view of Applesett. There was Iris coming out of the shop with little Stewart, no doubt loaded with the latest morsels from Mrs Dent. Hulking builders from the darts team were pointing a wall across the green and Big Alec Lund was racing his quad bike up through the village back to his farm. Billy Iveson was talking to Sam Burnsall outside the pub, as they had probably done most days for six decades.

I thought back over the year, unable yet to free my mind from the tangle of school, to Chris's shattered pottery and Mervyn's triumph in the quiz, to the Christmas party and the magnificent igloo. Then there was the great Egyptian mummy and our unforgettable trip to Whitby, along with the bottle rockets and Sports Day. So much had happened. Characters had emerged from the class: Yvonne, Vanessa, Bill, Guy, Nina and Hazel. And, of course, there was Sheena, who came in like a tornado and left silently in the night.

She had given me a lesson: that teaching wasn't easy and that life could be complicated even for a young child. A little wisdom had been passed on but with some pain. Yet she had improved, and there was a definite change in her: there was hope and a feeling that she could do well in her next school, if she kept up the medication and stopped battling those who were trying to help her.

Events at home had been momentous too: Barbara had learnt to drive and we had been blessed with a wonderful second son, the mighty Reuben, who kept us awake but melted our hearts. Then there were other memorable things: Mrs Boo, the village fair and bonfire before it, the miraculous Holly, and Tom's birthday.

One of the greatest joys was getting to know Adam and Ruth Metcalfe, who battled the elements and their stingy land every day to eke out an existence, and did so with such quiet dignity: they never complained and were grateful for everything they had. They too had taught the teacher.

A cry of 'Daddee!' from below caught my ear. There was Barbara, with Tom and Reuben in her arms. I smiled and started down.